THE MUSIC MONSTER

THE
MUSIC MONSTER

A Biography of James William Davison,
Music Critic of *The Times* of London, 1846–78

With Excerpts from His Critical Writings

Charles Reid

Quartet Books
London Melbourne New York

Line drawings appearing in the text reproduced
by courtesy of the British Library

First published by Quartet Books Limited 1984
A member of the Namara Group
27/29 Goodge Street, London W1P 1FD

British Library Cataloguing in Publication Data

Reid, Charles
    The music monster.
    1. Davison, James W.
    I. Title
    780'.15'0924   ML423.D/

ISBN 0-7043-2427-X

Typeset by MC Typeset, Chatham, Kent
Printed and bound in Great Britain
by Mackays of Chatham Ltd, Kent

For Louise and Stuart

Contents

Introduction

For the most part James William Davison wrote anonymously. This anonymity is easily penetrated, however. During his thirty-two years with *The Times* of London, he was that paper's sole writer on music. No problem there, then. *The Times* people were generous with space. His yearly flow ran to millions of words. Whether our need is with Richard Wagner, Hector Berlioz or Georges Bizet or, on the other hand, with such glittering and deathless native names as John Liptrott Hatton, Edward James Loder or Cipriani Potter, all we have to do is to set up the appropriate files on our desk at Colindale's newspaper museum and copy down Davison's prose until the closing bell rings.

Another of my sources is the weekly sheet he edited, the *Musical World*, long dead. His tenure here exceeded forty years; his output, when we consider copy he sub-edited as well as what he wrote himself, must have amounted to well over forty million words. Some of his pieces in the *Musical World* are signed by freakish or comic pen-names, as set forth in my Chapter 29, 'The Muttonians'. The rest are without signature. I have no difficulty in identifying them, however. In the first place there's the positioning. As editor, Davison naturally occupied the main section of the main editorial page – the position traditionally allotted to the 'leader' or editorial article. Furthermore, sidelights on what he wrote about from week to week and the controversies into which he pitched or insinuated himself are to be gleaned from fellow writers and musicians, as will be gathered from my bibliography, for which see Appendix.

Davison's great causes or obsessive fallacies were the supremacy of most contemporary British composers and the mediocrity of most foreign ones, Chopin especially. These were his recurring and loved themes. By these and by his tolerably rich, sometimes hilarious, prose, James William Davison is to be identified as plainly as if his signature were at the foot of every folio.

As to what was written about Davison, as distinct from his own writings, I should add that the biographical section of this work is an expansion and elaboration of the 'official' biography, which came out in 1912. Its title was 'From Mendelssohn to Wagner (etc.)'; its author Henry Davison, one of James William Davison's two sons. For my expansions and elaborations I have had recourse to over sixty volumes of reminiscences by musicians, and the like, of the same period who knew, or knew of, Davison.

PART ONE

1 The Actor-Parents

James William Davison (1813–85) was the music monster, nothing less. For over thirty years he was music critic of *The Times* of London, for over forty years editor of or contributor to the long defunct *Musical World*. In these capacities he ridiculed and flailed those whom he hated inordinately: the pre-eminent musical geniuses of his day and hour.

His prose had drollery and muscle. He never had to grope for a phrase. Chopin was 'a sickly schoolboy', 'a morbidly sentimental flea'; Schubert 'unpractised and overrated', Berlioz 'a vulgarian, a lunatic'; the mid-period, burgeoning Verdi 'a maker of wretched music for mobs'; Wagner 'patchy, puerile and poisonous'. Schumann concocted chamber music that was bad, symphonies that were worse. Liszt's music was 'hateful fungi'. Tchaikovsky turned out rubbish. These and a hundred more allergies and aberrations are quoted with dates and sources in the second part of this volume. Nobody has thought to disinter them before. They will, I am confident, be read with horror and hilarity. In Davison's day readers of *The Times* and the *Musical World* went to these prints as to founts of truth and good sense. Nor was his spell confined to his own day. It long survived him. Until middle age I myself spurned Chopin. From Chopin recitals I stayed away, explaining to Chopinite friends that I did not wish to be smothered with scented cushions. In the case of Liszt, sedulously remembered as a 'womanizer' and nothing else, I substituted for 'scented cushions' the phrase 'scented pillow slips'. Both gibes were reflections of Davison animosities which, dutifully culti-vated and spread, continued to hold sway during much of the following century.

3

My opening sentence spoke of Davison as a musical monster. There were, I must allow, redeeming glints, the brightest being his adoration of Mendelssohn, which is touched on in the biographical sketch that follows. It must be allowed, too, that he wrote of Handel, Mozart and Beethoven with veneration. But a critic is to be judged by his response to the music of his own day. Davison grew up and lived to the end in parallel with the efflorescence of Romantic music, one of the most startling and joyous chapters in the history of mankind. His hatreds and deridings of the Romantic masters were equally startling but a lamentable inversion of all that is joyous.

James William Davison was born on 5 October 1813, in Charlotte Street, off Fitzroy Square, Bloomsbury, where, some eighty years later, another critic, George Bernard Shaw, was to lodge and scribble. He had one congenital defect: a club foot. His limp was to be mimicked and mocked by enemies down the years. Of his father, James Davison, little is known; of his mother we have glimpses in this contemporary memoir and that. This is because of her acting career. She was born Maria Rebecca Duncan, daughter (according to Davison's earlier biographer, her grandson, Henry Davison) of 'respectable provincial actors'. Her own stage career showed marked versatility – Lady Teazle one week, Rosalind the next, the week after that star of some ephemeral song-skit that revealed her very striking vocal powers. These, says an early edition of the *Dictionary of National Biography*, 'almost' fitted her for grand opera. Maria Duncan, as she was billed by Drury Lane and other notable theatres, did not invariably achieve – and perhaps did not aim at – the 'respectability' with which Henry Davison credited her parents. The fact is that she put on male impersonation acts of a piquant and, according to notions current under George IV, distinctly unrespectable sort. We have an account of them from a notable witness, Leigh Hunt, who, in his *Critical Essays on Performers in the London Theatre* (1807), takes it upon himself to sermonize her. 'I have not a little lamented,' writes Hunt, 'to see [Miss Duncan's] increasing fondness for male attire . . . for tight waistcoats that imprison the waist merely to give greater freedom to the chest [Hunt's word for bosom], white silk stockings that make the leg want nothing but a pedestal to fix it for the eye of the connoisseur, and tight breeches through which [a lecture might be read] on the sartorian muscles.'

Was it not, Hunt continued, infinitely degrading for an English woman to strut and pose in public view, divested of 'becoming concealments', thinking of nothing but the cut of her ankle and the undulation of her hip, and making old men in her audiences gloat through their opera glasses at a display so refreshing to their memories? 'A slave in a West Indian market,' adds Hunt, 'could hardly undergo a more humiliating exhibition.' Maria was twenty-seven when this was written. She married five years later. Soon she had other things to think of than public undulations and transparent breeches.

As James William, her first-born, grew up, learning French with honours and much else at University College school, hampered by his club foot yet charging with umbrella aswing up and down Gower Street to the peril of other pedestrians, reading avidly in the British Museum library and at all times keeping an eye on girls, his mother regularly sang and played for him at home, nurturing a taste for music that had first been aroused in him by hearing William Henry Holmes's playing. Davison was then eighteen, Holmes a little older. In the end Maria made Holmes Davison's music teacher. Simple and guileless as a child, so modest that he addressed everyone as 'Sir', ladies included, and, on visiting a great house, would ring the servants' bell 'so as not to appear proud to the domestics', Holmes was nevertheless a pianist of the first order, with complete control of touch, tone and pedals. On taking over young Davison as a pupil, he seems to have been present at Maria's last lesson to Jim. He recalled this in a letter to Davison nearly fifty years later. He describes young Jim struggling through some piano sonata for left hand only by Kalkbrenner 'against a loving accompaniment of voice by your dear, good Mamma' – an odd experiment in *obbligato*, it would seem.

It was through Holmes that Davison, while still in his teens, made two lifelong friends: George Alexander Macfarren and William Sterndale Bennett, sedulous composers – of cantatas, oratorios, symphonies, concertos, operas and song cycles – ornaments both of that new British school which the chauvinistic Davison was to extol to the skies – or, at any rate, as high as one floor only beneath the great god Mendelssohn.

Meantime schooling and self-education were still making their

demands and instilling their prejudices. Davison was up to the
neck in great thinkers and others perhaps not so great: Aquinas,
Saint Augustine, Plato, Aristotle, Spinoza, Tacitus, Pascal – and
Shelley.

2   Shelley Worship

For some years the ferociously anti-Christian 'Queen Mab' was
Davison's intellectual joy and comfort. Henry Davison speculates
that he may have first come upon 'Queen Mab' in some
second-hand bookshop. Considering that the poem and accompanying Notes had been privately printed in a limited edition at
the poet's expense less than a score years earlier, this does not seem
altogether likely. Quickly Davison was immersed, absorbed and
conquered. Over thirty miles from the heart of London are
Thames-side woods where Shelley walked and pondered, his head
full of cantos, conceits and newborn stanzas. To these woods (near
Marlow, Bucks), Davison took Macfarren, Bennett and other
friends, to all of whom he gave or lent 'Queen Mab'. Their joint
suffrages and enthusiasms amounted, says Henry Davison, to
'something like a religion, with Marlow as its Mecca'. What form
did this quasi-religion take? The biography doesn't say. On
Shelley its note is respectful and reticent. Readers who have not
dipped into 'Queen Mab' may get the impression that in Marlow's
woods Jim Davison and the rest were lulled or enlivened by
Shelley's imagery, metre and 'music'. 'Queen Mab' is hardly that
sort of poem, however. In it we read of Christ's 'horrible
Godhead' in the shape of man and of the 'malignancy' of His soul.
The Christian tenets are savaged up to and including the
Crucifixion:

> I stood beside Him: on the torturing cross
> No pain assailed His unterrestrial sense;
> And yet He groaned. Indignantly I summed
> The massacres and miseries which His name

> Had sanctioned in my country, and I cried,
> 'Go! Go!' in mockery.
> A smile of godlike malice reillumed
> His fading lineaments. – 'I go,' he cried,
> 'But thou shalt wander o'er the unquiet earth
> Eternally . . .'

The same animosity surges and bristles from Shelley's prose. A single 'quote' from the Notes to 'Queen Mab' will suffice in proof of this: 'I am acquainted with a lady of considerable accomplishment and the mother of a numerous family whom the Christian religion has goaded to incurable insanity. A parallel case is, I believe, within the experience of every physician.'

Another of Shelley's points: mankind would be immensely more cheerful and strapping if it renounced meats and spirituous liquors, living instead on vegetables and pure water. One only had to look at Napoleon Bonaparte's face – his bile-suffused cheek, wrinkled brow and the yellow of his eyes – to read the entire Napoleonic tale of murders and victories and throne-snatching. Had he descended from vegetarian, water-drinking stock, there would have been none of this. Davison and his circle eagerly assented and conformed. G.A. Macfarren's biographer, Henry C. Banister, suggests that the vegetarian diet they adopted in the Marlow woods probably injured Macfarren's constitution for good. It is true he had never been robust. As to Davison, he soon dropped the regime, especially the forswearing of strong liquors. He is remembered from middle age onward as reeking of cigars and whisky at most hours of the day. Meantime, says Banister, they went defiantly on, worshipping Shelley's personality and opinions, the 'daring independence' of his life and the moral and other extravagances that were strewn along it.

Macfarren's father, George Macfarren, industrious playwright and interim editor of the *Musical World* before Davison took over, weighed up the teachings and preachings of the Marlow woods. He concluded, says Banister, that Davison was ringleader and his son's evil genius. A letter has come down to us which he wrote to Davison in the fall of 1834. He wrote:

> You are quick and apt, and there is no reason in the world why
> you should not excel greatly, except that you have imbibed

certain notions and philosophies which the world is not yet ripe
to tolerate, and which, I fear, either nullify, impede or at least
divide your attention . . . [You] will serve my son and yourself
and pleasure me greatly by giving him an example of
conformity to public, not private, opinion and the pursuit of
celebrity by a manly race along the beaten road rather than a
steeplechase of eccentricity which people tolerate, sometimes
laugh at, never admire.

During fifty years or more Davison wrote millions of words for
a variety of sheets. These I have combed. Also I have weighed the
handful of relevant private letters that survive. Nowhere in these
do I find any specific renouncing of the 'Queen Mab' poem and
Notes. It is true that in a hard-up, begging letter to his father
during that same autumn of 1834, Davison, having quoted
pentameters of darkling beauty from 'Alastor', puts in a word of
regret, styling Shelley 'the wildest of Utopians'. This is not
renunciation, however. Its purpose is placatory, its aim his father's
purse. In the same letter, written from Cheshire, where he was
staying with the pious Holmes family, he tactfully writes of the
family's evening prayers. There is nothing more beautiful, he
ends, than *sincere* religion, 'though, perhaps unfortunately, I am
not religious myself'.

Often his philosophical tinct was determined by that of the
person whom he was addressing. Thus with the shortlived *Musical
Examiner*, which expired, after something over a hundred issues,
at the end of 1844. In this case the person addressed was its
proprietor, Christian Rudolph Wessel, immigrant from Hamburg, holder of the English copyright (or equivalent) in Chopin,
of whom we shall have much to tell. My present point is that the
immigrant Wessel went in for religion, becoming a Congregationalist. To the *Examiner* of 24 December 1842 Davison
contributed a fervent note apropos of Handel which, without
deserting Shelley and Shelley's intellectual mentors, asserted faith
in immortality with an almost Congregationalist ring. He wrote:

Can Handel at this instant be but dust and ashes? Can the mind
of such a mighty being have perished with that grosser thing, –
his body? The notion is to our way of thinking preposterous –
and yet we are in no way straitlaced. We have had our freedom

of thought – we have doubted and disbelieved and still doubt and disbelieve much that is called canonical; – we have read our Hobbes and our Bayle, our Voltaire and our Vanini and our Diderot, and still read them and still intend to read them, tho they may be erring spirits, as in much we think they are . . . We are FREE THINKERS in a religious and moral point of view. But we also lay claim to some philosophy – and our position in philosophy leads us thoroughly to discredit the possibility, not merely the probability, of such a mind as that of Handel being other than immortal – and we cannot but think the faculty of creating such sublimities as *Messiah* an irresistible proof of our position and an unanswerable argument against the iron-ribbed obstinacy of materiality . . .

Back to Wessel. Since we shall be hearing more in a later chapter about him and his *Examiner*, a biographical point or two may not be amiss here.

Born in Bremen (1797) and dying at Eastbourne eighty-eight years later, he came to London in 1825 and set up as a music publisher with successive partners, including Edwin Ashdown, who later said of Wessel's investment in Chopin's works that in the beginning these did not sell and were for long 'a dead letter' (q.v., John Francis Barnett's memoirs). In letters to intimates Chopin dismissed him contemptuously, saying he was a 'cheat' and a 'windbag'. Of the 'silly titles' that Wessel put on his works he wrote angrily. The B minor scherzo became '*Le Banquet Infernal*', the F minor ballade '*La Gracieuse*', the rondo op. 5 'The Maid of Posnan' and the nocturnes either '*Murumures de la Seine*', '*Zephyrs*', '*Soupirs*', '*Laments*' or '*Consolations*'.

Do I detect Davison's hand here? Certainly, he had a wide and prompt French vocabulary. When left to himself in these matters, Wessel was capable of gross bloomers. His Chopin 'collections' or editions, included what is probably the most uproarious printer's error in musical history. It turned Chopin's polonaises into polonoises.

3 Honey-Dolby Dreams

Now a word about Davison's love dreams and miseries. This takes us back to his Marlow woods phase, and, more particularly, to his holiday with Billy Holmes's family in rural Derbyshire.

In letters home he babbles about *Honeysuckle* (his capital initial and italics). In the Holmeses' garden he found a most luxuriant *Honeysuckle* plant. Never had he beheld such a flower. 'I am quite in love with it. I pay it nocturnal visits as to some spirit in the shape of a flower to whom I may unload my soul.' To his brother he writes of Holmes's charming sisters, one of them most engaging – 'Were my heart my own I should be obliged to take care lest I lose it.' There was a Miss Sherrard, too. She lived not far from the Holmeses. He met Miss Sherrard at a tea-party – 'Her lovely eyes would be enough to melt the heart of anyone with a heart to melt, but, alas!, I can give not what men call love:–

> The desire of the moth for the star,
> Of the night for the morrow,
> The devotion the heart feels afar,
> From the sphere of our sorrow . . .

'Shelley again,' he concludes. 'You must pardon me, for he, of all poets, alone expresses my feelings.' Clearly his heart was pre-empted. A letter to him from Macfarren tells us to whom. The name is Mrs Honey. Addressing him as 'Sweet Honeysuckle Bee', Macfarren suggests that they walk as far as Mrs Honey's house the following Sunday. Henry Davison loftily admits that Mrs Honey's 'strange career' had inspired Davison 'with interest'.

There was nothing strange about Laura Honey's career. Her theatrical work apart, it was the career of a kept woman who didn't need to be kept. There is some account of her in an anonymous pamphlet printed in Lambeth in 1838 – *The Extraordinary and Secret Amours of Mrs Honey*. Coyly repudiating his title's promise, the anonymous author says: 'Of her amours, delicacy compels us to be silent, but she is at present under the protection of Lord Chesterfield.' Her acting career in some ways paralleled that of Davison's mother. In tinpot plays Laura played a string of juvenile parts, including, at the age of eleven, that of a midshipman in some production at Sadler's Wells Theatre, where she had been promoted from the wardrobe department. The Lambeth pamphlet describes her acting abilities as overrated. Presently she'd be off to Italy 'with the object of improving her vocal powers – and, one must add, she is greatly in want of it'. On theatre bills she figured as 'Honey Bee', singing cheeky ballads to much tossing of her dark corkscrew curls and winning loud acclaim – save at the St James's Theatre, 'a refined and aristocratic region', reported the periodical *Actors by Daylight*, in the spring of 1838, 'which found her act excessively vulgar'. She lived apart from her husband, a wastrel who milked her earnings and died in a boating accident. Davison babbled of her mopingly and hopelessly. To her he dedicated a song with text by a poet-chum; also a rondoletto for piano. At the age of twenty-seven she died – of what we do not know.

Meantime Davison had found a new flame – the singer Charlotte Dolby, for whom Mendelssohn was to compose the contralto numbers in his *Elijah* oratorio. Charlotte is said to have been not only a voice but a beauty. As Macfarren had accompanied Davison on his walks to Laura Honey's house, so he attended him on excursions to places where, with luck, Charlotte might be seen. We have an account of one such trip by Joseph Bennett, a musical journalist who for a time served Davison on the *Musical World*. In his reminiscences Bennett wrote:

> These love-lorn young men were in the habit of walking up and down in front of the dwellings of their respective damsels, Davison accompanying Macfarren to the abode of a Miss Bendison, with whom he was in love, Macfarren being 'best man' when Davison paraded before the dwelling of Miss Dolby.
>
> One day it came to the knowledge of Davison that Miss Dolby was staying as guest at a riverside mansion somewhere up the Thames . . . Miss Dolby's love, supported by

Macfarren, went upstream on the chance of seeing her. Having identified a house standing in large grounds the adventurers climbed the boundary wall and dropped down among some bushes, whence they worked round till the front of the mansion and the lawn before it stood revealed. Soon Miss Dolby appeared at a window looking on to the lawn and remained there some time, while Davison, concealed among the bushes, glutted his eyes with the sight of her, and Macfarren, having no personal concern, read a book. They were presently espied by a servant, a gardener, perhaps, who very properly demanded what they were doing there . . . They reclimbed the wall and regained the road.

Bennett adds that Davison later composed a descriptive fantasia for piano representing the whole story. He gave Bennett a copy. Between the staves there were descriptive annotations, such as 'Here Charlotte appeared', 'Here the Keeper came', etc.

4   The Catch Club Gluttons

Young Davison grew up and found his feet in a musical world strikingly different in some ways from that of our own time. Music was often the concomitant of drinking and nibbling. In some quarters, song graced gluttony. This we have from the singer Henry Phillips (1801–76), an impressive Caspar in *Der Freischütz* at Covent Garden and deviser of what he called 'table entertainments', in which arias and glees alternated with the roasts and the puddings.

Phillips's reminiscences deal entertainingly with the Antient Concerts Society (of which, from 1825 on he was principal bass) and their doings at the Thatched House Tavern, St James's, under the auspices of some gentlemen's and noblemen's catch club. One night in particular he describes with sprightly pen. There were performances by a couple of counter-tenors, with accompaniment, one called Terrail, the other William Knyvett who, in addition to warbling and fluting high above the stave, as is the counter-tenor's way, acted as conductor.

A facetious man off the platform, Knyvett was strict when on it. In accordance with the nomenclature of the time, his voice and all such were 'altos'. To them were given parts later sung by contraltos. Knyvett's singing and appearance were strangely at variance. When he and Terrail stood up to sing one would have imagined from their size that a voice like thunder would have shaken the very rafters of the ceiling; instead of which a still, small voice, scarcely audible 'stole upon the ear'. Instead of the trumpet-toned sound expected, a little squeaking voice came forth, something resembling a weak oboe. Phillips goes on:

And yet these singers, strange to say, appeared to require ten times more sustenance than men possessing ten times their power. In fact, they were monstrous eaters, an example of which I will give . . . I had leisure to observe what was consumed before the concert at the Catch Club, and, taking out my pencil, put down all our altos ate and drank during and before dinner. Thus ran my memorandum:

1, Plate of oxtail soup. 2, Plate of mock turtle. 3, Turbot and lobster sauce. 4, A few smelts. 5, Glass of sherry. 6, Salmon and lobster sauce. 7, The Cup (this was a silver goblet filled with beer, wine, nutmeg, lemon, etc., etc., extremely good and potent, a great favourite at the table, being continually passed up and down). 8, Roast beef and Yorkshire pudding. 9, Glass of Madeira. 10, Mutton pie. 11, Glass of sherry. 12, Glass of Madeira. 13, Bottle of soda water. 14, Two slices saddle of mutton and jelly. 15, The Cup. 16, Wing of capon and laver. 17, Glass of Madeira. 18, Marrow bone and toast. 19, Glass of sherry. 20, Marrow pudding. 21, Bottle of soda water. 22, Apple tart. 23, Glass of sherry. 24, Cheese and biscuits. 25, The Cup. 26, Two oranges. 27, Glass of port. 28, Ditto sherry. 29, Ditto claret. 30, Ditto port. 31, Two oranges. 32, Same of figs. 33, Glass of sherry. 34, Bottle of soda water, and a sly drop of brandy in it – quite necessary, I have no doubt.

During some of the glees, when the upper notes caused the eyes to start and the cheeks to swell with the difficulty, after dinner, of getting so high, someone observed: 'How gracefully Terrail is singing this evening.' On which another member of the Club, who had also taken note of the dinner served, commented: 'Yes, he's *bursting* with taste.'

The Antient Concerts were not, of course, confined to catch clubs and thatched taverns. When they functioned at, say, the Exeter Hall, royalty often attended; and, Phillips tells us, so did Townsend, chief Bow Street runner, whose office was to keep watch and ward over his royal charges. George III and George IV would go nowhere without him. He took special pains to dress much as these monarchs did in private and, till the day of his death, never altered his costume, which included a broad-brimmed white hat, flaxen wig and long drab gaiters or breeches. Always he carried a thick walking stick or cudgel. Every time the King's name was mentioned he raised his hat. At one of the Antient Concerts someone asked him whether he was fond of music. His reply: 'No, 'taint much in my line, but my missus is awful musical. I can't get her away from them horgans in the street sometimes.'

5   Enter Mendelssohn

Davison first met Mendelssohn in 1836 as a twenty-two-year-old. With Sterndale Bennett, two years his junior, who had some minor commission from Broadwood, the piano-maker, he journeyed to Düsseldorf for the Lower-Rhine Music Festival, where Mendelssohn conducted among other things his *Saint Paul* oratorio. They were there on Whit Monday and Tuesday or a little longer. Mendelssohn received them most kindly. He would call early 'to rouse the lazy Englishmen' at their hotel, play billiards, chat and make music with them. On that Whit Tuesday Bennett had just written the first bars of his *Naiads* overture. Mendelssohn was shown this scrap by Davison. He looked up radiantly from it and said 'in no uncertain tones' that he knew of no young German composer of Bennett's age with equal gifts. Mendelssohn, on occasion a skilled smarmer (as emerges in the Macfarren biography), may have been in earnest. On another morning he found Davison tormented by a headache. He'd been awake with it all night, said Bennett. Mendelssohn, all compassion, stroked Jim's head, saying 'Poor fellow, poor fellow!' – a memory that Davison frequently trotted out during half a century.

From Düsseldorf the two of them returned jubilantly, confirmed Mendelssohn militants for ever. Whenever Mendelssohn happened to be around their adoration was apt to take an aggressive turn. Consider the Philharmonic Society concerts of June 1842.

These were the cream and crown of English music-making, drawing the 'top people' to top-class performances. The programme had to be watched with censoring eyes, however, and subscribers protected against their weaker natures. At the seventh concert of that 1842 season Mendelssohn conducted his A major symphony, winning storms of applause. Then, on came Sigismund Thalberg, composer-pianist, and committed, as Davison would have put it, rather than performed, his 'dreadful' Bellini-tinted, Bellini-tainted *La Sonnambula* fantasia. Davison and Macfarren were there. Only one thing to do. They did it. When the pro-Thalberg clappings and clamours had died down they hissed violently, attracting general attention – and opprobrium.

The news got around that these two ill-behaved young men were composers – 'a disgrace', commented the *Morning Post*, 'to their profession'. There was a tit-for-tat sequel. At the rehearsal next morning for the eighth and last concert of the season, Mendelssohn again appeared. He sat down at the piano and was about to begin his D minor piano concerto when Davison and Macfarren appeared in the aisle, walking to their seats. They were spotted by the orchestral players, who instantly responded with retaliatory hisses that made Mendelssohn start up in bewilderment from the keyboard. 'Turn 'em out!' shouted the players. These shouts and hisses, commented the *Morning Post*, did the players credit.

Six months later, Thalberg's name having cropped up again, Davison wrote of him (*Musical Examiner*, 17 December 1842) with astonishing rancour, portraying him as out above all for 'stivers', earning £2,000 a year (a stunning salary in 1842), desperately anxious to turn his £2,000 into £4,000, and supplying in return for

these riches music that was quite calamitous. He had heard
Thalberg play one of his andantes, Davison went on. 'What an
affliction! We heard nothing so maudlin or monotonous, so
lachrymose and lackadaisical, so pitifully puling and positively
paralytic, or whining, whooping, whizzing, whirring, wishy-
washy, wallowing and warm-waterish, since the dear, delightful,
dead-for-durance days when dear old Aunt Tabitha seated herself
at the harpsichord . . .'

The world supplied critic Davison copiously, gratifyingly, with
musical rubbish, or what he took to be such. But how was he
coming on as a composer himself?

Davison entered neither music college nor academy. He had no
tutor and sought none. Apart from what he picked up in the
beaten way of companionship from Macfarren and Bennett, both
of whom were academically qualified, he was self-taught, as
anyone may be who knows how to read music and has a piano.
Henry Davison writes loosely of his turning out 'several overtures', but gives no list. In the British Library catalogue we find
but one, *The Fairy Tale of Fortunatus*. Davison's letters mention
two more – *Darnley* (which he liked 'much better') and *Amphitryon*, after Dryden's poem. We hear of *Fortunatus* being performed
in June 1835 'at Billy Holmes's concert', whatever that may have
been, and of *Amphitryon* as listed for 'the next instrumental trial',
presumably by the newly-formed British Society of Musicians.

For the rest, Davison's entries in the British Library catalogue
number sixty-two. There are songs, including some in alternative
editions, to words by Shelley (inevitably), Keats and Desmond
Ryan, who helped edit the *Musical World*; also sketches, tarantel-
les, bagatelles and mazurkas for the piano; and transcriptions of
arias or string quartets by the long-forgotten Woelfl and Thomas
Malleson Mudie. He was great on quadrilles (borrowed tunes
turned into sets of lancer-type dances performed at house-parties).

Of his quadrilles one set gave immense offence to the few who
came upon it. This was printed under the title *Bologna, Quadrilles
on Admired Themes by Rossini for the Pianoforte*. The offence was
that Davison took his themes, without acknowledging the precise
source, from Rossini's setting of the *Stabat Mater*. *Bologna* is not in
the British Library catalogue. All copies must have been chased,

traced and destroyed by Davison's family. Of *Bologna* we should have known nothing but for John Ella, violinist and scribbler, a contemporary of Davison, who, in his *Lectures on Dramatic Music*, tells how, at a great musical banquet in Stuttgart, he was asked whether the English did not dance to Rossini's *Stabat Mater*, a work that Ella held in awe. He repudiated hotly what, on reflection, he took for misplaced irony. Soon after his return to London, however, he received a copy of *Bologna*. It had an English publisher's imprint. Its contents outraged him. They were itemized thus on the flyleaf:

1 Pantaloon (Vocal Quartet) 'In amando Christum Deum'
2 l'Été (Quartet) 'Sancta Mater'
3 Parlé [?] (Quartet) 'Quando Corpus'
4 Pastorale (Tenor Solo) 'Cujus Animam'
5 Mazurka (Baritone Solo) 'Pro Peccata'
6 Finale (Chorus) 'Stabat Mater Dolorosa'

To the credit of the publishers, continued Ella, on being apprised of the source of this precious example of critical blasphemy, they had the plates destroyed. 'But,' he added, 'I have in my possession two copies of *Bologna*. Nothing ever created so much scandal and ill-feeling against English musical taste as the rumour of our dancing to liturgical numbers.'

What value did Davison put on his music? We have one bit of evidence, or pseudo-evidence, in the shape of a letter that he wrote much later, in the early 1870s, to the French composer, Charles Gounod, who, as an émigré from the Franco-Prussian war, was living round the corner from Davison in Tavistock Place. In this letter Davison declares that he has 'suppressed' almost all his compositions. His orchestral works and chamber music existed no longer even in manuscript; he wouldn't know where to lay hands on a single one, whether symphony, overture or quartet. Of three sonatas he rather liked the first – yet hoped that not a copy survived. The two others, thank God, had never been engraved. Of such of his compositions as had been engraved, he had given the plates to his brother (W.D. Davison), who had had other compositions engraved on their backs that were even worse – this was saying a lot – than his own. Nothing was now left of his *oeuvre* save a few *chansonettes* (comic patter songs). These he did

not wish to repudiate. The letter ends with a doggerel which he
ascribes to an unnamed acquaintance:

> There was a J.W.D.
>   Who thought a composer to be.
> But his muse wouldn't budge
>   So he set up as judge
> Of better composers than he.

6   Twelve-year-old Master

During the mid-1840s, Davison, while keeping up his critical
trade, set up in business for a while as concert-promoter, often
appearing on his own platforms. Some of his concerts were at his
rooms in Berners Street, which must have been commodious, to
say the least, since he accommodated audiences of up to a
hundred. He called these Berners Street events *levées*. They started
soon after noon and, incredibly, went on until after five. At one of
them Davison played piano in a Mendelssohn violin sonata with
Prosper Sainton, an immigrant violinist and orchestral leader of
high repute. At others the darling Dolby sang his Shelley songs.
Now in her middle twenties, she did not marry till fifteen years
later. This same Prosper Sainton was her choice . . . At the
Princess Concert Rooms, off Oxford Street, before 'an immensely
crowded audience', that included Mendelssohn, Offenbach and a
boy called Joseph Joachim, she sang the Shelley songs again,
winning 'a great ovation and a unanimous encore'. Three fellow
critics from the *Daily News*, *Morning Herald* and *Morning Post*,
went into raptures. Davison barefacedly quoted them in the
Musical World of 15 June 1844. They found his Shelley songs in
particular 'works of genius', 'full of melancholy charm', 'wild and
fitful in character' and of 'impassioned quality'. It was in this same
never-to-be-forgotten number of the *Musical World* that Davison
trounced, damned and dismissed Schubert as overrated and
unschooled.

Now as to the child Joachim. He played the fiddle and was from Hungary. Between him and Davison a friendship sprang up that lasted till the year of Davison's death, a friendship roughly paralleled, as we shall see, by that of von Bülow, pianist and conductor, first husband of Cosima Liszt. As well as playing concertos and violin-piano duos and leading his own string quartet, Joseph Joachim composed to busy, if not immortal, purpose. Lists of his compositions survive in various reference books. Among them are orchestral overtures to *Hamlet* and *Henry IV*, after Shakespeare. He was clearly a man of versatile interests. Many photographs have come down to us. In his thirties he was clean-shaven, with forceful and very Slavonic brows and mouth. In his fifties he was engulfed by one of those obligatory Victorian beards. In his sixties the beard was elegantly fringed with white.

He first came Davison's way at a Philharmonic conducted by Mendelssohn in May, 1844, one month and one day before his thirteenth birthday. Musical prodigies were supposed to be banned from Philharmonic solemnities. The rule against their admission to Philharmonic programmes was unambiguous. Mendelssohn laughed. When further challenged, apparently, he gave a guarantee that in young Joachim's case juvenility was 'an accident'. At twelve, it seems, the boy already commanded uncanny maturity. In this Davison was heart (as usual) and soul with Mendelssohn.

There was no maturity about young Joseph's appearance, of course. He came on to the platform for the Philharmonic rehearsal in a short jacket and turned-down collar, as distinct from 'stand-up' with stock. One jacket pocket was 'unbearably full'. What was in it? Chocolate lumps, bull's-eyes, treacle-toffees? In the audience sat a small, singular tribe: women organists who held posts in the City. One of them, Ann Mounsey (she presided over the organ at St Vedast's for nearly half a century) stared obsessively, concluding that Joseph was still boy enough to over-indulge his sweet tooth. While conducting, she noted, Mendelssohn repeatedly turned to the young soloist with a bright smile of pleasure, following his tempi dutifully. She adds: 'Mendelssohn's own subordinate position seemed to give him a degree of amusement. But it was very beautiful to see the pleasure it gave him to regard the boy at his side not only with admiration but with honour.'

It is Davison who brings us back to the evening's serious business, Ludwig van Beethoven. His *Musical World* critique says that Joachim's reading of the Beethoven concerto

> was astonishing . . . not only as coming from a comparative child but as a violin performance, no matter from whom proceeding . . . Young Joachim attacked it with the vigour and determination of the most accomplished artist. No master could have read it better; no finished artist could have better rendered it. Tone, execution and reading were alike admirable – and the two cadences introduced by the young player were not only tremendous executive feats but ingeniously composed . . . consisting wholly of excellent and musician-like phrases and passages from the concerto.

After the performance there was prolonged and rapturous applause. Young Joseph's success was complete and triumphant. Since the year was 1844, nobody seems to have harrumphed or made other dissentient noises over the intrusive cadences, as Davison spelled 'cadenza' after the dying fashion of his day, or even to have inquired from whose hand they came. These intrusions for solo violin were regarded by all as a justifiable, nay, learned and gracious adornment of Beethoven's soaring though profound score. If anything of the sort were revived in our own time, our purist critics would suffer spasms of apoplectic rage. Suffice it that in 1844 cadences were enough to show off young Joachim's uncanny brilliance.

Later on he never breached taste. During that first visit, however, he was capable of unseemly straying. At his London début two months earlier he had performed – or perhaps one should say committed – on the Drury Lane stage, between the first and second acts of *The Bohemian Girl*, Ernst's Grand Variations on a Theme from Rossini's *Otello*. The occasion was a 'benefit' night for Alfred Bunn, the theatre's manager.

During that first London visit, the 'wonderful little Joachim', the 'marvellous little Joachim' (these phrases pepper all the *Musical World* accounts) played in chamber music and as soloist (in the latter capacity committing one more adored indiscretion, a rondo 'Russe', sunk without trace, by the forgotten Beriot) at five concerts before crammed, fashionable gatherings in stylish halls and theatres. Particularly striking was the last concert but one, which again brought Mendelssohn and Joachim together.

This was advertised, what is more, as one of Messrs Macfarren's and Davison's Concerts of Chamber Music. Instead of writing an account off his own bat, Davison, prudently tactful for once, reprinted the critique of the *Musical Herald*, from which I take salient phrases:

> The Princess's Concert Room was crowded . . . Every seat occupied . . . London's most eminent musicians and dilettantes were there . . . Altogether it might have been a Philharmonic night, no less . . . With the composer at the piano, little Joachim led Mendelssohn's trio in D minor . . . A spirited, fresh, brilliant performance, unapproachable by any other artists . . . Then the Mendelssohn string quartet in D op. 44, this again superbly led by the little Joachim . . . The more frequently this gifted lad plays the more extraordinary does he appear. Boy as he is, it does not seem that he has more to learn . . . He has all the energy, feeling and judgement of the matured musician . . .

Then came the goodbye. The *Musical World* of 20 June tells how, seven days earlier, this most startling of prodigies had sailed for Hamburg on his way to Leipzig for lessons with a contrapuntist, one Hauptmann. He had been having lessons with Macfarren. 'Does he better himself,' the note continued, 'by leaving Macfarren? . . . Little Joseph's departure will cause many a heart pang. He is as much loved for his amiability as for his most wonderful talent. He has had no reason, we hope, to feel discontented with his reception in England.'

Things were going so swimmingly for Davison that he was bound to come a cropper. In July 1846 the *Musical World* advertised a series of 'Grand Concerts' under its own auspices in London's principal concert hall, the Hanover Square Rooms, with Julius Benedict (already eminent) as conductor and an imposing string of solo artists (fourteen in all, including yet again Dolby and pianist Davison) at an admission charge of 7/- or 10s/6d for reserved seats. As well as the usual Davison and Macfarren pieces, music by Bach, Mozart and Beethoven was proffered. The first concert of the series pulled in 1,200. It looked as though the

Musical World and Davison were on to a good thing. What of their outgoings? Can it be that the string of solo artists had been induced to perform gratis or for a nominal fee?

We are invited to this conclusion by Henry Fothergill Chorley, music editor of the *Athenaeum* weekly, a dandified eccentric who heard every musical note half a tone sharp, a thing that seems to have worried him needlessly. He and Davison became notorious enemies. The *Musical World* grand concert, so called, sparked off their first conflict. That concert had done grave injury to music, wrote Chorley. He continued:

> When the editor of a critical periodical, to render his journal attractive, lays himself under heavy pecuniary obligation to those whom he criticizes – as is the case before us – what chance is there of his duty to Art being performed without fear or favour? What prospect have his readers of getting at the truth with regard to any musicians likely to offer or withhold a contribution to the programme?

Davison's retort (*Musical World* 18 July 1846) combined impudence with bluster. 'No-one,' he wrote, 'reads the musical articles in the *Athenaeum*. I never conversed with any regular reader of it who was aware until we informed him that the *Athenaeum* printed musical articles . . .'As to Chorley's reproaches, it was not to be overlooked that he himself,

> a man of SUPERHUMAN VIRTUE . . . would have been proud to consider the same assistance accorded to us by artists whose names adorned our programme as a matter of personal regard – for with the majority of them we are . . . on terms of the most friendly intimacy. Let the *Athenaeum* project a concert on the same scale: and what a failure it would end in!

In 1846 Felix Mendelssohn-Bartholdy paid his ninth visit to England, in 1847 his tenth and last. On each occasion he rehearsed and conducted his new oratorio *Elijah*, before which musical England fell on its face ecstatically – as, all things considered, it had much reason to. The 1847 visit in particular entailed for Mendelssohn exacting labour. He conducted five daylong rehearsals and, within a fortnight, six public performances in Birmingham (which had staged the 1846 première), Manchester and London. In the *Musical World* Davison spread himself elatedly, reprinting his *Times* number-by-number analysis and paean. His original piece ran to 3,500 words. From this *The Times* cut roughly 1,500 words. Back into the *Musical World* went the rejected 1,500. One key sentence may be quoted from Davison's raves of or about this time:

> Let me state my firm conviction . . . that Mendelssohn is nothing inferior to any of the most distinguished men that have influenced the progress of the [musical] art and that his name, placed by the side of Bach, Handel, Haydn, Mozart and Beethoven – the hitherto Unapproachable Five – will shine as bright and endure as long as any of them.

This was Mendelssohn's most exalted hour. Yet he was a stricken, smitten man. It was his *Elijah* labours – aggravated by a swarm of chamber music assignments and private organ-playing for Queen Victoria and Prince Albert at the Palace – that ended him. That face which H.F. Chorley had exclaimed over as one of most beautiful ever seen – 'No portrait could do it justice' – was now hollowed and careworn; the 'lustrous, unfathomable eyes' (poet Bayard Taylor's phrase) were dulled, yet sometimes they wrinkled with irritation and petulance. He had become sensitive, unstable, agitated by the most trifling circumstances. The wavy black hair was thinned, with touches of grey and partial baldness. He was but thirty-eight. Yet he still had a mind for practicalities. Nobody was suffered to sort out the *Elijah* band parts into their order of distribution on the players' stands. He did it all himself, under the side windows of the Hanover Square Rooms. He stooped. He shambled. He was inattentive to his clothes. Conducting an Exeter Hall (London) *Elijah* he showed an enormous hole under his armpit every time he lifted the baton high. Yet his thoughts were often of others, not of himself. Davison travelled back in the train with him after a Birmingham *Elijah*. Mendelssohn's talk was much of Sterndale Bennett. 'Ah!' he said, 'Bennett ought to come out with some big work and say: "Here I am! I am Bennett!" For he is so gifted.' Early in May he journeyed home. Friends begged him to stay a little longer. 'I

fear,' he replied, 'that I have stayed too long. One more week of
this unremitting toil and I should have been killed outright.' He
had but six months to live.

7   Shock, Agony, Babble

As much, perhaps, because he loved the French language as for
any professional obligation, Davison dearly relished a week or
two, better still a month or two, in Paris. He made fast friends
there. One of them was a fellow music critic – A.P. Fiorentino, of
Italian stock way back, who did a weekly *feuilleton*, some 3,000
words long, covering opera and opera singers mainly, in a stylish,
four-page literary-cum-political sheet, *Le Constitutionnel* – well-
funded work, since Fiorentino was scruple-free. Any singer,
fiddler or pianist about whom he was to write would call upon
him ritualistically, not forgetting to leave 'something on the
mantelpiece'. About this 'something', Joseph Bennett tells us,
Fiorentino was exacting. If it failed his expectations, the singer (if
it happened to be a singer) would probably read in the
Constitutionnel that, while he had sung with his usual ability, there
were signs that his memory wasn't what it once was. Fiorentino
used to ask Davison why he didn't follow the same tack. 'I shall
die rich,' he would say, 'and you will die poor. What better are
you for your poverty?' Later, Davison and another were to be
accused – and cleared of – like corrupt practices.

Sharp critical practice doesn't seem to have taken the edge off
Davison's liking for Fiorentino. In the midsummer of 1847 he
received from him a hospitable note. Addressing him as *esprit de
l'enfer*, he invited him to Paris, bidding him come quickly,
quickly, as he was yearning to grasp him by the hand. Davison
promptly made the journey – which then took three days – and
busied himself among other things with the doings of a Miss
Birch, who seems to have been the soprano equivalent of
Charlotte Dolby, on Paris platforms and stages. Hell Sprite duly
shook hands with Bribe-Master. They had rollicking times
together. Then came a shattering blow. Fiorentino narrated it in

the *Constitutionnel* of Sunday 14 November. It read thus:

I do not remember where we were the other evening. One half of the party was musing, the other half smoking. We had exhausted all possible subjects of conversation, and, not knowing what more to say, we had recourse to music. Our interlocutor, Davison, one of the most accomplished critics of the English press, exercised his biting irony and inexhaustible wit against our modern composers, whose art, he said, consisted either of fracas and orchestral noises, or of puerile and gross imitations.

'Ah!' he cried with rising exaltation, 'you alone, you who are grand in thought, grand in style, grand in the boldness of your conceptions, in your large and powerful execution, yes, the most rich, the most varied, the most erudite genius of erudite Germany – when shall I see you again, enfold you in my arms and declare once more all my admiration, all my enthusiasm – my friend, my brother – Mendelssohn!'

Suddenly his looks, drawn as it were by some magnetic influence to a journal that lay half open on the table, read these terrible words:

FELIX MENDELSSOHN–BARTHOLDY IS DEAD

It is impossible to describe the cry of agony that escaped him. He rose – and fell immediately. His eyes were filled with tears, his face was ashen pale, his lips trembled, and during three hours he was attacked by successive convulsive fits, broken only by heartrending sobs and unconnected phrases, until he was brought to the verge of delirium and fever. Would that I could recount to you with the same familiar ease, the same impetuosity, all the charming traits, all the noble actions, all those details so touching and simple in the life of Mendelssohn such as I heard them one by one from the lips of my distracted friend.

Gradually his grief subsided. He was given the salient facts. After recurrent heart attacks Mendelssohn had died on 4 November. He had no wish to go on living. The stroke that killed his sister Fanny five months earlier had robbed him of all life incentive.

Davison found succour in his pen, mailing thousands of words to the *Musical World*, which came out with mourning borders, memorial verse, projects (which came to nothing) for a Mendelssohn statue in Hanover Square – a statue of 'that great and good man whose death, a lamentable catastrophe, has plunged intellectual Europe into despair. Mendelssohn dead! Let music put on a suit of mourning, let the sons and daughters of Music weep. The lute on which the breath of Heaven was wont to play is silent – its strings are snapped asunder – its harmony is melted into air – Eternity has drunk it up. Echo will pine away for the loss of its most loved companion. Alone upon his shoulders, Atlas-like, he had sustained the burden of high art.'

Where to find the new Atlas? Here Davison drops into fatuity. Three names come to him, no more. Spohr? His had been a noble mission. That mission was now fulfilled. Sterndale Bennett? He had ceased to write, alas. Most of his time was taken up by teaching at the Royal Academy of Music, where he was to become Principal. As for Macfarren, unable to prosper in his homeland, he had gone to seek his livelihood in the United States: which, apparently, disposed of him for good.

Thus, in the end, Davison reverted to occlusion and banality. This should not, however, deter us from saluting the deep emotional resonance of his memorial prose to Mendelssohn. This has almost the ring of greatness.

8   Chopin Blackballed

Never in any branch of criticism since the art won toleration has there been a face-about to compare with Davison's on the subject of Chopin and his *oeuvre*. In the autumn of 1841, writing in the *Musical World*, he had dismissed Chopin as 'an enthusiastic schoolboy', 'a maker of sickly melodies', 'a morbidly sentimental flea'. Less than two years later came an astounding volte-face, the anonymous *Essay on the Works of Frederic Chopin*, a lavish hymn of praise, sheer tub-thumping hyperbole that went on for 10,000 words. The morbidly sentimental flea has become 'an illustrious example of pure, unwordly genius'. At the end, exploding into capital letters, Davison exalts him as 'THE MOST ACCOMPLISHED PIANOFORTE COMPOSER THAT EVER EXISTED'. In the official biography, Henry Davison affects to laugh off this blatant self-contradiction, contending that his father chose to shroud his true opinion in a 'satirically humorous surge of words'.

What was Davison's motive for the Chopin *lie*? Henry Davison offers no clue. The answer is simple. He was moved by *interest*. The *Essay* was printed by his patron Wessel, publisher of Davison's own compositions or 'arrangements' – the latter including, believe it or not, three sets of Chopin mazurkas, four of the nocturnes and four *grandes valses*, all listed in the *Essay* with opus numbers. In what way Chopin's piano music may have been considered to need 'arrangement' by Davison is not explained. It was enough for Davison that he had his name alongside Chopin's in the *Essay* and in Wessel's advertisements. In a letter to the magazine the *Orchestra* getting on for a quarter-century later, John Ella recalled the *Essay* (long known among Chopinites, because of its covers, as *The Yellow Book*) as 'an abusive, insincere piece of writing that contradicted its author's convictions and contained much that had better never seen the light'. (Excerpts from *An Essay* are printed in the second part of this book, following Davison's Chopin denunciation of 1841.)

Davison was twice in Chopin's presence. The first time was during his 1847 visit to Paris. He then caught the merest glimpse. He was with a companion in the crowded and joyous Boulevard des Italiens on All Souls' night, the most animated and brilliant spectacle (he later wrote) that he had ever seen: 'an anthill, a beehive aswarm with careless, happy multitudes bent on pleasures and joys . . .' But suddenly a thin, pallid figure crossed his path, wan and worn, frail and stooping, with melancholy smile and step as silent as a ghost's, unobserved and unobserving, a living phantom. 'There,' said his companion, 'goes Frederic Chopin.' The marks of tuberculosis and death were upon him.

His second sighting of Chopin happened in the spring of 1848. Chopin, never a rich man, came to England for money's sake, giving recitals at twenty guineas a time for dowagers and duchesses in their Park Lane and Eaton Square mansions. Daniel, his valet, curled his hair and generally dandified him every

morning. When they reached the great houses Daniel would carry
him like a babe up staircases that his lungs and legs could no
longer cope with.

As well as giving recitals, Chopin gave the dowagers' and
duchesses' daughters piano lessons, charging a guinea a go. One
pupil took nine lessons, then disappeared into the country without
paying a penny. Davison's version of these transactions is that
Chopin picked and chose; he had to be 'induced' to give lessons –
and gave but few. Always his fees were high. In a biographical
note he added: 'Happy the lady of rank who could count on a few
lessons from Chopin, idol of drawing rooms and boudoirs, alone
and uninterrupted.' In one way or another Chopin earned about
£300 in three months, enough to keep his head above water. At
the keyboard he knew respite. He would walk to the piano feebly,
'like a half-opened penknife'. Once there, strength and prowess
came back on brief, wondrous lease. He played in the drawing
rooms of the Duchess of Sutherland, Lord Falmouth, Lady
Rothschild, Mrs Sartorius (formerly the actress Mrs Kemble) and
others, his repertory including the ballade in A flat, the B minor
scherzo, the andante spianato, the nocturne in E major, the
berceuse and groups of études, mazurkas and waltzes.

Picking on the two recitals for Mrs Sartorius, Davison declared
gratuitously that he had been at neither – 'and therefore have
nothing to say on the subject'. (For some reason he added *Vivat
Regina!* – perhaps a snide reference to Victoria's amiability when
Chopin was presented to her.) Here we have another barefaced
fib. It was exposed as such nearly sixty years later by Walter
Macfarren (composer, conductor, pianist, like his brother George
Alexander) whose memoirs (which came out in 1906) say that,
having heard Chopin at the Broadwoods' place, he had the
unimaginable felicity of hearing him again at the Sartoriuses' – in
Davison's company.

Davison's contempt for Chopin is further proved by his *Times*
taboo. *The Times* carried not a line or word about Chopin's 1849
recitals, events that people will want to go on reading about as
long as reading and music persist. But, as to music, *The Times*
didn't give a fig for future or, when it came to Chopin, current
affairs. With Davison's blackballing of Chopin it was in tranquil
accord. The official *History of The Times* for the period 1841–84,
which came out in 1939, mentions that the Chopin concerts were

in private houses. It adds bluffly: 'It is no part of a critic's duty to attend society functions in the pursuit of musical genius.' To which an apt reply would be that it is the critic's duty to pursue musical genius wherever it alights for the delight, solace and wonder of mankind. If Chopin had chosen to play in an igloo, a coalface canteen or in a corner of Farmer Murrain's barn, the critic's duty would have been to be *there*, all ears, mind and marvel, ready to rush out at the end and catch the edition with his quickest and choicest prose.

The finger of death was on Chopin, plain for all to see. Davison felt no compassion – not a pennorth, apparently. His thoughts were still centred on the great god Mendelssohn. It came to his ears that eminent musicians living in Paris had sent to Mendelssohn's widow a memorial of sympathy. Owing to some misunderstanding they had sought Chopin's signature. Chopin reluctantly declined on grounds of protocol: 'Coming as it does from Germans who are speaking for all German artists living in Paris, how can you expect me, a Pole, to sign it?' In a private note he spoke of 'poor Mendelssohn's widow'. Clearly, he did not exclude himself from the memorial through coldness, indifference or professional rancour. Davison put it down to thickheaded chauvinism. Insolently describing Chopin as a piano player who, he believed, had written some dance tunes and mazurkas, he couldn't for the life of him see why Chopin declined to co-sign anything that Germans signed, since they were clever at composing exactly the same sort of trivialities as he.

Mendelssohn never, he was happy to say, wrote mazurkas or waltzes. In the *Musical World* he continued:

I have been reproached by some persons for the *bitterness* which dictated my observations last week apropos M. Chopin and the late Felix Mendelssohn-Bartholdy. The reproach is unjust; no bitterness gave birth to those remarks but respect to the departed master in whose single person was concentrated the essence of all music and whose death is as though from now to a century forward were to be a blank in the progress of the art. The musician who fails in respect where respect is so magnificently due – nay, I will go further; the musician who does not merely respect but revere, worship, idolize the name of Mendelssohn – I do not, I *cannot* consider a worthy follower of his art, and, therefore, owing him no respect I pay him none . . . If not to admire the music of M. Chopin be proof of a bitter spirit, let me for ever be called 'bitter'. I like it not, nor can I like it . . . If to think that M. Chopin forgets himself in not readily paying homage to Mendelssohn – who, in comparison to the Polish pianist, is as the sun to a spark flickering in a tinder box – entitles me to the charge of bitterness, once more I am content to be styled bitter and, strong in faith, exult in my bitterness.

Towards the end of 1848 Chopin was back in Paris. Less than a year later he died. Davison went to Paris for the obsequies. He writes of the black hangings emblazoned in silver with the initials 'F.C.' which draped the porch of the Church of the Madeleine and the catafalque before the altar. The Madeleine is roomy and it was crammed to the doors. Yet, in the *Musical World* (10 November 1949) Davison persisted that Chopin was neither a popular name nor a popular talent. 'Time will show,' he went on, 'whether his high reputation as a composer was wholly or partially merited, or whether his genius and influence have been greatly overrated . . . Chopin, by some means or other, was able to acquire the name of a musician at once profound and inventive.'

Once, at least, Davison paltered and reluctantly praised. In 1860 Boosey and Sons brought out a Davison edition of the Chopin mazurkas – including those very mazurkas which, a generation earlier, he had so brutally lambasted. Some, he wrote in his preface, were gems as faultless as they were attractive . . . '[not] one of them is wholly destitute of points that appeal to the feelings, surprise by their unexpectedness, fascinate by their plaintive character or charm by their ingenuity'.

Again one cannot but wonder whether these compliments may not have been dictated by interest. In old age Davison reverted to his 1841 line. Current attempts, he insisted, to magnify Chopin, a sentimental drawing room composer, into a colossus were absurd and nauseous.

Written in December 1876, this was Davison's last word on Chopin.

9   Berlioz Bullied

Soon after joining *The Times* in 1846, Davison covered one of the
century's most lustrous and unforgettable musical occasions: the
first performance of Berlioz's 'dramatic legend', as it has been
styled, *La Damnation de Faust*, at the Opéra Comique, Paris. His
notice appeared on 23 December at the foot of a column, with
'Musical Intelligence' as its highly debatable introductory phrase.
In it Davison narrates among other irrelevancies Meyerbeer's
tinkerings with his latest opera, the rumoured marriage of Liszt to
a Hungarian peasant girl and a torchlit serenade to the singer Jenny
Lind by students in Heidelberg. *Faust* he heartily slammed and
damned, finding it lengthy, tedious and incoherent, with scarcely
any melody and, whatever the phrase may conceivably mean, no
decided rhythm, a work depending for its effect on massive
orchestral combinations and a vast chorus. His *Musical World* piece
(26 December) expands these misjudgements and embroiders
them brutally. *Faust*, he concludes, is a tissue of monstrous
absurdities and impotent ravings.

All this was written in December 1846. During the ensuing year
an astounding thing happened. Berlioz and Davison became
friends. It is to be assumed that Berlioz did not come upon
Davison's anti-*Faust* scrawls and that they were kept out of his
way. They were, in any case, anonymous. Davison went so far as
to assert that, on reaching Paris in September 1847, getting on for
a year after the *Faust* première, he had never set foot in the city
before, the implication being that of *Faust* he hadn't heard a note.

No sooner was the friendship sealed than Berlioz shot off to
London, travelling alone, to conduct a Gluck-Mozart-Donizetti
season under Louis Antoine Jullien's auspices at the Theatre
Royal, Drury Lane and concerts of his own and other music at the
Hanover Square Rooms and another long-vanished venue, Exeter
Hall. Berlioz's mistress, Marie Recio (his second wife-to-be),
joined him a month later. It was Davison who escorted her to
London. A fragment of commonplace book survives among

Davison's papers. The date is 6 December. It vividly tells of their journey. Arriving at Boulogne in the evening, Davison dined on ham and brandy, rose at 7.15 a.m. and met Marie in dreadful rainy weather. The steamboat journey took seven hours, both being fearfully seasick; then three hours by primitive railway to London, where Berlioz met and whipped them off in a cab to the Drury Lane theatre where there were mobs of musicians and busybodies to shake hands with.

Jullien, the man who had invited him over, promising six months' conducting work per season for six seasons, was a highly improbable person, French like himself, a conductor, too (of sorts), ringleted, scented, braided, frizzed, frogged, patent-leathered and so fetchingly moustached that the moustache looked as though it had been stuck on. In the Surrey Gardens and other public spaces, he would conduct a band of 400 in British Army quadrilles, the 400 being supplemented by four Guards bands who marched in successively, playing among other things 'God Save the Queen' with cannon shots marking each bar. Sometimes he rose above his 'dance-concerts' to higher things. From a conductor's desk sustained by a gilded seraph, he would direct odd movements from Beethoven, Mozart and Mendelssohn, using a jewelled baton which had been ceremoniously carried to him, by a menial wearing white kid gloves, on a silver salver. Occasionally there would be a poetic touch. Rehearsing the fifth piano concerto of Beethoven, he halted the orchestra at a certain point in the andante and asked for more delicate tone, saying 'Hush, hush, gentlemen – angels are coming down!'

At times the poetic touch turned freakish. Jullien had an estate in Belgium. Davison was once a guest there. Walking one day in the grounds, Jullien talked obsessively of 'the deep, underlying tonic note of the universe'. Darting to a tree, he clapped his ear to its bole, then beckoned Davison, telling him to come and bear witness to the universe's pedal-point.

One is not surprised to hear that he ended his days in a lunatic asylum. In 1848 he got no further than the debtors' prison. It turned out that he had launched the Drury Lane season without funds or credit. By March the season had disintegrated. 'Once I am at the end of my resources,' wrote Berlioz from his Harley Street lodging, 'there will be nothing for me to do but sit in the gutter and die of hunger like a stray dog – or blow my brains out.'

Under Jullien's auspices, at the end of January, there had, however, been a concert, including *Faust* excerpts, which in Berlioz's phrase, 'went off like a train of gunpowder'. To his friend Auguste Morel he wrote: 'Davison did an article about it for *The Times* which, for want of space, was cut by half. But I don't know what he really thinks. With opinions like his one must be prepared for anything.' With Davison himself, Berlioz was more circumspect, however. There is a letter of this time which tells how, at the Exeter Hall an evening or two earlier he had searched for Davison 'as for a diamond in the sand'. The occasion was a performance of Mendelssohn's *Italian* symphony. About this he adds a note that must have rejoiced the recipient (Davison's) heart: 'I want to assure you of what you are already aware, that this symphony is a masterpiece, struck as gold medals are struck, all of a piece, at a single *coup*.' The letter's main purpose had to do with the Jullien fiasco and the threat of poverty. Would Davison be so kind as to ask the editor of *The Times* whether he would consider printing in his paper hitherto unpublished articles (intended for his distinguished *Journal des Débats* series), done into English by Davison himself? Nothing came of this.

Berlioz conducted one other concert, this time at the Hanover Square Rooms – the *Faust* excerpts again, preceded by the *Roman Carnival* overture and the *Harold in Italy* viola concerto; also, be it noted, two movements from a Mendelssohn piano concerto. Davison's advance and after-the-event account have the rapt publicity ring of a much later age. Never were there such butterings up. Berlioz's works (he wrote) were of the highest order, without precedent anywhere, their originality such as to mark their author as one of the most remarkable men in music's history . . . 'Overpowering vigour and excitement . . . magnificent . . . sublime . . . poetic . . . daring . . . And the man's manners, both on the platform and off! These were as winning and gentlemanly as his talents were remarkable.' There was never a phrase, however, to convey that any single work by Berlioz had truly possessed him, charging his soul with quintessential visions and dreams.

This is tolerably clear from his obituary article (*Musical World*, 13 March 1869). In this he relishes Berlioz's prose, praising him as 'a great musical thinker'. But was he a great composer? Davison dodges the issue barefacedly: 'Now is not the time to criticize

Berlioz as a composer . . . Apart from his music, to know the man
was to love him . . . Good, right-hearted to the core, eminently
sincere . . . Berlioz, whatever views may be entertained about his
music, was truly wonderful . . . Those who may have conscientiously objected to his general notions of music . . . could not do
other than respect him.' The truth is, in short, that in 1869, as in
1846, Davison considered Berlioz's music worthy of and destined
for the dustbin but contrived – or at least tried – to convey the
point elegiacally.

After 1848 Berlioz paid four more visits to London. Of these
two only need detain us here: that of May-June 1853, when he
conducted his opera *Benvenuto Cellini* at Covent Garden, and his
concerts with the New Philharmonic Society in the summer of
1855, his programmes then including *Romeo* fragments and, once
more, *Harold in Italy*.

The *Cellini* night (25 June) was one of the most disastrous,
perhaps *the* most disastrous, in operatic annals. Every number was
booed, hissed and catcalled even before the singers had opened
their mouths, by groups that appeared to have been placed
strategically in all parts of the house. Many had brought whistles,
doorkeys and 'other instruments of sibillation', as Davison
described them. The sibillations were especially wounding. At the
conductor's rostrum Berlioz must have suffered agonies. After the
calamitous final curtain there was to have been a supper-party
backstage for the composer, singers and friends. Shrugging off his
distress, Berlioz appeared punctually. So did Davison. The singers
stayed away 'out of needless embarrassment', as Jacques Barzun
puts it. The two friends, swallowing their emotions, stayed on,
sitting at the head of an otherwise empty banqueting table and
seem, in spite of all, to have enjoyed each other's company.

Davison put down the anti-*Cellini* terror to an Italian cabal.
Writing in the following issue of the *Musical World* he ascribed this
to Italian impotence and jealousy: 'There is not an Italian
composer of genius living and writing today. None of Verdi's
operas succeeds in this country . . . Italians tremble for their
supremacy after long reigning and monopolizing. There are,' he
continued, modulating into the farcical vein, 'at least 500 Italian
composers in and about London with one, or two, three or more
operas in their portfolios – say 2,000 operas in manuscript.' For
once Davison was swimming against the stream in a noble cause.

In the end, his native ineptitude triumphed. A month earlier *Rigoletto* had had its Covent Garden première, an opera, opined Davison, that could not live: 'It may flicker and flare for a few nights . . . but it will go out like an ill-wicked rushlight, leaving not a spark behind. That is our prophecy for *Rigoletto*' – a work that has persistently and perversely gone on being sung ever since at all the world's key opera houses, Covent Garden included.

10   A Friendship Foxed

I come now to the summer of 1855 and Berlioz's concerts with the New Philharmonic Society (see above). London had also an *old* Philharmonic Society, more illustrious and lush than the new one. For its 1855 season the old society had taken unto its bosom a fellow firebrand of Berlioz, Richard Wagner. In the eyes of right-minded, wrong-headed and comfortably off concert-goers, Wagner and Berlioz were commonly conjoined as musical maniacs. Curiosity got the upper hand, however. People imperiously wanted to see, watch and, perhaps, listen. Both lots of concerts, New Philharmonic and Old Philharmonic alike, went well, with cordial, nay, thunderous applause at the end.

Meantime, during Prosper Sainton's supper-party, at his house off Manchester Square, Sainton had the two geniuses at table as sole guests. Hitherto they had seen little of each other. Now, face to face, each saw in the other a brother soul. They talked eagerly, mutually echoing and supplementing, plumbing their joys and bitternesses, their soarings and sorrows. The talk went on for five hours. On parting they embraced as comrades, with a warmth of understanding rarely given to genius encountering genius. Soon afterwards there was another meeting, this time at Wagner's lodging in Portland Terrace, north of Regent's Park, where a carpenter had built him a tall work-desk at which, with quantities of multi-staved music paper before him, Wagner was getting on, in his spare time, with the third act of *The Valkyrie*. That night others were there, Sainton among them. Marie (now Madame

Berlioz) reclined elegantly on a sofa. Champagne-punch stoked lively conversation. The party did not break up until three the following morning. Again there were protestations of undying friendship between Berlioz and Wagner, the latter stressing his devotion with stampings; he had tears in his eyes.

Davison may have known of the rapprochement, or sensed or surmised it. At that time he loathed Wagner's music to a point not far from insanity. The summer musical season was ending. Soon the two of them would be gone. Before they went the rapprochement must be stamped out for Berlioz's sake. Davison thought of a way. For the *Musical World* he had commissioned a translation of Wagner's essay *Oper und Drama* that was to run for months, often at two pages an issue. His motive was to let Wagner's own pen expose him as a laughing-stock for the *bien-pensants* and right-minded.

Serial publication of the essay had already begun. It contained much anti-Berlioz matter. Davison waited upon Hector and Marie with a pocketful of stabbing quotations. These he read aloud to the couple, roaring with laughter as he did so. In his essay Wagner analysed what he took to be the effect on Berlioz of Beethoven's ninth symphony. This sublime music inflicted giddiness upon him: 'A witchlike chaos danced in wild confusion before his eyes. In his dazzled condition he thought he perceived fleshy, tinted forms. These were phantoms toying with his fancy . . . a hobgoblin illusion from which he emerged (as one emerges from the stupefactions of opium) to an environment of frosty empti- ness.' And so to the climax: 'In the end Berlioz as an artist had to descend to mechanics. He had become a wonder-working, imaginative fanatic, obliterated by materialism, converted into an object of deep sympathy because, in the end, he lay buried beneath the wastes of his own orchestral machinery.'

One can readily imagine Davison throwing back his head for a final bellow of mirth at the ceiling. Much that Wagner had written supported Davison's own diagnosis of Berlioz's artistic failings. For the moment, however, his target was Wagner's tortuous, often woolly, thinking and prose. He was printing that prose in the *Musical World* not for trenchancy but for its news value. For one reason or another Wagner happened to be in everybody's mind, restless, loquacious, compelling.

During Davison's reading Hector seems to have remained

impassive, occasionally smiling. It is improbable that *Oper und Drama* was new to him. A French translation had been published a year or two earlier. One of Berlioz's biographers, Boschot, suggests nevertheless that Davison's performance brought about a certain coolness between them and that they never again knew the cordiality they experienced at Prosper Sainton's table. The episode is certainly significant as illustrating Davison's tendency to irresponsibility and mischief, of which examples will be adduced in a later chapter.

A year earlier Berlioz had paid Davison a high compliment, dedicating to him his newest overture, *Le Corsair*. Eight years later he mailed him from Paris a copy of his opera *Beatrice and Benedict* (after Shakespeare) and gave him the latest news about another 'opus' of his last phase, *The Trojans*. The letter to Davison that accompanied his gift says:

> I live like a man who may have to die at any moment, who no longer believes in anything and who acts as if he believed in everything. I am like a warship on fire, whose crew let things take their course. Oh, I do wish I could see you and open my heart to you! I was a long time getting to know you, and I now understand you. I like the stuff you are made of, both as artist and as man.

When Richard Wagner landed in England early that year for the 'old' Philharmonic Society's concerts, Davison was heard by Ferdinand Praeger to say: 'I have read some of Wagner's literary works. In his books he is a god. But so long as I hold the sceptre of music criticism, I'll not let him have any chance here.' Wagner was to conduct eight programmes including all the Beethoven symphonies except the first and second, a couple of symphonies by Mozart, Mendelssohn's *Italian* and *Scotch* symphonies, sundry overtures and concertos – and five Wagner items: the *Tannhäuser* overture plus excerpts from *Lohengrin*. Although overshadowed by Wagner's later music, these works of the early period (*Der Fliegende Holländer* as well) have stayed on in the repertory of all nations and the affection of millions down the decades. For Davison, they were patchy, puerile and poisonous – hideous and detestable into the bargain. Wagner was a worker of musical evil. How would such a one cope at the rostrum, baton in hand, with the music of the Elect? Let us pass in review Davison's notices in the *Musical World* from March to June 1855.

Never, if we are to believe his testimony, was there such a display of perversity and self-confident incompetence:

> This short, spare man, capacious of forehead, has the oddest way with the baton, beating up and down indiscriminately. So many quickenings and slackenings of tempo . . . Nothing like it was ever heard before . . . Beethoven's *Eroica* symphony all at sixes and sevens. It threatened to tumble to pieces . . . First movement of Beethoven's ninth? Higgledy-piggledy, untidy . . . Sometimes this man is less a conductor than a tormenter of the band. Did we ever hear such slips, messes, perversities in a single evening? Could we possibly hear anything worse? . . . Beethoven's B flat symphony? A catastrophe fatal to the renown of the orchestra was only just averted by the decision of the performers themselves . . . Mendelssohn's *Italian*? A more coarse, monotonous, uniformly loud and at the same time rigorously frigid performance never left an audience as un-moved and apathetic in any concert room. Wagner's reading of Mendelssohn's music may be signalised in a sentence – *Get to the end as quickly as possible* . . .
>
> Overture to *Euryanthe*? [Weber] Went off like a shell at Sebastopol – fizzed and screamed. Audience stared at each other aghast . . . Mozart's E flat symphony? This defied description. First allegro was drawled, not played. The andante had the most commonplace performance ever heard. The minuet unutterably dreary. Finale went off like a rocket, ending before we had reconciled ourselves to the beginning . . . Mozart's *Jupiter* symphony? A fantastic, old-maidish, sentimental read-ing, almost killed by Wagner's caresses. First allegro murdered outright, andante just ridiculous, the minuet slow as a funeral march. In the finale the orchestra took matters into its own hands and set all Wagner's tempo attempts at defiance . . . We venture to say [this after the last concert] that Wagner leaves London convicted of one of the profoundest failures on record . . . Another such set of eight concerts would go far to annihilate the [Philharmonic] Society.

11 Polycacophonous Wagner

Not until the following October did Davison see *Tannhäuser* on
the stage. This was in Cologne where, as he admits, the work
scored a considerable success, being much applauded by a full
house, presumably of musical dunderheads – certainly not,
according to Davison, of musicians. Musicians, he wrote, would
never tolerate *Tannhäuser*, a tuneless, polycacophonous carnival
from first to last, the orchestra in continual ferment, anything like
a plain vocal phrase being promptly obliterated by 'raging seas of
tone'. Never before had an opera orchestra made such a fuss to so
little purpose.

'*Tannhäuser*,' he continued, 'is three parts declamatory recitative
which, long before the end, becomes tedious beyond endurance . . . The chief tenor, soprano and bass are made to roar and
scream with scarcely an interval of repose . . . In listening we pity
both artists and audience, for, if on the one hand, the voice cracks,
the ear splits on the other. A few bars of Wagner's music are
enough to make us aware that he has never studied the elements of
music . . . Never was a cooler imposition upon the world than
Wagner's operas and the theories on which they are based.'

Wagner's letters from London have occasional references to
these or like ravings. In a detached way, Davison amused him. He
wrote to Minna:

Quite funny tales are told me of Davison. It is quite certain that
he has been bought by Meyerbeer [see below] to pull me down
and prevent my making my way here. I have been assured that
Davison was positively enraptured by the libretto [as distinct
from the music] of *Lohengrin*. A few days before he had told a
friend: 'The man who wrote this poem must be a very
demi-god.' Now, what is one to make of this? Praeger says it is
just like him; he can be quite transported by a thing one day and
tear it to pieces the next.

Notwithstanding tremendous tirades against his music in *The Times* and that 'sad rag' the *Musical World*, Davison had, he continued, left a *door open* [my italics].

> He has been waiting for me to take some kind of step to win him over . . . People assure me that it would have cost me nothing further than according him some kind of acknowledgement. The greater, naturally, has been his anger at my doing nothing of the kind. They tell me he is keeping the door open even yet, to change front as soon as I take 'the smallest notice of him'. But nobody, I hope, will expect that of me; it would be a poltroonery for which I could never forgive myself.

There is a touch of ambiguity here. For precisely what kind of acknowledgement was Davison keeping his door open? We get an answer in the *Musical World* of 22 September 1855. This quotes a letter from Wagner to some friend, written the day after his penultimate Philharmonic concert, which, according to Davison, found its way into a Dresden newspaper and a week or two later into a Berlin sheet. Neither newspaper is named by the *Musical World*. In this letter Wagner alleged outright that Davison and other London critics 'only proved by their attacks on me that I had omitted to bribe them. Indeed, it has always amused me to observe how they left the door open in order, upon the slightest approach by me, to change their tactics – a step which, of course, I never thought of taking.'
To which libellous surmises Davison replied with racy sarcasm:

> The most extraordinary thing is – taking into account an author's natural longing to have his works praised and his full knowledge of journalistic venality – that he should have omitted to bribe the music critics in the first place. Was there ever such folly and stupidity? We do not exactly know the price at which each individual critic can be bought – our own terms can be known from private inquiry at the printing office – but we have no doubt that a few thalers tendered out of hearing of the editor (*entre nous*, the editor sometimes goes 'snacks' with the critic) – would have made the writer place *Lohengrin* beside *Fidelio* and have rated *Tannhäuser* with *Don Giovanni*. Would that have satisfied Herr Wagner? Never was money more

foolishly kept in pocket! . . . The next time Herr Wagner comes
to London, we strongly recommend him to bring with him a
little money or a little better music. In the event of his becoming
an honest convert to the good old bribery system, he may be
induced to speculate on the virtue of a few thalers. Should the
critic refuse the money, as there's no knowing what these
obstinate and malignant dogs may do especially if they fancy
they have been cheated out of their lawful due, we advise him to
try a dose of real good music . . . Herr Richard Wagner may
even now buy them. We only fear he has got neither the music
nor the money.

Some twenty years later Wagner and Davison met briefly face
to face. On that occasion Davison was to stand on his head in a
manner of speaking, all sweetness and light.

12   Coup d'État

Weighing up Davison's merits and failings, the 1841–84 volume of
the official *History of the Times* admits that his misjudgements were
conspicuous and that his honesty was sometimes questioned. It
lays emphasis, however, on his excellence as a reporter, 'a quality
shared by few music critics, who in general are so anxious to
express their views that they neglect to make clear to the reader
exactly what it is they are writing about'.

Davison's supreme reporting feat for *The Times* hardly concerned music at all. Menace and musketry were the themes. In the
winter of 1851 they sent him to Paris, which may be termed his
holiday town, for *Le Château de la Barbe Bleue*, by a young nobody
called Limander at the Opéra Comique, and for two productions
at the Théâtre Italien – Verdi's fifth opera, *Ernani* (after Victor
Hugo) and *Don Giovanni*, with the admired Jeanne Sophie
Cruvelli as Elvira. This latter was sung on Tuesday 2 December,
the day on which Louis Napoleon, nephew of Napoleon
Bonaparte, sprang the *coup d'état* that raised him to the presidency

of the republic and ultimately to the throne of a recobbled empire.

For *The Times* he wrote off the cuff some two and a half
thousand words describing one minor, though engrossing, aspect
of this event. The article appeared in *The Times* of 6 December
and, 'since it will probably have some interest for musical readers',
the *Musical World* carried a four-page reprint of it one week later.
Although peppered with unnecessary bits of French, it is a striking
piece of work. In his official biography Henry Davison deals with
it but cursorily.

On Monday the first there had been few overt signs of the
troubles to come. For *Bluebeard's Castle* the Opéra Comique was
crowded to suffocation. 'All Paris was there,' we read, 'and the
feuilletonistes looked as grave and attentive as if they were to write
their critiques as usual and as though, if written, they were to be
printed and, of course, if printed, read.' Like many other routines,
the regular sequence of scribble and print was to be dislocated for a
while and given a brutal shake-up. With an eye prescient (as it
were) after the event, Davison noted in the audience two
politicians hostile to Louis Napoleon – M. Thiers and M.
Cavaignac, the former seated, strangely enough, alongside M. de
Morny, Minister of the Interior, the only minister persuaded by
Napoleon to affix his signature to mandatory decrees which,
already printing through the night on secret presses, were to hoof
out one administration and welcome another.

By the evening of the following day, with Louis Napoleon's
decrees pasted up all over the city, 'giant forebodings' (Davison's
phrase) had spread far and wide. At the two opera houses packed,
brilliant and ornately dressed audiences listened as attentively as
they could, fighting off, to the best of their ability, restless
curiosity and insidious fear. Interval bells rang. This time the
audience neglected the foyer. Their foyer this night was the
boulevard. Between acts they hurried out into the darkness and
cold to see and hear what was happening. What they saw was a
sullen crowd, the amorphous citizenry. What they heard were
monotonous cries of '*Vive la République*' from this group and that.
After watching and hearing, they returned to their seats and tried
to put the threatened crisis behind them. After all, it was supposed
to be Cruvelli's and Guasco's night, not to mention Mozart and
Verdi.

In the days that followed, days of chaos, cannonfire and

frowning soldiery, Davison took refuge in a café from time to time. Most newspapers had been suppressed. Customers consoled themselves with dominoes until the small hours. A right-wing sheet, *La Patrie*, printed copiously, however. Men were rowdily selling it in the streets. Some of them, comments Davison, were 'more obstreperous than usual'.

Stragglers returning from late reunions were ordered off the great thoroughfares and compelled by military pickets to take circuitous routes home. If anybody uttered a word of protest he was threatened with immediate arrest. There were pickets at the entry to every street and passageway. Comings and goings were watched, checked and, usually, redirected. Gloom began to settle on the faces of the mob, whose pro-Republican shouts and cries, hollow and at rarer intervals, assumed a tone of menace 'as though a storm were not far away'. Along the boulevards, shops and cafés, the Tortonis and the Maisons Dorées, put up their shutters; swarms of smaller places, too. 'Anything more desolate and blank than their appearance when deserted,' wrote Davison, 'can hardly be imagined.'

With a friend he ventured as far as the Boulevard du Temple. On the Tuesday there had been plenty of *blouses* and *ouvriers*, as Davison called the proletarians. Their numbers had, indeed, been vast. These 'ancient abettors of revolution' were now exceedingly thin on the ground. 'Scarcely one was observed. To some this brought confidence, to others fear. Those who feared thought, not without a show of reason, that the *blouses* and *ouvriers* must be gravely occupied elsewhere. This by no means improved the prospect of what was likely to happen on the morrow.'

They ran into a group flying from a newly closed café. They listened to a gabble of news. Two of 'the people' had been killed in an encounter with a military patrol. Their bodies had been carried about protestingly by the boldest among their comrades, who tried thus to excite public commotion and anger. Presently the two bodies were snatched by a military squad and despatched by ambulance to the nearest hospital. An attempt was made, under the direction of the Mountain (a left-wing political group) to erect a barricade in the rue Sainte Marguerite. It failed disastrously. Two more were killed here, both members of the Mountain.

13   Rondo for Muskets

Reporter Davison or, as a later age would have described him, Our Special Correspondent James W. Davison, continued with sharp eye and questing ear. The faces of the soldiers, worn and fatigued by short commons and want of sleep, grew more serious and anxious. *Carabiniers, cuirassiers* and *gardes* no longer put on a gay and showy pageant, glittering effigies in a gigantic puppet show. Now, he wrote, they meant business. They had become a threat and admonition to the crowd who, in the faces of the soldiery, whether mounted or on foot, found no sympathy and read no hope. The streets having been cleared by infantry pickets, the populace had no choice but to watch from the windows and balconies of their homes which, from bottom to top of building after building, were alive with observers trying to take in the inexplicable evolutions of military detachments that soon filled up every prospect from that point along the Boulevard des Italiens where Davison was posted. He continued:

> That something of consequence was about to be enacted was evident to every looker-on. Circulation, which had been partially allowed, was at length imperatively forbidden . . . The rapid passage to and fro of heavy artillery directed to unknown parts, the sound of distant cannon, which told an undeniable story, the *croquemorts*, as those are called whose business is to carry away the dead and wounded, the army surgeons in their regimental guise, incessant departure and return of the (military) *guides*, all at the gallop – these and other appearances no less suggestive were insufficient to drive the people into their houses. The windows and balconies continued to be busily occupied.
>
> At length, however, two or three successive motions of the hand by the general who was supervising the manoeuvres . . . gave warning that danger was at hand, and the greater number of the curious retired from the windows. Those on the *balcon* of

the Café du Cardinal failed to take the hint, and it was not till tremendous volleys of musketry made the boulevards ring again that they became aware of the peril to which they stood exposed and scrambled through the windows of the *premier étage*.

Those who have been to Paris will remember that the Café du Cardinal forms the *rez de chaussée*, or ground floor, of an enormous house, half of which faces the boulevard and the other half the rue de Richelieu. The remainder of the house, from the ground floor upwards, belongs to M. Brandus, the most extensive music publisher in Paris, who has recently leased the premises and constructed perhaps the largest and handsomest *magazin* of its kind in Europe. It was on the *balcon* which appertains to this *magazin* that I was stationed with seven or eight others, watching the evolutions of the troops, the magnitude and variety of which surprised everybody in a quarter of the boulevards from which, usually, little danger is anticipated in revolutionary times. To our astonishment and no small discomfort, our escape from the balcony of the music shop of M. Brandus had merely interposed the walls and windows between our persons and the threatened danger.

The fire was now immediately directed against the house in which we were. The smashing of windows immediately below speedily invited us to a move upstairs, where, it was imagined, we should be out of immediate peril. No such thing. Musket shots penetrated even the bedroom of M. Brandus. The consternation was as general as the cause of the aggression was incomprehensible. In the short time that everybody was doing his best to get out of the reach of shot, the screams of servants in the lower department of the house [one wonders why they had been unchivalrously left below] announced a fresh event, and the shouts of a hundred voices outside crying '*Ouvrez! Ouvrez!*' exposed the intention of the military to enter the building. No one daring to descend to obey this summons, the door was broken open, and a number of soldiers rushed upstairs and, demolishing every obstacle, searched each room in succession, until they reached the *quatrième étage* where M. Brandus and his friends had repaired for safety. There information was given that a shot had been fired from the house upon the troops and that the business of the invaders was to visit every apartment and examine the persons of all present.

The scrutiny proved unavailing, but the soldiers insisting on the fact of a shot having been fired, the whole party was arrested and taken before the general in command on the boulevard. One of them, luckily, happened to be M. Sax, the well-known inventor and manufacturer of the instruments that bear his name. Being recognized by the general, the protest of M. Sax was accepted and the party allowed to escape into the nearby Passage de l'Opéra – but not to re-enter the house. In that agreeable *locale* we were compelled to wait, penned up like beasts of burden until the military had evacuated the Boulevard des Italiens, when each was allowed to find his way home as well he might, amid bustle and confusion.

It afterwards appeared that the suspected shot was attributed to the house next door to that of M. Brandus and subsequently to the Café Anglais, which was subsequently almost de-molished. Whether on such a shallow pretext the house of a peaceful citizen ought to be destroyed, the lives of its occupants endangered and a heavy loss entailed upon the proprietor for repairs, I leave for those whom it concerns to answer. I speak as a looker-on, ignorant of the cause of so imposing and grandiose a display of military tactics, which will doubtless be explained to you by a more competent authority. The search for arms could surely have been effected without shattering the windows of a house *en fusillade*. How contemptible must the invaders have felt when they found nothing other in the whole building than a rusty *fusil*, unfit for use, which had served M. Brandus in 1848, when he officiated as one of the most zealous and active officers of the Garde Nationale and helped to maintain the peace and tranquillity of the capital.

There remained the little matter of getting back to London. In the hope of grabbing business, hotel keepers were saying that all railroads had suspended business. Davison did not believe a word of it. Leaving his luggage in his hired room he went on foot in search of a *cabriolet*. What he found was a *coupé* on the Boulevard des Capucines. The driver said, yes, for fifteen francs he would take him to the Gare du Nord, but, owing to traffic snags consequent on the *coup d'état* Davison had better fetch his luggage himself. This Davison did. At halts on the way to Calais he learned that the provinces were not, as expected, marching on Paris. Somewhere near St Denis two men had cut the electric telegraph wire. Both were instantly put to death . . .

London at last: muddy streets, swathes of smog. A month or two later Berlioz appeared. At the Exeter Hall he conducted many classics, among them Beethoven's *Choral* symphony; also movements from his dramatic symphony *Romeo and Juliet*, that wondrous distilment of beauty from sorrow and pain.

14   J.W.D. and Arabella

In the twenty years or so that followed Davison's sighings over Laura Honey and Charlotte Dolby he never seems to have squandered a thought on women. Such, at any rate, is the impression which the official biography gives, false though this may be. Then Arabella Goddard happened. In Henry Davison's book there is an unconvincing lithograph of Arabella at the age of four. She has pensive eyes, cherub's lips and a sleek cap of hair ending in ringlets on the nape . . .

At that time she was already a prodigy pianist. At four and a half, in St Servan, near St Malo, Brittany, where her parents lived, she played somebody's fantasia on tunes from *Don Giovanni* at a charity concert. Her parents were English. At seven she is said to have played before Chopin and George Sand in Paris, at eight before Queen Victoria and Prince Albert. In a fashionable sense, these sessions 'made' her for life.

Fleeing before the 1848 Revolution, the Goddard family settled in England. There Arabella resumed her career, surviving a couple of bumps early on that might have deterred a less resolute spirit for good. A few weeks before her thirteenth birthday, with five other soloists, all much older than she, Arabella started out on a concert tour managed by a retired army captain that was planned to take in the entire British Isles but got no further than the Home Counties, ending in disaster. Typical was Brighton. Here two concerts had been fixed for the same day. The afternoon concert drew seventeen persons, the evening concert thirty-five.

Two years later Arabella ran into misadventure of a more personal sort. At a recital in the Hanover Square Rooms, she broached a technically challenging Mendelssohn piece, the fourth *Morceau Charactéristique*. When two-thirds of the way through she stopped and put a troubled finger to her brow. Her memory had failed her. The audience cheered vociferously, as audiences will in such situations. She signalled to the concert manager, asking him to bring on the copy. The manager declined, bidding her in dumb show to start the piece again. Arabella complied – and stopped at the same place. The cheers this time were positively tumultuous. The manager brought on the copy and set it on the piano desk. Arabella started again. Paying the copy little attention, she played the *Morceau* at a speed and with a precision never heard before. Such, at all events, was Davison's judgement. He wrote:

> Arabella Goddard is too admirable a player, . . . and is already too great a favourite with the public not to have created a certain amount of antagonistic feeling in certain minds . . . An anxious desire to take the piece at the tempo indicated by the composer – which she and few beside her *can* do – and the nervousness naturally consequent thereon were no doubt the cause of her forgetfulness.

The extract is from the *Musical World* of 26 June 1852, which accorded to the fourteen-year-old's recital a 2,500-word spread (as compared with only half that space allotted in the same number to another 'star' recital, that of the distinguished French pianist, Marie Pleyel), including reprints running to two pages of Arabella's notice in other London dailies.

From that season on, wherever and whenever Arabella played, Davison flew into dithyramb: 'Unprecedented success . . . Her powers and her execution marvellous . . . At the age of fourteen she is surpassed by very few pianists of either sex or any age . . . Thunderous applause . . . Encored boisterously and persistently . . . At fourteen has proved herself the best pianist in England, if not in Europe.'

Nor were Arabella's physical graces overlooked. Her appearance was 'highly prepossessing . . . Grace of carriage . . . Intelligent, handsome features . . . Although she is entirely unassuming, she could not fail to win the most casual observer at a glance . . . Very tall for her years; slight rather than thin . . . Her dress at once simple and elegant . . .'

She impressed German audiences in much the same way. We read of the storms of cheers that followed her playing of Mendelssohn's G minor concerto and Weber's *Invitation to the Waltz* at Wiesbaden in the autumn of 1855 (the season in which she first appeared also at the Gewandhaus, Leipzig). After that concert some forty singers of the Saint Cecilia Society marched with lighted candles in their hands to the hotel where Arabella was staying and serenaded her for an hour. Never before had a musician been fêted thus in Wiesbaden.

Her first teacher-trainer was that Herr Thalberg whom Davison years before had publicly hissed in the concert hall and ridiculed in print. Her early programmes, while giving due weight to the graver masters, had, not surprisingly, been decidedly Thalbergian in their trimmings and operatic tartings-up, ranging from *Lucia* and *Masaniello* to *l'Elisir* and *Don Pasquale*. With Sainton she had made the empty-heads gape with a fiddle-and-piano entertainment based on Meyerbeer's best-seller, *Les Huguenots*. More exasperating still from Davison's viewpoint, she drew copiously on Chopin for encores, often obliging with two waltz 'extras' on the same night. All this had to be put a stop to.

On the recommendation, singularly enough, of Thalberg himself, Arabella's formative teaching was transferred to Davison, 'the real master and former of her taste', who, for particular studies in harmony and counterpoint, put her under Macfarren.

At fifteen she was booked by the Philharmonic Society for a concerto date, a notable feather in any prodigy's cap. It was left to her to decide what concerto to play. Egged on by Davison, she was ill-advised enough to choose Macfarren's third in C minor. This was a year of quarrel (about which she cannot have been primed) between Macfarren and the 'old' Philharmonic's conductor, Michael Costa. Arabella was asked by the society's directors to drop the Macfarren piece and pick instead a concerto by one of the accepted masters. She refused – and went to play the Macfarren for the 'new' Philharmonic instead, to the critical plaudits of Davison, who did not spare the 'old' Philharmonic Society his digs and damnings.

It must be allowed, however, that while she was still in girlhood

Davison guided her to one of music's great mountain ranges: the five last piano sonatas of Beethoven. These had never been heard publicly in England before. To most listeners of that day they were obscure and freakish. There was a Frenchman who had dared to cope with op. 106 (the *Hammerklavier*), leaving frowns of puzzlement in his wake. The pundits judged it 'extraordinary' and 'impracticable'. At her first performance of it in London Arabella did the first three movements from memory, presumably for greater freedom of touch. Under her hands it seems to have commanded not a little awe. And so with the remaining four sonatas – Arabella played them all with mastery and passion.

15 'Transposed from G to D'

As to passion of another sort we get not so much as a hint in Henry Davison's pages. He lifts without date a doggerel from *Punch* reporting that Arabella's key had been transposed from G to D and cites, without textually quoting it, some reference that Jullien made to arrangements for the marriage in a letter of June 1858.

In such a case the biographer has but one recourse: to the public register office. There I find that Arabella Goddard, daughter of Thomas Goddard, gentleman, and Anne Goddard, was married in the presence of her parents, on 12 May 1859, to James William Davison, bachelor, gentleman, in the parish church of Saint Pancras. The pair's ages, singularly, are not given. All the certificate tells us is that both were of 'full age'. The truth is that Arabella was twenty-one, Davison forty-five.

As well as the discrepancy of age there was another that bred constant trouble: the discrepancy between Davison's marital loyalty and his critical function. A case in point cropped up not more than two years after the marriage.

The case involved a stolen twenty-pound note. An under-waiter in a Leeds hotel, where touring concert artists chanced to be staying, lifted the note from a fellow scullion's pocket. It was later paid in part exchange for a fifty-pound note from Mrs Sims Reeves, wife of the most celebrated English tenor of his day. Mrs Reeves handed it to her husband, her husband handed it to Davison, Davison paid it into his bank, and, on police advice, the bank stopped it.

These transactions were described when the under-waiter appeared before the Leeds magistrates, charged with theft. The case was, of course, reported in the local papers. Sending clippings to *The Times*, a northern professor of music, whom Henry Davison does not name, aspersed Davison pointedly: 'The twenty-pound note sent by Mr Sims Reeves to Davison looks like a sop thrown to a hungry dog to stop him barking and may account for the extravagant praise bestowed on Mr Sims Reeves's singing when he has been confessedly out of voice and greatly out of tune.' Equally absurd encomiums, continued the professor, had been conferred by Davison on another singer, Herr Formes (the operatic baritone who used to amuse his friends by mimicking Davison's limp). The professor went on:

> Those encomiums might be attributable to the same cause as in Mr Reeves's case. While almost every other musical critic denounced his singing as positively disgraceful and unworthy . . . the critic of *The Times* bestowed on it unqualified praise. Miss Arabella Goddard's pianoforte performances are on all occasions praised to the skies, whilst many others, of equal talent, are scarcely noticed. Unfortunately I have not so many twenty-pound notes to give away as Mr Sims Reeves, and therefore I do not receive a similar amount of adulation.

At *The Times* the affair was taken care of by Mowbray Morris, the manager. Morris wrote to Davison that a plain insinuation had been made against his character, adding, 'You cannot allow that insinuation to go unnoticed.'

Davison at once invoked Sims Reeves. Reeves wrote explaining that the twenty pounds, paid into Davison's account for convenience's sake, was for professional services rendered by Arabella in connection with one of Reeve's concert tours. Mowbray Morris found the explanation quite satisfactory but thought it would be well for Davison to let Arabella henceforth look after her own money matters.

Torments continued, however. What no rival pianist could forget was Davison's strident praise of Arabella before he married her; how according to him she ranked as the finest pianist in England – nay, conceivably in Europe. How could he fail to go on puffing her up at their expense?

The official biography has the draft of a letter from Davison to his editor, John T. Delane, which shows the journalistic straits to which he was reduced. 'Instead of lauding Arabella Goddard's performance . . .' he wrote, 'I have for more than a year past, on almost every occasion when writing about a concert in which she took part, carefully avoided any expression of opinion, confining myself to the pieces she may have played and on the reception they met with from the audience.'

To readers who had written to Delane alleging that his praises in print of Arabella's recitals were instigated by 'unworthy motives', he retorted that his reputation for integrity had been put gratuitously at stake. He asked that one particularly offensive letter should be left in his own keeping in order that he might immediately place it in the hands of his solicitor: 'I am acting only in self-defence. It is of the utmost consequence to me that I should possess the *unreserved* confidence of those who honour me in the positions I hold and which I have now, for nearly fifteen years, held with a perfectly clear conscience.'

Musically, then, the Davison-Arabella partnership invited squalid imputation and involved a great deal of bickering. Nor does it seem to have been much of a marriage in the deeper sense. One reads in Henry Davison, with much astonishment, that from the early sixties on Davison lived with his younger brother, William Duncan Davison, in the same house as 'their very old friend', Henry Jarrett, a horn player turned musical agent. (With Davison in 1843 he had played in the Beethoven horn sonata at a concert in Chappells' music shop, Charlotte Dolby adding one of Davison's songs to the menu.) The trio continued under the same roof, at Tavistock Place, Bloomsbury, for nearly twenty years.

Jarrett is credited by Joseph Bennett with 'peculiar tastes'. He was among other things a snake lover, permitting snakes to nestle in his bosom, even at the dinner table, 'where their writhings excited mingled feelings among the guests'. One cannot envisage Arabella fitting into such scenes and diversions, still less presiding at them as hostess. Nowhere, indeed, does Henry Davison report that she ever did so. His reticences are such that one inclines to the view that Arabella and James lived apart. In the biography a photograph is reproduced of her. Dating from a much later period, it shows a strong mouth, resolute chin and an air of musing melancholy.

16 The Strong Mouth, Resolute Chin

It is from quite other sources than Henry Davison that we learn of Arabella's most singular and strong-chinned feat: her world tour which, occupying most of three years from 1873 to 1876, took in Australasia, the Far East and the United States. During this whirligig she gave scores of recitals, always to adoring applause and positive bombardments of bouquets. Concert halls were jammed, with hundreds turned away at the doors.

During those three years she earned much money: a fortune, indeed. Also she enjoyed the flattering attentions of Their Excellencies the Governors General of colony after imperial colony. These eminences and their wives and aides-de-camp graced her concerts and the bumpers of celebratory champagne which often followed.

Having spent the preceding Christmas week 'with friends in the vicinity of Liverpool' – the phrasing, which I quote from the *Musical World* of 19 January 1873, appears to preclude husbandly company – Arabella sailed from Southampton for Australia via the United States at the end of April, disembarking at Sydney a month or two later. Up from the hold they craned the Broadwood grand piano that she had brought with her from London; then went into conference with Williams, her tour manager, and Smythe, her business agent, whose wife, a soprano, was to join Arabella on platforms as far off as Ceylon.

At her opening concert in Melbourne she triumphed with a programme which, a century or more later, makes one scratch a puzzled ear, the main attractions being Thalberg's fantasias on Verdi's *Masaniello*, *The Last Rose of Summer* and *Home Sweet Home*.

For subsequent dates she had Beethoven's op. 26 (the *Funeral March* sonata) and Woelfl's *Ne plus ultra* sonata up her sleeve. Shuttling between Melbourne, Sydney and Brisbane, she frequently played to 3,000-dollar houses, clearing in four and a half months between 50,000 and 60,000 dollars.

Then she went to India, with an excursion to Ceylon on the way. It had been hoped that she would stay in Ceylon for a whole month. The demand in more populous places was such that she cut her stay to a fortnight, giving the Ceylonese a single concert, with tickets at 'fabulous' prices. In Madras there were six concerts, each before an audience of 2,000; in Bombay six again, all largely patronized by rich Parsees and English residents; in Calcutta eight concerts plus a 'benefit' night whose every rupee of revenue went to Arabella's account . . . Next, she went to China. In Hong Kong there were five concerts, all highly profitable; in Shanghai's Lyceum Theatre six more to English-American-French audiences, with tickets at 'three dollars gold' each – worth the money for Handel's *Harmonious Blacksmith* alone, which had them starry-eyed and rowdy.

Saying goodbye to China she put on three concerts each in Manilla (Philippines), Singapore (Malay Peninsula) and Batavia (Isle of Java), the latter being under the Governor's patronage in his summer palace up in the mountains. Arabella was not allowed to leave Batavia without taking part in a 'grand concert' which the residents had organized in her favour. This was 'remunerative' in the extreme . . . In the fall of 1874 she was back in Australia, playing farewells, which usually ended with bouquets showered on to the platform from the audience's front rows. At Ballarat she received a silver trowel from the mayor. With this she token-smoothed mortar on the foundation stone of Ballarat's rising Academy of Music. Beneath the stone lay enclosed Arabella's signed testimony that she had duly performed the ceremony, which was officially celebrated with ceremonial champagne at the Royal Hotel across the way.

While bringing in packed audiences, with people standing at the back and down the sides, as well as heaps of money, Arabella's tour was not without its tribulations. On four occasions her strong mouth and resolute chin proved serviceable. A year after first landing in Melbourne she used the P & O liner *Baroda* for her comings and goings along the coast. Smallpox broke out aboard.

She was quarantined for a fortnight. Then, two days after landing in Colombo, she contracted severe fever, ascribed, as fevers often were in those days, to sitting in a draught, or, to particularize, on a veranda exposed to dangerous land breezes. Only through the unremitting attention of two doctors was her life saved. After this an attempt was made to rob her. Having played to the general delight in Madras, she drove miles from the Capper House hotel, where she had stayed, on the next stage of her tour. Going through her things on the way she missed a bag that had contained 400 rupees. She went back to the hotel. The manager knew nothing of the bag's whereabouts. At once she went to the police, who conducted a search at Capper House. The bag and the rupees were found secreted in the wardrobe of another room.

The most perilous and exciting event, however, was the grounding in the summer of 1874 of the Royal Mail Steamer *Flintshire*. Arabella and her pianoforte were aboard. Charles Blondin was a fellow passenger – the tightrope walker who footed his way over the Niagara Falls once blindfolded, once pushing a wheelbarrow and once with a man on his back. They sailed from Townsville, Queensland, for Sydney. Twenty miles out the *Flintshire* ran on to a rock and stuck there. Somebody called out that the ship was sinking and lost. Boats were lowered. Three or four men, the ones who had shouted, panickily slid down into them and were ordered out, on threat of death by two passengers with revolvers. All women passengers, Arabella included, were got into the boats, husbands and friends following. A deluge of rain began, quickly soaking the boatloads. The deluge went on for nine hours when, thanks to the oarsmen – who included Williams, Arabella's business manager – the lights of Townville were sighted. Ashore they went. Most hotels were full. They had to sleep on sofas. What of the Broadwood grand? Arabella was on the point of saying goodbye to it when glad news came. Empty watertanks fitted into watertight compartments below deck had saved the *Flintshire*, despite further damage by heavy seas. With just enough coal left, she hobbled on to Sydney, where Arabella and her pianoforte were restored to each other.

Most of her last year abroad she spent in San Francisco, New York and Washington, where her successive appearances were praised to the skies by an admiring, nay, rapt, New York weekly in its first year, the *Touchstone*, whose critic could not have written more fervently had he been in love with her – as who is to say he wasn't. For him Arabella was:

> The most beautiful and accomplished of women . . . This great artiste whose genius has illuminated every land and who stands unrivalled before the world at the present moment . . . Her London concerts are a gigantic success . . . a great idol of the English people . . . an incomparable pianist and the greatest interpreter of Beethoven living . . . When approaching the zenith of her glory Madame Goddard toured the Continent and swept all Germany . . . Then this wondrous creature sailed for Australia . . . then to India . . . her visit to Calcutta [being] a much more important event than the arrival of any crowned head . . . In Batavia [and neighbouring countries] she was the great central star, princes and potentates vying to do her honour and the entire *élite* of cities conspiring to make her sojourn among them worthy of the splendour of her attainments.

Amid the worship occurred a sentence or two about cash matters. On arrival in California, says the *Touchstone* writer, she signed a three-month recital contract with a leading entrepreneur for $15,000 in gold which committed her to seven concerts in as many months while residing in a beautiful San Francisco property she had bought. Presently she would be forming a company to tour the rest of the United States and Canada. After that she and her Broadwood grand would sail for England.

She owned property not only in California but in Australia, London and Boulogne, too; and was estimated to be worth between $300,000 and $400,000. Among her possessions, by the way, is believed to have been a trick piano. The 'Arabella', as this instrument was named by its makers – 'in honour of the fair pianiste of that name' – had a second row of hammers which, worked by an extra pedal, produced the sound of an octave upon the striking of a single note and of a double-octave if an octave was struck.

Around the time *Touchstone* printed its love lyric, as we may call it, other 'transatlantic' sheets, as the *Musical World* styled them, were coming out with stories that Arabella's intention was to pay a mere year's visit to England, thereafter returning to the United States and making the sumptuous San Francisco house her permanent home. It may be that some reporter had heard her thinking aloud before changing her mind. When she returned to England it was soon made clear that London was again to be her base. At St James's Hall in October she gave two recitals to crammed houses. 'Our great English pianist was received with the enthusiasm to which her merits entitle her,' reported the *Musical World*.

The thunderous plaudits were not only for her felicities of touch and the brilliance of her scalework. They were an acknowledgement that Arabella of the strong mouth and resolute chin had proved herself a tough and highly individual feminist in an age, that of Florence Nightingale, when feminism was more effectively in the ascendant, perhaps, than today.

Arabella had to bide her time and keep her place. She lived on for more than half a century, dying in the land of her upbringing at Boulogne-sur-mer, little noted, certainly unfamed.

17   Meyerbeer Foul . . .

In dealing with Arabella's recitalings I glanced at a *Huguenots* fantasia for fiddle and piano that she played with Sainton. During thirty years, the gracious, insinuating and astute Giacomo Meyerbeer (born Jakob Liebmann Beer), composer of *The Huguenots* and much else, crammed the opera houses of two continents with works that, to most modern ears, are of patchy musical quality, though telling enough in theatrical effect. His *L'Africaine* came out at the Paris Opéra in April 1864. Before the year ended it had been sung to excited acclaim by picked voices in other capital cities on both sides of the Atlantic. Most of his career had been of similar sway and glamour. In London, pubs were named after his *L'Étoile du Nord*, casually translated, of course . . . 'Shall we have a whisky in the North Star?'

Davison would have none of this. In the *Musical Examiner* of 6 December 1842, with scornful not to say insolent pen, he had written:

What [not Who, it will be observed] is this M. Meyerbeer about whom such a fluster is made by half-educated amateurs, paid *claques*, would-be *cogniscenti* and poetastical penny-a-liners? M. Meyerbeer has flimsy pretension as a harmonist and contrapuntist . . . Bombastic strivings after originality . . . *Robert le Diable* is third-rate, clumsily executed, deserving perpetual and merited obloquy . . . Consider, too, *Les Huguenots*, that cumbersome drawl of monstrous commonplace and vulgarity dressed up as a species of importance by the most vapid and inflated grotesquerie . . . Meyerbeer is a fellow of not a solitary new idea, whose invention is a bath for commonplaces to swim about in . . . committing a shower of vulgarisms, as melodist null, as harmonist *nuller* still.

In later issues of the *Examiner*, he held that Meyerbeer was not fit to hold the napkin while Rossini was washing his fingers:

Or, put another way, a spoonful or two of Rossini's bottle rinsings would be the making of Meyerbeer . . . The more we know of Meyerbeer the more we do not like him. Like him we never did. Like him we never can. The *Huguenots* music is dullness ineffable. What melody there is – alas! to call it melody! – is largely in the style of the most maudlin, sickly, languishing Italian *cantilena* . . . The opening chorus for a gathering of French nobles, flower of the nation's chivalry, is of a kind that would appear too vulgar if introduced at a debauch of costermongers . . . quite hideous, tiresome, indefinite, confused and noisy . . . Meyerbeer is the most overrated composer of the present day and, perhaps, of any time.

On Meyerbeer there was to be a change of wind – and tune, however.

In 1845 Davison was in Bonn, Germany, for the festival attended by the world's musical notables to inaugurate a new Beethoven statue and other memorials, including the launching of a Rhine paddle-steamer, the *Ludwig van Beethoven*, and an oil painting of the composer at his desk in the throes of the Mass in D while angels laid laurels on his brow.

Before telling of their meetings, a word or two from Davison about how the festival jogged along, brooded over by the Image.

In a hall with five long tables in it, busy small men and men of genius munched and chattered. Davison spotted among others Berlioz, Robert Schumann 'with his clever spouse' (not as clever, though, as Davison later proclaimed Arabella to be) and, a hundred feet further down, Franz Liszt, one of whose preoccupations was how to elude the notorious Lola Montez, 'the eccentric choreograph', as Davison styled her.

'Champagne,' wrote Davison,

> was the order of the day. The cigars were indifferent enough, the coffee indifferenter, the champagne indifferentest, smacking of gooseberry wine. Up in the gallery at the far end of the room a band dispensed quadrille music and waltzes. Over the band hung another portrait of Beethoven which, as the night wore on, could not be seen for the smoke of indifferent cigars, two or three hundred of them.

The inauguration of the Beethoven statue invoked from Davison prose of a more reflective sort. It had a touch of bitterness:

> Long and loud were the huzzas and cheers of the multitude – of that multitude which cared not a straw for Beethoven while living whom now they apotheosized when dead. There he stood, the great Beethoven, simple, undaunted, unmoved in effigy as when the blood flowed to and from his heart and the pulse beat impetuously with the measure of his never-ending melody, unmoved by the hollow vociferations of the mob. Silly mob – quackish mob – empty mob!

The mob had their share of festival pleasure, of course. They could buy tiny Beethovens in gingerbread or jelly, Beethoven pipes to smoke and Beethoven cups to swig from. The age of commercial exploitation had untimely dawned. Thus, nobody was left out – not even Meyerbeer, once so haughtily despised by Davison.

The two men were introduced to each other on the morning of 15 September 1845 by a French writer with musical leanings, Jules Janin. Davison seems to have been bowled over, in a personal sense. He found Meyerbeer

a most agreeable person . . . As you become more intimate
with him his face and figure betray a fund of intelligence. His
manners are remarkably courteous and gentlemanly, his choice
of language elegant and apt . . . I must confess myself agreeably
disappointed in Meyerbeer, whose polished manners and
absence of all affectation cannot fail of winning him a host of
friends.

The festival ended. But before homing Davison had two more
meetings with Meyerbeer at the latter's invitation, one at
Coblentz, the other in Cologne.

Their new relationship notwithstanding, Davison continued
with his anti-Meyerbeer tirades for a few years more, picking
holes in Meyerbeer's scores and wrinkling a fastidious nose. His
notice of *Robert le Diable* at Her Majesty's Theatre (*Musical World* 8
May 1847) not only damned the music, it also had personal
touches of a distinctly uncomradely kind. In it he referred to
Meyerbeer's sensitiveness, 'which verges on the ridiculous. He is
never satisfied. Fifty rehearsals of an opera are not enough to
satisfy him.' The massive fulness of the man's orchestration
offended him. It called for lungs as well as instruments of brass.

As a musical score, he went on, *Robert* exhibited dryness and a
false show of depth:

a vapid inflation without melody or soul . . . feeble and insipid,
displaying a worthless contrapuntal ingenuity . . . Impression-
able as water – and as unstable . . . In his hands a melody that at
first sight may appear to be but a vulgar tune affects a kind of
exclusiveness on the strength of a quaint turn of cadence or an
unusual chord or two . . . These endow the whole with a
distorted something which is not originality but its shadow . . .
His efforts are, like the images which delirium paints upon
darkness, vague, incoherent and without manifest purpose.

18 . . . Meyerbeer Fair

Gradually a change of wind occurred. Quickly the wind became a gale of flattery. For Davison Meyerbeer suddenly became 'the greatest musician living and writing'. True, there was, in Davison's book, another great living composer, Gioacchino Rossini. But Rossini was writing no longer, having prudently retired from all operatic battles and triumphs. In the *Musical World* (14 July 1855) he proclaimed that the composer of *Les Huguenots* – trounced during his *Musical Examiner* days as 'dullness ineffable' – had proved himself a man of superior force and intellect by signally triumphing over incidental 'emptinesses' in the libretto . . . He went through the opera ecstatically, episode by episode . . . In this particular scene beauties blossomed of the first order . . . In another scene he found profundity and pathos unparalleled in the whole range of operatic music . . . For twenty years the *Huguenots* has been universally hailed as the Master's *chef d'oeuvre*. 'What an immensely powerful piece!'

In the case of *L'Étoile du Nord* flattery became lavish, even slavish. 'Upon closer examination of all M. Meyerbeer's works,' he wrote, 'there is no other, in our opinion, which carries so unmistakably the stamp of originality, which is so equal in its parts and which betrays so surely the marks of a thinker and a purely musical genius.' That quotation is from Davison's critique in the *Musical World* of 25 August. The same issue has a leader that launches Davison on a poetic flight. In *L'Étoile*, he writes, melodies come and go as fast as swarms of fireflies, each resembling –

> The beam-like Ephemeris
> Whose path is the lightning's.

The quotation is, of course, from Shelley. The entire opera, he goes on, was conceived and sketched by Meyerbeer during a stay in the Belgian countryside where 'all these tunes, so evanescent in

themselves, descended upon him, petitioning the Master to
receive and clothe them in harmony, that they may endure to
delight the world and not for ever remain invisible . . . Meyerbeer
catches melodies among the trees to sing a child to sleep or rouse
people to fight for liberty.'

But to Meyerbeer-worshippers of Davison's temper or pseudo-
temper, the ultimate, the delirious acme was *Le Pardon de Ploërmel*
or, as the Royal Italian Opera (Covent Garden) preferred to name
it, *Dinorah*, the composer's penultimate piece, a homely, pathetic
legend of simple, lovable peasant souls, with just one wicked soul
among them. The first night at Covent Garden went on till
quarter to one in the morning, prolonged by repeats not only of
elaborate vocal ensembles but of the overture, a quasi-symphonic
poem that took up quite twenty minutes. Meyerbeer and his
singers were called to the footlights at the end of each act.

Owing to the lateness of the hour, all that Davison could get
into next day's (or rather, the same day's) *Times* was a paragraph
about operatic splendours as yet unsurpassed in London, and, for
M. Meyerbeer, another triumph. On the following day (28 July
1859), the man who had declined to grant Chopin a line in *The
Times* came out with two and a half columns opposite the leader
page, stupefyingly dull, in small type, without a single cross
heading. At a quick glance (and it didn't deserve more) his *Dinorah*
notice looked like a particularly soporific Lords debate on Corn
Laws or the new transatlantic cable.

Its encomiastic phrases were predictable. A subject apparently
hostile to M. Meyerbeer's genius, crowed Davison, had been
turned by Meyerbeer into the basis for one of his most admirable
works, thus giving another proof that his talent was as versatile as
it was original. He had painted the story, in a musical sense, with
coherency, avoiding all violent contrast and rough edges . . .
'Orchestration picturesque, varied in colour and masterly from
end to end . . . The music is pure Meyerbeer . . . Unfailing skill
. . . Wonderful consistency . . . exquisite felicity . . . one melody
especially delicious, among the loveliest melodies conceivable –
fascinating, a masterpiece, anything more delicate or original in its
way could hardly be imagined . . . So many florid, sparkling,
brilliant tunes . . . '

What could have been more gratifyingly fulsome and laborious?
Meyerbeer's response was prompt, gentlemanly – and generous.

It was written on the day following Davison's 3,000-word spread and is worth quoting in full:

> July 29, 1859. – My dear M. Davison, I cannot leave London without seeing you and personally expressing my deep gratitude for your admirable article on *Dinorah* and at the same time my admiration at the astonishing spontaneity of your perception, enabling you, after one single hearing of such a complicated opera, to penetrate with eagle glance into the very marrow of the score, so that no detail escapes you, every aspect of the composer's meaning being interpreted to your readers with absolute lucidity of style and language. Such criticism constitutes a *second creation*, and I am proud and happy to have obtained the approbation of a man as eminent as yourself. But you would double my obligation to you if you would kindly accept the accompanying little souvenir, continue your valued friendship for me, and remember me to the charming Madame Goddard-Davison
>
> Yours very sincerely,
Meyerbeer
>
> P.S. – At twelve noon tomorrow I will knock at your door. Please instruct the janitor of your sanctuary to permit my entrance.

As usual the German-born, multilingual Giacomo (alternately Jakob or Jacques) had written to Davison in French, France being his country of adoption. The letter's salient phrase in the original text was *le petit souvenir ci-joint*. One wonders how *petit* the souvenir was. To the 'souvenirs' that composer friends showered on Davison we shall return in a few pages. Meantime the point must be made that Meyerbeer had substantial grounds for gratitude. Apart from his newfound praise for every item and most aspects of Meyerbeer's *oeuvre*, Davison eagerly sprang to Jakob-Giacomo-Jacques's side in the hour of controversy.

Thus four years earlier Davison's enemy John Ella, having praised in print Richard Wagner as man, scholar, poet and musician, was judged by the *Musical World* to have implicitly traduced Meyerbeer, whom Wagner 'hated and loathed', using against him as essayist, a pen 'nibbed with a dagger and dipped in poison . . . Wagner has been exposed to no calumny. He has been

condemned in England, by the best judges, as a composer
[employing] false principles.' Again, in the *Musical World* of 7 and
14 July 1855:

> Meyerbeer has an immense popular following in this country.
> He has deserved it *universally*, since the *fiendish* subtlety of the
> sophist Wagner, however he may analyse, dissect, cut it to
> pieces or grind to powder, cannot get over this difficulty – that
> Meyerbeer has given delight to thousands in every town and
> city where there is a lyric theatre. His melodies have become the
> property of the crowd – which there is no danger of ever being
> the case with *Tannhäuser* and *Lohengrin*.

After a long and gruelling intestinal illness, about which
Davison was kept well informed, Meyerbeer died in the spring of
1864. Within mourning borders Davison gave himself up to
typographical sobs which almost recall those evoked in him by
Mendelssohn's passing:

> Meyerbeer is dead. The hand that traced the *Huguenots* is cold;
> the spirit that directed that hand is fled . . . Yet another great
> genius is departed from among us . . . He had lived to secure
> for himself an undisputed niche in the Temple of Fame . . .
> Peace be with his soul! . . . His death calls for a tear as well as a
> tribute.

Occasionally, a music-lover, having done a bit of heavy
digging, sets up a Meyerbeer score or two on his piano desk. This
I have done myself – not entirely without aesthetic reward. But
for musical folk at large Meyerbeer lies deep and unstirring, not
the only immortal crowned by Davison on whom the world has
turned its back.

We must, I fear, conclude that Davison was insincere in his
crowning gestures. In later years he often scoffed at Meyerbeer's
expense, remarking that, notwithstanding his brilliant position,
the composer of *Les Huguenots* would grovel in the dust before the
most insignificant journal or journalist.

19 The *Rigoletto* Howler

The backturning was largely accounted for by another name that had newly risen and was to go on rising for decades more, that of Giuseppe Verdi, most 'hooking' of melodists and a man with an eye for librettos that purported to be – and sometimes were – as gripping as contemporary melodrama. Let the reader turn to Part Two of this work, the Verdi section, where he or she will find one of the critical howlers of the century, possibly of all time.

In the summer of 1853 *Rigoletto* had its première and five succeeding performances at Covent Garden. Here is an expanded text of Davison's reflections on the subject:

> With all that has been accomplished for *Rigoletto* by the directors of the Royal Italian Opera, it cannot live. It may flicker and flare up for a few nights, fed by the oil of [baritone] Ronconi's genius and blown into momentary vitality by the soft breathings of [tenor] Mario; but it will go out like an ill-wicked rushlight and leave not a spark behind. Such is our prophecy for *Rigoletto*!

Consulting the appendix of Harold Rosenthal's *Two Centuries of Opera at Covent Garden*, I find that by 1953 *Rigoletto* had been performed there 281 times, no mean achievement for a piece that is supposed to have been scorned and snuffed out a century earlier. It was the same with leading opera houses the world over. As Brockway and Weinstock report in *The World of Opera* (1963), *Rigoletto* was a contagious hit from its first performance at the Fenice theatre, Venice, in 1851, lifting Verdi, who had hitherto been merely 'well-known', to pre-eminence. After running like wildfire from top to toe of Italy, it was heard during the next four years in Austria-Hungary, Germany, England, France and the United States. As these authors remark: 'Everywhere it remains a true staple of the operatic repertoire.' It marked, indeed, the opening of Verdi's markedly enriched second period.

Verdi and Davison had been born within a week of each other. They had no other affinity. There is no word that they ever met; but Davison maintained a lively awareness and characteristic misappreciation of the grocer's son who, from hovel, illiteracy and a Duchy of Parma hamlet, was already soaring to something like domination of the world's lyric theatre. The first Verdi opera Davison saw seems to have been *I Masnadieri*, with its tortuous and tragic, not to say anarcho-pessimistic libretto, based on *The Robbers* of Schiller, about a nobleman's two sons, one the foulest of forgers, the other an amiable brigand who, repenting, kills his sweetheart to spare her sharing his life of shame. Commissioned to write *I Masnadieri* by Benjamin Lumley, yet another of the impresario breed, for Her Majesty's Theatre, he settled in London lodgings in the summer of 1847 with his pupil, Emanuele Muzio, getting up daily at five in the morning and working on his multi-stave score until six in the evening. The lodging had been fixed by Muzio, who seems to have been something of a bargainer. The landlord, he says in one of his letters, wanted five pounds a week for three rooms. He opted instead for two rooms at a lower price, contenting himself with a bed put up in the parlour. Verdi was much discomfited by London's smoke. This he hated. There was a perpetual, pervasive smell of coal. 'It is like being on a steamboat,' he told a friend. But the look of London, its elegant streets, its lordly Bank, even the docks, enchanted him. 'If only London had the climate of Naples,' he added, 'there would be no need for paradise.'

The *Masnadieri* opening night (22 July 1847) was socially the most glittering imaginable. Lumley had organized it with lordliness and cunning. He contrived to get the Queen and Prince Consort there; also the Queen Mother, the Prince of Wales, Prince Louis Napoleon, the Duke of Wellington and lesser dukes by the dozen. Verdi conducted. As soon as he appeared in the orchestra pit the handclappings and shoutings began and went on for a quarter of an hour. At the end he was repeatedly called to the stage, either alone or with the singers, and pelted with flowers. The din comprised compatriot yells. Muzio mentions cries of 'Bietifol!' – as near as his compatriots could get to 'Beautiful!' In *The Times* Davison offhandedly pronounced *I Masnadieri* anything but a

first-rate work. It was nothing of *that* kind. What did impress him
were Lumley's schemings. He wished Lumley well in his resolve
to win for Her Majesty's Theatre, with Verdi's prestigious aid, the
rank of 'first theatre in the world'. While acknowledging Verdi's
prestige, on the one hand – he unhesitatingly salutes him in one
context as 'a man of the highest reputation' – Davison makes no
bones, in another context, about Verdi's alleged melodic impotence. Here is what he wrote (*Musical World* 31 July) of the
Masnadieri première, leaving his critique incomplete – a mark of
contempt, no doubt:

> The personal superintendence of the composer and his presence
> in the orchestra added to the *éclat* of the whole; and the failure of
> the opera is solely attributable to its want of merit . . . The
> rising of the curtain is prefaced by an instrumental fragment for
> the orchestra . . . destitute of musical form and interest . . . We
> were not astonished that Verdi should have refrained from
> attempting the composition of an overture. The few essays he
> has made in that style have sufficiently displayed his inability to
> write a movement of any length or regularity of design, which
> (we must not shirk the consequences) is to declare at once that
> he is ignorant of the main principles of his art.

This is followed by a postscript in brackets from Desmond
Ryan, at that time the *Musical World*'s sub-editor, in private life
something of a poetaster. He appears in Henry Davison's pages as
early as 1841. Then a medical student, he composed verse for three
of Davison's songs – 'Sweet Village Bells', 'The Lover to His
Mistress' and 'I Have Wept Mine Eyes Tearless'. Four years later
he was working on an opera libretto for Macfarren. A 'gay and
genial Irishman', he was nevertheless capable on occasion of the
barbed phrase. One man's face he defined as 'four kicks in a mud
wall'; the eyes of another were like 'boiled gooseberries put in
with dirty fingers'. Henry Davison doesn't tell us who the men
were or what the context was. Here, then, is Ryan's parenthesis:

> The above fragment of the opera notice was left by the Editor,
> who has quitted town without completing it or leaving
> directions for the completion. I should have attempted it
> myself, for, though I have not heard *I Masnadieri*, I am

sufficiently well acquainted with Verdi's music to guess with probable accuracy at the merits or demerits of a new work from his pen; but I have just learned that Verdi has departed in high dudgeon at the ill-success achieved by his work; discontented with Mdlle. Lind and [the other] singers, discontented with the orchestra, discontented with the audience and, above all, discontented with himself. It is best, therefore, under the circumstances to defer the analysis until the Editor returns next week.

Hopefully I leaf through the *Musical World*'s pages for the following week and weeks after that. There is writing on every subject under the sun, including much on lofty non-musical themes – Shakespeare's House, Flowers and Women, the Queen and the Poet, Drama in Liverpool and Manchester, a Treatise on the Affinities of Goethe, and reams about the French actress Rachel, the 'incomparable Rachel', who never harboured or emitted a musical note. His pen, confessed Davison, hesitated to trace the words, but alas! they must be written. Rachel the incomparable had taken her leave of the English public the previous night and almost immediately would quit the shores of England. Matters of high moment, no doubt. But of Giuseppe no further sign or syllable in the *Musical World*'s pages. Davison had other things to think about. He was on the point of shooting off to France. Giuseppe had been dismissed from Davison's mind, but not from Benjamin Lumley's, however. Lumley asked Verdi to stay on at Her Majesty's Theatre for three years as musical director, composing one new opera a year.

'Why only *one* a year?' grumbled Verdi, conscious of cornuco-pian capacities. For each new piece, he countered, he must have 60,000 francs, for his duties as conductor a further 30,000 francs; also a carriage and a house in the country. By this time Verdi had left London and was in Paris, on his way home. Lumley showed a certain coolness. The project dropped. Verdi continued on his way.

20   Verdi Ruffled . . .

We are now overdue for another of Davison's hops from loathing to bland, not to say buttery, approval.

Verdi was back in the spring of 1862 for one of those subordinate festivals by which the Crystal Palace Exhibition of 1851 hoped to perpetuate its memory. Her Majesty's Commissioners for this self-perpetuating exhibition asked him to grace the occasion with a special composition and come over to conduct it himself. What they wanted precisely was an orchestral march. Three other composers had been invited to assist. Sterndale Bennett was to contribute a setting of a poem by the Poet Laureate Tennyson; Meyerbeer an overture and Auber another march. Why two marches? Taking into account Meyerbeer's martial-melodic proclivities, it looked as though the outcome might, in effect, be *three* marches.

After consulting Auber in Paris on his way to London, Verdi resolved to ignore Her Majesty's Commissioners' wishes and turn in a cantata. In the course of an article on the imminent exhibition festival, *The Times* (19 April 1862) wrote ominously – and, it seems, inaccurately: 'The various pieces of music which Auber, Meyerbeer and Bennett have composed are in hand, but Verdi's contribution has not yet been received.'

Now Verdi was already in London. He had taken a comfortable lodging, with pretty garden attached, in Alpha Road, on the outskirts of Regent's Park which, in letters, he called Regent Saint's Park. From 43 Alpha Road he wrote to *The Times* a correction which, since it is from the hand that later gave us *Aida*, *Otello* and *Falstaff*, is, I think, worth quoting in full:

M. Verdi and the Great Exhibition
To the Editor of *The Times*

Sir, – Just arrived in London, I hear that in one of your articles of the 19th inst., it is stated that of the four composers who are to write each a piece for the opening of the International

Exhibition, I am the only one who has not yet sent in mine. I beg to say this is not the fact. On the 5th inst. a gentleman appointed by me wrote to the secretary Mr Sandford that my composition was in his hands completely finished and at the disposal of Her Majesty's Commissioners. I have not composed a march as it was first arranged, because Auber told me in Paris that he was composing one for the occasion. I composed instead a vocal solo with choruses which Tamberlik himself kindly offered to sing. I thought this change would not have displeased the Royal Commissioners, but instead they intimate that twenty-five days (sufficient time to learn a new opera) is not enough to learn this small piece and refuse to accept it. I wish to state this fact not to give importance to a transaction in itself of no consequence but only in order to rectify the mistake that I have not sent in my composition.

I shall be very much obliged if you will make this public in your most valuable paper.

I am, sir,
yours truly,
G. VERDI
43 Alpha Road, Regent's Park, April 23

Now for the statutory reversal of engines – Davison's engines, that is to say. Having for years bemoaned the affliction he suffered in listening to Verdi's wretched music – so feeble, so puerile, so destitute of invention and power – in ideas so poverty-stricken, its debased tunes so redolent of the barrel-organ – Davison modulated into wholehearted, verbose praise, declaring himself emphatically against Her Majesty's Commissioners and wholly on Giuseppe's side. Expunged in particular were the 'hideous' *Traviata* nights from which he had stridden in pious dudgeon.

In *The Times* of 30 April 1862, he wrote that Verdi – 'assuredly the Rossini of his day', which was to say the foremost Italian composer – had been asked by the commissioners to supply a mere march. Instead he had obliged with a cantata for voices and orchestra, comprising tenor solo, rife with Italian patriotism and modern Italian inspiration. He continued:

Signor Verdi's cantata –. But why speak of that which, having been written in such good faith and with a feeling not less honourable to its distinguished composer than complimentary to ourselves – has been unceremoniously rejected? We should be only too happy to place on record how worthily Italy – the land of song, the cradle and nursery of music – has done her part in this great festival. But that pleasing task has been denied us – not by Signor Verdi (to his credit) but by Her Majesty's Commissioners.

Davison developed his theme with even keener edge in the *Musical World* of even date:

We hope Signor Verdi will understand the deep disgust which the news of the rejection of his kind, sympathetic co-operation has aroused among the musical and general public of London. Our opera houses are not endowed with money by Government, as is the case in many other countries; and Signor Verdi, however much we may admire his music, could never hope to receive in London anything like the myriads of roubles which the Emperor of Russia gives him simply as an honorarium for having written *La Forza del Destino* for the Opera of St Petersburg. Nor do we imagine that Signor Verdi attaches any undue importance to such pecuniary trifles. But he probably expected to find the Commissioners of the Great Exhibition endowed by Providence with . . . some capacity for appreciating art and the intentions of artists. We are sorry for his sake, as the most popular composer in Europe, and for our own, as Englishmen, and the compatriots of disreputable commissioners, that in both these very natural expectations he has been disappointed.

The burden was taken up by Desmond Ryan, a spirited coadjutor, in the *Musical World* of 10 May. In a leading article Ryan spoke witheringly of the 'wisdom or spleen' that had prompted the Royal Commission to reject a work by one of the most popular of living dramatic composers – a work ordered by themselves and rejected without a shadow of reason. He went on:

Fortunately, the whole feeling of the country . . . is with the Italian Maestro and against the commission. The cry has gone forth from one end of the kingdom to the other of the grievous wrong he has been done, and restitution is imperatively demanded. What can make amends to Signor Verdi for the extinguishment of his hopes? . . . No doubt Signor Verdi was deeply offended at the conduct of the commissioners. No doubt his vanity was probed to the quick by the refusal. It may be that he considered himself lowered if not degraded in the eyes of Europe. Outwardly, however, the popular composer seems to have borne the indignity thrust upon him with philosophical composure . . . All Art England has made joint cause with Signor Verdi, and his popularity will not moult a feather from the ruffling it has received at the hand of the Royal Commissioners.

From the said commissioners not a word. It was as though, harried not only by *The Times* and the *Musical World* but by the entire London press, they had wrapped up, put in ear plugs and gone to ground. It seems likely in the light of modern research that they were not the true culprits. The musical director of the 1862 exhibition festival was Sir Michael Costa. Wherever and whenever Costa ruled the roost all things went or were bent his way. In short, it is now surmised by some that Costa turned down Verdi's composition with an initial veto all his own. Objecting that it did not comply with the original terms of the commission, he is considered by some researchers to have been actuated rather by rivalry, even jealousy, he too, being an Italian conductor-composer – and a markedly inferior one at that. Nothing for it, then, but to have Verdi's *cantica*, as its composer styled it, performed elsewhere and under other auspices. Its title was *Inno delle Nazione – Hymn of the Nations*. The text had been furnished by Verdi's young protégé Arigo Boito who, a decade or two later, was to win pre-eminence with the *Otello* and *Falstaff* librettos. About Boito's share Davison was disdainful. He brushed him off as a poetaster and his stanzas as 'bombastic'. In both *The Times* (May 26 1862) and the *Musical World* (May 31) he exclaims sarcastically at the cantata's sub-title: 'Chorus of the People of *All* Nations' (Davison's italics), pointing out that only three nations were invoked in either words or music, namely, England, France and Italy, the national hymn of France, moreover,

being ingeniously put forward under the familiar guise of the revolutionary *Marseillaise*. This is probably the true reason why Her Majesty's Commissioners, after having solicited the cantata . . . were virtually disabled from including it in the musical performances at the opening of the [festival]. We cannot help saying that if they had owned as much they would have screened themselves from no small share of obloquy.

21. . . . And Appeased

In the end, of course, the *Inno delle Nazione* got the public hearing that was Verdi's due, whether in theatre or in concert hall. The cantata was by nature, of course, a concert hall piece. It was a theatre that came to Verdi's rescue, however – Her Majesty's Theatre, naturally. Mapleson put on the cantata one Saturday night as an extra after Rossini's *Barbiere di Siviglia*. By unanimous desire, Davison tells us, the *Inno*, which ran for fourteen minutes, was performed twice over, Verdi, who conducted, being called back for rowdy ovations three times after the first performance and twice after the second. For some reason the solo bits, originally written for tenor (Verdi had Signor Tamberlik in mind), were transcribed for soprano. In the mouth of Mlle Titiens they sounded as if they belonged there – 'They might,' commented Davison, 'have been written for a woman in the first place.' There was much goodwill backstage and between the wings. Suffice it to say that the entire company and four star singers of Her Majesty's 'lent their assistance', giving professional weight and keenness to the chorus of amateurs.

In so far as the cantata reflected Verdi's political leanings – he was fervently pro-Cavour and, in Italy, at any rate, much against crowned heads – Davison's critiques were on the wary side. He mentions in particular Boito's 'rhapsody of sorts about peace, intermingled with reflections on a wholly supposititious past, when war and universal misery were rampant'. This number was, however, pleasingly sung by Mlle Titiens. For Davison, as for the rest who packed Her Majesty's auditorium, it was the music that 'made' the cantata. Boito's words incidentally and savingly, saluted England as queen of the seas. In *The Times* notice Davison asserted that a more flattering reception was never accorded to a new work.

> The popular composer of *Il Trovatore*, *Rigoletto* and so many other operas which have elicited universal favour in England and elsewhere, achieved a legitimate and brilliant triumph. Signor Verdi's work is not merely effective but, in every sense, good . . . As an artistic production, the cantata is extremely happy and may lay claim to unqualified praise . . . There is warm commendation for the solo-and-choral finale, which first stated 'God Save the Queen', a nationalist Italian air and the *Marseillaise* all at once 'in the fugued style, of which Signor Verdi has already afforded us an inkling in the introduction to *Un Ballo in Maschera*; and, lastly, restated independently with a felicitous ingenuity . . . That he should have combined [these three airs] so efficiently is greatly to his credit as a musician . . . The termination of the cantata, in which . . . the opening theme is given in unison with that pomp and splendour for which Signor Verdi has long been renowned, is as telling and effective as the rest – a climax, in short, which fully answers expectation.

Nowhere in his reflections on the *Inno delle Nazione* does Davison give us to believe that he clutched any part of the music to his bosom. He was civil, he was cordial, he was almost warm. But his judgement has about it a touch of the hustings. Verdi had composed the *Inno* as Europe's 'most popular composer'. What was the point of trying to swim against so tumultuous a stream? He may still have thought in his heart of hearts that Verdi's purpose and practice was to write wretched music for mobs. With a shrug he accepted the democratic vote, however.

22 Bribe Bids

Henry Davison has two passages purporting to defend his father against the allegation that occasionally he accepted bribes. We read:'Auber, Rossini and especially Meyerbeer are flattering in their politeness and hospitality. From time to time one may give him a snuff box or a diamond pin or some shirtstuds, which accumulate and survive him, an apparently untouched and neglected collection.' The other passage reads: 'The bribery to which London critics were susceptible does not appear to have been of a very gross kind. The dinners, boxes of cigars and trinkets of which Davison was not infrequently the recipient from those who were more or less his personal friends could scarcely be regarded as instruments of corruption.'

In the first passage the auxiliary 'may' is to be noted. Evasive grammar argues guilt. In accordance with the styles and elegancies of the time, the studs and trinkets that came Davison's way were probably of gold and silver which, as with diamonds, cost money – and may be sold for money. The upshot is that Henry Davison, admitting that his father accepted such bribes, affects to make light of them. By this time Davison's power was formidable. He loved the exercise and feel of it, as one of his Paris friends, the distinguished Théophile Gautier, acknowledged with almost brutal brevity. On the eve of a singer-friend's London début Gautier wrote to Davison: '*Faites sa fortune avec trois lignes, je te prie.*' Henry Davison seems to reason that, since his father conferred fortune so infallibly on others, he could be excused if he kept a bit of usufruct for himself – so long as mere silver, gold and diamonds were the currency involved. Banknotes were quite another matter – often the squalid source of misunderstanding and distress, as we have seen in an earlier chapter. Sometimes, it is true, distress was avoided and giggles ensued.

Joseph Bennett cites two such outcomes. In both cases banknotes were proffered by composers of oratorios and other sacred music.

One of the composers was Henry Hugo Pierson, a little-known Englishman who chose to spend most of his life in Germany. In 1869 Pierson was billed for the Norwich festival. Numbers from his unfinished oratorio *Hezekiah* were to be performed.

A night or two beforehand Davison and Bennett were at dinner in their hotel when a servant handed him two visiting cards, one bearing Pierson's name, the other that of a local gentleman. With the cards came a message. The maid said: 'They say they'd like to speak to Mr Davison.' Without putting down his knife and fork, Davison returned: 'My compliments to them, Anne, but I am at dinner with a friend.' Within minutes Anne was back with a renewed request from Pierson and his friend for an interview with Davison 'downstairs' for a few moments. This irritated Davison: 'Tell the gentlemen I cannot possibly see them,' he snapped. Anne came back yet again. She handed Davison a letter. From the envelope he drew banknotes (for what amount Bennett does not tell us) and, to his companion, read out the accompanying note, 'the purpose of which was by no means obscurely stated'.

That night, continues our narrator, the banknotes went to London, presumably by railway letter-parcel, and were delivered to *The Times* office. Next morning the would-be bribers were asked by the Editor to call upon him in person and receive back the sum for which they had thought his musical critic's honesty could be bought. They never did call, 'and the money, if I remember rightly, was paid into the coffers of a charity'.

The other instance involved that tireless anthem-writer Samuel Sebastian Wesley, great-nephew of Methodism's founder, John Wesley, and, among other things, a cathedral organist.

One afternoon when Davison and Bennett were busy getting copy away for the ensuing edition of the *Musical World*, Wesley appeared on the editorial threshold with a brand-new edition of his *European Psalmist* under an arm and, upon his tongue, a request that Davison might be so kind as to accept it for review. It was clear, however, Bennett goes on, that their visitor had more to say. Davison having motioned him to a chair, 'he moved restlessly in his seat and looked in my direction, jerked his head towards the door and at last made it evident to the critic of *The Times* – not merely the editor of the *Musical World* – that a private interview was desired'. Whereupon the two men passed into another room:

A little later I heard the front door close upon the visitor, and Davison reappeared laughing. He told me that Wesley, after remarking that a review of *The European Psalmist* in *The Times* was especially desirable, said he could not expect Davison to spend time and labour upon such an article without remuneration. Forthwith he took a banknote from his pocket and placed it in Davison's hand. At once the critic placed it in the pocket it had been drawn from and joked the whole transaction away . . . presently dismissing his visitor with a promise to notice the edition briefly as soon as opportunity offered.

In summing up, Bennett scorns the many tongues that, now and again, busied themselves with Davison as bribe-taker. These tongues, he said, babbled nothing but lies. But again, in Bennett's mind, bribes were banknotes, nothing more and nothing less. As to the 'presents' that came Davison's way there is a revelatory passage in *The Times* official history. This tells us that Francis Hueffer, who ultimately succeeded him as *The Times* music critic, had to engage a four-wheeler [cab] to carry back to musicians the presents which, in accordance with previous practice, were brought to his door. It adds that under Hueffer the suggestion of corruption to which Davison had laid himself open entirely ceased.

Joseph Bennett

23   Costa the Enemy

Some time in 1853 an attempt was made by musical bigwigs 'to bring about a rupture' between Davison and his chiefs at Printing House Square. This we have from Joseph Bennett. The bigwigs included John Ella, contemner of the *Bologna* quadrilles, and a scribbling rector from Bishopsgate, the Reverend Edmund Cox, who made a hobby of music criticism. They were led before the Editor, John Delane, by Michael Costa, director of the Covent Garden Opera and of the Philharmonic Society who, as we have seen, thought little of Davison's friend Macfarren's third piano concerto.

Brought up on and for music in Naples, Costa came to Birmingham at the age of twenty-one to conduct some contemporary Italian opera and, owing to an uproarious misunderstanding, found himself singing the tenor lead instead. Said to be of austere temperament, staying aloof from most fellow musicians, he anglicized himself thoroughly and loyally. Baptized Michele, he ended up as Sir Michael Andrew, a skilled builder, trainer and conductor of orchestras, himself a tireless confectioner of operas, oratorios, masses, symphonies and ballets which will never see the rostrum lights again, if they ever did, and most of them didn't.

What the delegation put to Delane is not reported by Bennett. There is reason to suppose, however, that the gravamen was bribe-taking on Davison's part. In the *Truth* libel case a quarter of a century later [see infra] Davison recalled the delegation and how it was confounded. The charges made against him at Printing House Square were, he said, fully investigated, the investigation lasting ten days or a fortnight, during which *The Times* printed none of his articles. At the end he was informed by the management that there was no foundation whatever for the charges, and his articles continued as before. Editor Delane finally saw the delegation off the premises with typical weight and style. Rising from his chair he said, 'Well, gentlemen, I have listened carefully to your observations and now have only one thing to

78

say, that I think it will be better for you to let me run *The Times* in
my own way. Good morning, gentlemen!'

In those days the Conductor Cult had not begun. Costa
anticipated it. One cannot but conclude that in leading his fellow
bigwigs to Printing House Square he may, in part, have been
actuated by a sense of personal affront. In 1854, public music-
making in this country had been given a great boost by the
transfer of the Crystal Palace, that prodigy of metal and glass,
from Hyde Park to the heights of Sydenham and its rededication
to great choruses and orchestras. For the inaugural concert Costa
had levied 1,700 singers and players. The programme included not
a performance but an inflation of the 'Hallelujah' chorus from
Handel's *Messiah*. Davison wrote:

> The 'Hallelujah' was taken so slow that some parts of it might
> well have served as a dirge. Moreover, the new brass band of
> foreigners, [sub-conducted] by a foreigner, Herr Schallen, was
> seldom in time and always out of tune with the choir; and parts
> for all sorts of brass instruments, added to the score by some
> bold, uncompromising hand, helped rather to mystify than
> augment the effect of Handel's tremendous paean which, had an
> English musician been appointed conductor, would have been
> left alone in its glory. In one place, we thought, the brass band
> came in a bar too soon . . .

There is a touch of tentativeness about the last point. Davison
adds, indeed, that the premature brass entry might have been 'an
error of judgement or a fault of hearing'. There is an ancient
journalistic saying: 'When in doubt leave out.' Davison's failure to
leave out smacks almost of malice. But who can predict or plumb
the mysteries of critical conscience?

In later life Costa seems to have forgotten Davison's caning on
account of the 'Hallelujah' chorus. What he remembered – and
regretted – was the Printing House Square plaint. Joseph Bennett,
diagnosing remorse, suggests that he may have tried to make up
for it. He writes: 'Costa was accustomed, during the years which
lay under my observation, to invite J.W. Davison and his wife . . .
to an annual dinner at his house in Eccleston Square . . . It may
have been that Costa's annual hospitality to Davison was an act of
expiation.' Incidentally, this is the only after-mention of Arabella

in any contemporary reminiscence of Davison and his doings
upon the London musical scene.

24   Dickens wasn't Amused

What manner of man was Davison in these later years? How did
he look? More importantly, how did he sound?

The Crystal Palace saw much of him, either in the critics'
gallery, directly facing the platform, or, between performances, in
what became known as the critics' bar, one of a series that gave on
to the music room. Here he relaxed good-humouredly and
domineeringly, a man of medium height, spare of frame, careless
as to dress, clothes put on anyhow, hair in wild condition, 'all that
goes to a man's make-up in a disarranged state' (J. Bennett). One
of Bennett's critical colleagues, Francesco Berger, said he had a
plebeian look. He was always a centre point. Fellow critics, most
of them younger than he, swallowed his dicta whole, picked his
brains, accepted his drinks (he was a liberal replenisher), roared at
his jokes and nodded approvingly at his comic asperities. Of the
latter I have no direct record from his Crystal Palace days but take
the liberty of drawing upon what he is quoted as saying on other
occasions. Of the Meyerbeer faction: 'It stuck at nothing. Actually
paid people to *snore* through *William Tell*.' Of a young piano
recitalist: 'Most promising. But he *will* like Chopin.' Of Verdi: 'A
prince – what am I saying? – no, *the* prince of operatic
mountebanks.' Of the first London performance of the much
unloved and laughed-at *Tannhäuser* overture: 'Sterndale Bennett
was sitting by me. "Why," he exclaimed, "this is Brummagem
Berlioz, no more, no less." '

Thus he went on, sipping, gulping, forgetting to flick his cigar
ash, until bells signalled the end of the interval and he returned to
his seat, spouting and gesticulating all the way, inveterately
voluble. Let us sit in on two of his performances.

He was invited to dinner during a spring concert season by
friends in Bruton Street, already fashionable with people who

made a point of not leaving cards north of Oxford Street. Among fellow guests was Charles Dickens. At table he and Dickens sat facing each other. What befell is told by the unfailing Joseph Bennett:

> The two men were not friends, nor were they enemies. In a personal sense they scarcely knew each other. But Davison was quite aware of the fact that Dickens could, when in the mood, talk brilliantly, even as himself. Scarcely had the napkins been unfolded before the great musical critic 'took the floor'. What his subject was I have forgotten, but his wild and sometimes daring fancies held the company to listen at length. Knowing what was intended, I watched Dickens curiously . . . The illustrious novelist, at first obviously surprised, seemed to detach himself from what was going on. With face 'laughless', he attacked the course before him, sometimes addressing a quiet word to the lady he had brought in. Davison, having secured the advantage, held on to it, which was easy enough, for Dickens ate his dinner and made no sign. He seemed, indeed, to drop into the sulks. So Davison carried off the honours, and the achievement mightily elated him.

Now for Davison's second oratorical performance. It ended less gratifyingly for him than the one in Bruton Street.

On this occasion his host was the immensely popular and illustrious Sims Reeves. For power, quality and fire there was no tenor of the day who could touch him. Whether as Captain Macheath in *The Beggar's Opera* or as Faust (Gounod's, to be sure, not Berlioz's) or in any one of the oratorios (conspicuous among them *Saint Paul*, *The Hymn of Praise* and *Elijah* of the adored Mendelssohn) to which he devoted the essence of his later career, Reeves commanded well nigh regally the influential few, flattering crowds and a deal of money. A man of marked vitality, Reeves, having lost his first wife at the age of seventy-seven, married again, chosing one of his pupils, whom he took the following year on a concert tour, officially described as successful, of South Africa.

On the heights of Norwood he had a gracious house and there entertained the great, the glittering and, as occasionally turned out, the erratic. The heights of Norwood are not far from those of

Sydenham and its then Crystal Palace. Having a Saturday
afternoon concert to attend at the Crystal Palace, Davison decided
it would be no bad thing when the music was over to call upon
Reeves at Grange Mount and sample the great tenor's hospitality.
His wish being conveyed to Reeves, the reply came that Davison
would be most welcome, his young colleague and friend Joe
Bennett also.

At Reeves's table that evening there were two other notables,
both in their twenties and at the beginning of their careers. One
was Frederick Clay (1838-89), composer of a string of light operas
and a couple of cantatas, one of which, *Lalla Rookh*, contained a
vocal solo, 'I'll Sing Thee Songs of Araby', which outlived all
sheet ballads, surviving (as did two other Clay numbers, 'The
Sands of the Dee' and 'She Wandered Down the Mountain Side')
well into the 1920s. The other youngster was the incomparable
Arthur Sullivan. Already he had to his credit – or discount – the
delicious *Cox and Box*, one flop (another theatre piece, *La
Contrabandista*) and *The Prodigal Son* (oratorio) in which Reeves
had sung and saved the day. For what happened that night Bennett
is again our authority:

> Of the five men at table, three were noted *causeurs*. The only
> danger was that Davison . . . would resent the rivalry of his
> juniors and either sulk or talk them down. However, the dinner
> went off excellently well, and Reeves was radiant. Only myself,
> perhaps, knew how likely it was that there would be trouble in
> getting Davison away. Always difficult to move on such
> occasions, the great critic thought nothing of keeping his host
> out of bed through all the small hours of the night, himself
> going home with the milk.
>
> Towards eleven o'clock Reeves announced that he would
> send us to London in his carriage, and, a little later, a servant
> brought the news that the vehicle was at the gate. Now began
> the tug-of-war. Davison bestowed no manner of notice on the
> twofold hint but, glass in hand, poured forth story after story,
> with witticisms and paradoxes in wasteful profusion. Nor did
> the stream cease to flow when his fellow guests put on their
> overcoats and stood ready in the hall. The hour was far too
> early for the breaking up of a merry party and the dispersal of
> the genial atmosphere in which most of our friend's most

enjoyable moments were spent. Sullivan prayed and Clay entreated, while Reeves, who, as host, could not very well do the like, looked on imploringly at his passive resister. Nothing, however, could move J.W.D. from the spot where, still glass in hand, he stood like Tennyson's tower, 'four square to all the winds that blow'. Time went on. The horses in waiting could be heard pacing up and down as a precaution against the chill of the night, and Mrs Reeves no longer sought to hide her vexation.

At length Reeves came to me as I stood watching the struggle. 'You have more influence with Davison than anybody,' he said. 'Do what you can to get him outside.' To that end I did my best, at length, by quiet reasoning and a little

Arthur Sullivan, early a *Musical World* hero, is here caught at the piano by Charles Lyall. *Cox and Box* is behind him, *HMS Pinafore* two years ahead and a dozen other W.S. Gilbert comic opera libretti to conquer and adorn – *Musical World*, 12 February 1876

gentle compulsion, to get my friend's feet over the threshold. That accomplished, Reeves closed the door with a bang.

Meanwhile Sullivan and Clay had retreated into the carriage. Along two miles of the way home our great critic was plainly out of temper. He fell to rating poor Sullivan and Clay. 'You call yourselves composers!' quotha, and then, with a contemptuous finger-snap, 'Pooh, pooh!' Yet the adventures of that night did not end without an outburst of Davison's restored affection for the youngsters . . .

The next stop was at Davison's rooms in Tavistock Place. I saw my friends into the sitting room and remained there while the coachman consumed a liberal allowance of whisky and soda

. . . Neither Davison nor I ever dined at Reeves's again. I well remember the critic once wiring to the tenor: 'Bennett and I will come to you from the Crystal Palace tomorrow.' To this came a reply of two words: 'Please don't.' We didn't.

25   Nights at the Albion

In this memoir and that we get glimpses of Davison's day-to-day routine and environment. At Tavistock Place he did not always have rooms of his own but shared, now with his friend Jarrett, snake-charmer and theatrical 'fixer', now with his brother, William Duncan Davison. It goes without saying that Jarrett was the more dynamic of the two. At Her Majesty's Theatre (Haymarket) he had been appointed acting manager under John Henry Mapleson, who, without justification, often called himself Colonel Mapleson. On top of his Haymarket salary, Jarrett milked Mapleson's singers of a salary percentage as their theatrical agent at all times and in all circumstances.

In December 1867 he was helping the 'Colonel' to organize a Christmas operatic season when, late on the night of the seventh, Her Majesty's Theatre caught fire. It is significant that Mapleson, faced with disaster and possible ruin, sought Jarrett's help at once. In the middle of the night he knocked on the Tavistock Place door. It was Davison who opened. Mapleson explained that Her Majesty's was burning down to the cobbles. He must speak with Jarrett at once. Jarrett was already abed and snoring. Davison went into his bedroom and shook him awake. Davison outlined the crisis. Jarrett, head on pillow, mused for a moment or two, then said: 'Go away, Jim. I want to think.' He mused for some moments more, then jumped out of bed, dressed, and, with an agitated Mapleson, left on what looked like a hopeless mission.

By dawn (according to Joseph Bennett) he was back. All was well, he told Davison. He'd tell him more later. Then, getting into bed, he had his sleep out.

What had happened was this. Jarrett had made a beeline for the home of one J.B. Chatterton, lessee of another Theatre Royal, that of Drury Lane. He had Chatterton roused. With tact and skill he talked the dressing-gowned Chatterton into conceding Mapleson a sub-lease of the Drury Lane theatre from the following March until July, precisely the period Mapleson had in mind for the staging of a string of Italian pieces, with the right to renew the lease before its expiry. Jarrett came in for jubilant backslappings at Tavistock Place when he'd had his sleep out – especially when the news leaked that, on hearing belatedly of the fire at Her Majesty's, Frederick Gye, manager of the Covent Garden opera house, had rushed round to Chatterton, an hour after Jarrett left, futilely offering a sweetener of £200 a week to bar from Covent Garden 'Colonel' Mapleson and all his doings and schemings.

Twice a week, in his later years, Davison edited his *Musical World* from Tavistock Place, a routine much interrupted by duet playing on the Broadwood grand, where Joseph Bennett broke off his sub-editing chores to partner him; and by a multitude of callers, who infallibly sparked off Davison's solo talk perform- ances. It is true that some of the callers were kept away by Davison's 'dragon of a housekeeper', as she was called by his friends – a hardy, humourless old woman who had two stock answers for anybody she knew to be unwelcome: 'Mr Davison is hout' and 'Mr Davison's abed.' Often this second speech was no offhand excuse but a valid reason. On days when he wasn't getting copy away, Davison rarely rose until 5 p.m. Never did journalist persist more stolidly in reversing the normal clock hours. Many, probably most, days he homed to Tavistock Place with the milk or first sunshine. For this we must credit – or blame – the Albion Tavern, a conveniently central place of resort just wide of Drury Lane, where music critics and drama critics alike came after curtain-fall to write their notices for the morrow's London dailies and not a few weekly sheets.

There has been no parallel to the Albion in later times. The only conspicuous absentee was Henry Fothergill Chorley, the 'ladylike' critic (as one colleague called him) of the *Athenaeum*. At the foot of its main inside stair opened a snug front room with mahogany tables and horsehair seats. Here the dozen or so leading critics, musical or dramatic, scribbled quietly and intently night after night. They regarded this room as very much their own. Had a

stranger looked in about midnight, we are told, he would have
retired promptly before the dart of resentful eyes.

Until old age approached, Davison was a sure and rapid writer.
In the Albion scribblers' room he would turn out a column of
copy at a speed that made his juniors stare enviously. Off the copy
went by cab to Printing House Square. In later life he wrote
haltingly, often so revising his manuscript that only a few words
of the original remained. 'And even then, were I present,' testifies
Bennett, 'he would ask me to read his copy with a severe eye.'
Once copy was away the time came for pleasure, that is to say for
alcohol and oratory.

The Albion was officially styled a coffee and chop house – but
nobody drank coffee there. Davison's tipple was whisky. At the
Albion, having drunk his fill, he expanded even more liberally
than in the Crystal Palace bar. The misnamed coffee house had an
L-shaped main section with 'boxes' for eaters, drinkers and talkers
along either length. Whatever box Davison sat in, there the talkers
would gather and the laughter be loudest. His familiars regularly
included not only fellow critics and a minor author or two but also
one of music's journeymen, John Pitman, Covent Garden's
rehearsal accompanist, officially known as the 'maestro al piano'
(he also played the organ at the church in Lincoln's Inn), a small
man usually with a steaming glass of punch before him, his face
webbed with wrinkles and given to barking laughter. With
Pitman would usually be found one of the new technocrats, a
photographer from Regent Street called Banables, often to be seen
with Davison at the opera, whom Bennett describes as an
instigator of alarms and excursions when a bore, having taken
possession of the box, had to be cast forth. The oddest portrait
from the L-room, however, is that of a person known as the Turk,
about whom nobody knew anything, his looks, apparently, being
enough: rotund, middle-aged, smooth of skin, with the fresh face
of a boy, who sat in one or other of the 'musical' boxes with intent
ears, missing no word and beaming all the time through
gold-rimmed spectacles.

The Albion's head waiter had a majestical name: William
Paunceforte, known to seasoned customers as William. As well as
head-waiting, William was the pub's manager, concerned, among

other matters, with opening and closing times. He had the greatest difficulty in persuading his customers to go home. Midnight was the official closing hour. After midnight no fresh customers were admitted. Those already there went on drinking. At 12.30 William made a round of the boxes, putting on a firm business mien: 'Time is up, gentlemen, if you please.' The drinkers pretended not to hear, engrossed by Davison, occasionally exchanging a dialectical shaft with him, bellowing always at his humorous turns of punditry. At the Albion, in Bennett's borrowed phrase, Music had its Sir Oracle – 'When I ope my lips let no dog bark.' The company in the main music box drank everything in avidly, storing up Davison's erratic or eccentric witticisms for iteration and laughter that continued into the 1900s. At 1 a.m. William turned off the lights over unoccupied boxes. At 1.30 a.m. he said: 'Gentlemen, please, if you please! We want to close the bar.' All lights were then reduced to half power. Perhaps because eyes were beginning to prick with sleepiness, William's third appeal had some effect. 'Very sorry, gentlemen,' he said with finality 'but you *must* go.' 'Then the symposium ended – sometimes, as I can testify, at 4 a.m.' (Bennett); and off the company cabbed or trudged homeward reminiscently chuckling.

Invariably Davison's box attracted a 'central group' of critics who, as to enthusiasms and hates, are said to have acted very much under his influence. Bennett names them: Desmond Ryan, music critic of the *Standard* and assistant editor of the *Musical World*; Howard Glover (*Morning Post*) musical composer as well as critic; Sutherland Edwards, who succeeded Glover on the *Morning Post*; and Campbell Clarke, whose critical 'stable' I have not traced. 'These, with smaller men,' Bennett tells us, 'were more or less intimate friends of the great man of *The Times*, who had over them the natural and inevitable, not to say legitimate, influence which a man of marked personality and great powers must exercise upon his fellows.'

On one occasion, at least, the 'great man of *The Times*', possibly owing to his immersion in Albion delights, did less than his duty by that august and thunderous organ. Henry Davison prints a letter to his father, bearing the date 6 January 1866, from John Thaddeus Delane, the editor, which says in part:

I am informed that your copy on Boxing Night, or rather, on
the following morning, was not delivered until nearly three
o'clock, and I need not tell you how exceedingly inconvenient –
in fact, disastrous – such a delay is. I have just looked at the
article you then wrote, and I can see in it no reason why the
whole should not have been written the day before or, with a
few words added, after the performance, so that the copy might
have been in the office before one o'clock.

Delane admitted that Boxing Night was a night 'sacred to
nonsense'. All the more reason for prompt copy-service on
Davison's part.

26   A Second Enemy . . .

Another of Davison's fellow drinkers at the Albion was Charles
Lewis Gruneison, once a disdained enemy, now a firm and
irresponsible friend. 'Green-eye-son', as Davison called him in
former days, needs a chapter or two all to himself. Not that the
man was irresponsible all the time or exclusively pursued his own
caprices. It is rather that he encouraged irresponsibility in Davison
– an irresponsibility that took the detestable form of practical
joking or, using a briefer and perhaps better word, pranks. In a
moment I shall be describing two of their pranks at provincial
music festivals. In both they plumbed the depths of paranoiac
hilarity.
    First, however, some account of Gruneison, who seems to have
been the busiest of journalists, with a capacity for sitting in two or
three editorial seats at once. Born in Bloomsbury, son of a father
from Stuttgart, he was schooled by a private tutor at the
Pentonville Academy, rounding off his education in Holland. By
his mid-twenties, he was a sub-editor on the *Morning Post* and
manager of that paper's 'foreign department'. At the age of
thirty-one he joined the Carlist forces in Spain as a war
correspondent, taking part in the advance on Madrid and in the

subsequent retreat. Captured in a skirmish, he was lined up with combatant prisoners for execution at the rate of every tenth man along the line. One of the doomed tenth men stood next to the teller of the tale, who had been saved by the count. Gruneison would narrate this adventure on the slightest encouragement. 'His accounts,' drily comments J. Bennett, 'varied occasionally.'

Bulky, blustering and on occasion overbearing, he ran into George Smart (organist, composer of anthems, chants and glees, later to be knighted) in some Bonn restaurant and described with relish a recent quarrel which ended in Gruneison 'drawing his glove' across his opponent's face, an assault which the said opponent (described as a gentleman) chose not to resent. From this Gruneison crowingly passed to another 'disagreeable episode', recounting which he found himself with yet another quarrel on his hands, presumably with some fellow diner. By this time Smart and his friends had had enough. In consequence of the turmoil they left the restaurant.

After his adventures and trials with the Carlists, Gruneison returned to London and, apart from a trip to Germany with Queen Victoria and her Consort, this time as correspondent of the *Morning Herald*, settled down to music criticism, off and on, for this daily paper and that, as well as for two successive weeklies, the *Maestro* and the *Great Gun* (facetiously renamed by Davison the 'Pop Gun'), a serio-comic sheet which he seems to have both founded and conducted. 'How it came to pass that Gruneison joined the ranks of music critics I am unable to say,' confesses J. Bennett. 'Anyhow, he did become a critic, and an aggressive one.'

Against Davison he aggressed in good time. In the spring of 1844 Davison appeared at a public concert as accompanist, accompanying what or whom does not appear in Henry Davison's quotation from the relevant *Maestro* page, written by Gruneison, of course. What we do gather is that Gruneison's notice dismissed as so much idle cant the perpetual preachments by Davison and his followers of English talent and English symphonies, especially those of Sterndale Bennett, 'that elaborate copyist of the school of Spohr'. Gruneison went on:

We remarked with astonishment the very inefficient, nay discreditable, manner in which several of the artists were accompanied on the piano; and on demanding the name we

learned that it was Mr. J.W. Davison who, in conjunction with
another, hissed Thalberg a few seasons ago at the Philharmonic
[see above, Chapter 3] . . . If Mr Davison intends accompanying at other concerts . . . we most strenuously advise him to go
to the Royal Academy of Music and take lessons in piano
playing. He would make an admirable scholar. We cannot
understand how the *bénéficiaire* could engage so utter a
nonentity, who frequently did anything but assist the artists
who entrust themselves to him.

This was the opening round in a journalistic slanging match of a
kind virtually unknown in the musical prints of our own day. In
successive issues of the *Musical World* (27 June and 1 August 1844)
Davison remarks that, in noticing for the *Morning Post* a
symphony by one Cipriani Potter, Gruneison had spoken of a dog
coming on to the Philharmonic Society's platform and wagging
its tail, implying that the *Morning Post*'s critic welcomed such
frivolous irrelevancies as easier to write about than key signatures,
recapitulations, harmonic sequences and other arcane matters that
are the music critic's true concern. He goes on, without naming
Gruneison but clearly identifying him:

He knows nothing of music abstractedly and less than nothing
of art generally . . . He would scarcely know an arpeggio from
a jew's harp, or a duet from a fiddle . . . It is discreditable to a
respectable paper to admit of such a dangerous anomaly, in its
redaction. If an educated critic write, it is true that he may err –
but at all events he can give a reason for the faith within him.
Not so one wholly uneducated. He gropes about in the dark and
hits here and there, smiting sometimes one who deserves the
blow, as often, or oftener, one who merits it not. His praise is
worthless because it has no foundation – and is merely the
offspring of unaccountable caprice, a personal obligation or the
grateful memory of an excellent dinner – or the savoury
anticipation of a capital supper – or something of the kind. But
though his pains and blames are alike worthless and equally
despised by men of reflection . . . still, morally speaking, he
does a large injury to art . . .
    He does not know a symphony from a drumstick – yet we are
sure he has a dictionary of terms musical out of which he selects

some dozen or so for every article. Of these terms he ordinarily makes a strange misuse . . . It is one thing to write ungrammatically of a skirmish and another thing to write intelligibly of an art. A civil war and a Philharmonic concert are wholly irrelevant matters – there is little kin between a cannon and a symphony – and a Spanish legion bears no relations to a comic opera . . . He commits stale eulogies of Mendelssohn, about whom he knows as much as a Lapland whale of the Pyramids of Egypt . . . Well, let the poor man write. Certes, he knoweth not a horseshoe from a dotted crotchet.

To this Gruneison replies in the fourth issue of his *Great Gun*. To begin with he pretends lofty absent-mindedness about Davison and his set. 'Who,' he inquires, 'is this dolorous pianist who appears in dismay when he has struck a wrong chord? How dismal is his music – how loud his moans . . . Unhappy youth! He is rejected on all sides.' Then he remembers. Of course, of course – he is:

The great J.W.D., who wails for the world's wrong. He makes himself generally useful and is in ecstasy when allowed to turn over the leaves of some great lion. He pours forth the froth of Frith Street and glorifies all music provided it be 'on the Square' [The references are to addresses, including Soho Square, where Davison's sheets were published or printed.] He is a kind of Diable Boiteux with all the malignity but not the wit of the club-footed imp?

To which the *Musical Examiner* retorted virtuously that a writer who reproached men for odd looks, club feet and other endowments of Providence that were hardly to be reckoned as sins was degrading his calling and perverting his pen, nothing less.

What if he, Davison, were to round on Gruneison in similar terms, lampooning him as the Devil in Spectacles – '*le diable louche, un gros bonhomme qui a un oeil un peu de travers*' [the squinting devil, a fat fellow with one eye rather out of true]?'

Gruneison's final volley dismissed Davison's 'rhapsodies and ravings', in the 'Muck' (*Musical World*) and the 'Investigator' (*Musical Examiner*) as emanating either from intense intoxication or irreclaimable insanity.

To be dispraised by some writers is no mean praise. Men of
frank and manly character may pass muster when assailed by
the railer at Royalty and the apologist for Atheism. If we chose
to pollute our pages with extracts from the 'Muck' and the
'Investigator' we could expose the vile writer. We could
unmask a profligate professor foaming with frantic passions,
culling the flowers of St Giles and Billingsgate. But we will not
proceed now – *'le jeu ne vaut pas la chandelle'*.

27 . . . Turns Co-prankster

Then, of a sudden, some time in 1847, all was over, says Henry
Davison. Hands were shaken and peace permanently concluded.
(The official biography, incidentally, tells little or nothing of the
verbal punch-ups that I have quoted.) Says J. Bennett: 'Journalistic
feuds seldom last long, and the fierce combatants of the 1840s
were good friends in the 1860s. At provincial festivals they
chummed up invariably.' Chumming continued in Paris.
Together they strolled companionably from boulevard to boulevard, theatre to theatre. Henry Davison has Gruneison listening
while Davison takes part with Carlotta Grisi and other operatic
eminences in readings from the poems of Voltaire.

Given Davison's mischievous cravings it was natural that the
comradeship should breed pranks. Who should the first victim be?
Why not pick on some viola player?

Davison had never forgotten a certain historic hissing – not his
and Macfarren's of Thalberg but one much graver, a hissing of the
hallowed Mendelssohn. Turning up twenty minutes late for a
Philharmonic rehearsal, Mendelssohn sparked off the fury of a
violaist who, having precisely timed lessons scheduled for later in
the day, not only hissed the venerated man but, using 'vulgar,
commonplace language', hurled grotesque and noisy insults at
him. In reporting this offence, Davison as usual drew a high-
toned, absolutist moral.

'We boldly say,' he wrote, 'that genius is, or ought to be,

despotic. It is so rare a thing. It is so absolutely the presence of God in humanity – so supremely above all else – that he who reverences it not, obeys it not, appreciates it not, is little better than an *animal*, without reason, a creature without SOUL.' How to deal with such misfits, with such anomalies? There was only one fit course. They must be deported.

Davison did not, at the time, name the offending 'viola-holder', as he so contemptuously styled him. The man may very well have been the distinguished Henry Hill, in much demand at provincial music festivals, a member of the Queen's private band and soloist in the first London performance (1848) of Berlioz's *Harold in Italy*. Certainly, Hill was the surname (the accompanying forename has not come down to us) of the man picked on for a prank that he and Gruneison carried out many years later at the Hereford music festival.

Again our source is J. Bennett. The prank was elaborately prepared. Signing himself Joab Gas, Davison wrote to Hill's private address saying how glad he was that Mr Hill had been engaged as principal viola at Hereford and that he would call on him to discuss 'a matter of importance'. When Hill reached his Hereford hotel the girl at the reception desk handed him Joab Gas's card and a message of regret that Mr Hill had not yet arrived. Joab continued to call at the hotel, his calls invariably coinciding with Hill's absences with viola on festival platforms. Finally Joab's card was passed to him while actually in the orchestra, executing some pious glee accompaniment or other. The accompanying message said: 'Most important. *Must* see you now. Cannot you come outside for a minute or two?' Hill waited till the end of the concert. There was no sign of Joab Gas in the hall or its precincts. Next morning he wandered from hotel to hotel in search of Joab Gas. Finally he heard the town crier's bell and message: 'Mr Joab Gas, being about to leave Hereford, will await Mr Hill at the west door of the cathedral at the conclusion of the morning's festival performance.'

The concert over, Hill sped to the west door. In or about the portico no sign of any Mr Gas. Hill patiently waited – and at length spotted Davison and Gruneison watching from the far side of the street. They were laughing uncontrollably, as pranksters will – and, perhaps, must.

Another prank victim was a fellow member of Davison's craft: a music critic. J. Bennett tells us what happened to him but doesn't give his name. About the man's status, however, he is biting. He was a talentless writer, it seems. At Norwich festival a year or two earlier he had opened his introductory article as follows: 'Walking about the streets of this ancient city, I noted the following points of interest,' continuing with page upon page transcribed in summary from an out-of-date guide book. Clearly he had no glimmer of talent: reason enough, one would have thought, for sympathizing with rather than plaguing him.

The plaguing was highly ingenious. A day or two before some other provincial festival was due to open, the local superintendent of police received a call from two visitors, one lame, who explained as a precaution that a friend was visiting the festival who, though actually harmless, was subject to violent 'outbreaks' which if not restrained might hurt himself or others. He suggested that a plain-clothes constable be instructed to shadow this friend when he was away from his hotel. A description of the victim was supplied by the pleasant lame gentleman – Davison, of course, with an occasional confirmatory phrase by, presumably, Gruneison, who accompanied him. For two days the shadowing was carried out ruthlessly and conspicuously. It presently dawned on the victim that he was being followed. At last he expostulated, asking the plain-clothes man: 'What the devil do you mean by following me wherever I go?'

'It's all right, sir. Pray don't excite yourself. Keep cool, keep cool.'

'What's your name, fellow? Reply, or I'll call the police!'

'Then call *me*, sir. I'm a policeman.'

'Oh, that's it, eh? Take me to the police station at once. This must be seen to.'

J. Bennett adds: 'And seen to it was, the police superintendent producing the cards of the two visitors and relating what had been done at the instance of the Pleasant Lame Gentleman. It was, of course the Pleasant Lame Gentleman who soothed the irritated nerves of the police and their victim. He left the police station amid roars of laughter.'

The police of the day revelled in jokes, even practical ones, with the gentry. In our day Davison would have left the police station with a summons for obstructing the police in the exercise of their duties and a prospective fine in the magistrates' court of up to £200.

Bennett strikes me as a dependable reporter, and I feel confident that he dependably reported Davison's story of the shadowing incident. But, even in Victorian times, the police did not, I am sure, laugh uproariously at elaborate infringements of the law. If the shadowing fell out as Davison told Bennett it did, he surely would have been clapped in the local magistrates' court without delay and fined substantially for wasting police time. What a rolling of eyes and holding up of the hands there would have been!

28   Gruneison: a Coda

I cannot conclude this tale of escapades without adding a touch to my portrait of Gruneison, a man who, if his writings are to be credited, always came out on top conversationally and in the hour of trial. Early in 1874 he lectured in the Shire Hall, Hertford, to the local literary association on his adventures in Spain. After the retreat from Madrid he had a talk with the Infante Don Sebastian, son of the Pretender to the Spanish throne. It is a connoisseur's piece:

> 'The game, your Royal Highness,' I remarked bitterly, 'the game is up, all is lost.'
>
> 'Ah,' replied the Infante, 'you always look at the black side of everything.'
>
> I replied: 'When a monarch marches on his capital and retires without a battle, his case is hopeless.'
>
> There followed an interview with the Pretender himself, Don Carlos. He advanced and shook hands with me when I was about to leave the room. 'Have you anything more to say – anything I can do for you?' he said.
>
> 'No, your majesty,' I replied. 'But there is one word in the Spanish dictionary I should like to see taken out, for it is the curse of your cause.'

'What do you mean?' retorted the King.

'I mean the word *mañana*, for your servitors always put off till tomorrow what they should do today.'

Later the Nacionales captured Gruneison. He was sentenced to be shot. He describes how, when alone, he wept a little. Then they bound him. 'I believe there was not a movement of a muscle nor a vibration in my frame. I stated I was ready.' Would he have a priest to confess him? He replied: 'To God much, to man – nothing.' The colonel in charge abused him. Gruneison, throwing off his bonds, sprang at the colonel's throat and held him over the precipice, with the intention of throwing the colonel and himself into the depths. The colonel pleaded for mercy. Gruneison freed him. The colonel said: 'You are a brave man. I love you.' General Espartero (Army of the North) later declared that Gruneison had done more harm with his pen than any sword of the Carlist generals.

Resettling in London and immersing himself in music, Gruneison eventually succeeded falsetto Chorley as music critic of the *Athenaeum*, holding that office until death. I cannot close this chapter without touching on a streak of devotion in the man. Its object was the Royal Opera House, Covent Garden, as it became known. Without seeking a pennorth of personal gain, he drew up a plan of management for the house that satisfied financial backers. A manager-cum-chief director of Gruneison's choice was appointed who, with encouragement and stimulus, was to produce works of the greatest composers, without distinction of country.

But here, a singular thing. Everything was to be sung in Italian, French and German masters included. This was because Italian, preached Gruneison, was the best language in which to sing works of all masters, no matter what their language of origin.

'This,' he added, 'was my suggestion as the only system calculated to spread the universality of art.' A swarm of workmen, night shift as well as day, rebuilt the inside of Covent Garden, with tier upon tier of boxes, in a matter of four months. In the new house, as in the old, Italian singers held exclusive sway. For some reason Meyerbeer handed his *Prophète* score, with its French libretto, to Gruneison, 'relying solely on my good offices to secure an adequate execution'. Gruneison took the score to Costa.

They had the libretto italianized in short order: 'Costa nobly kept faith with me by securing a magnificent rendering of the opera.'

The forgoing and other relevant 'quotes' are from a pamphlet of selected press cuttings reprinted by Gruneison in 1869. By then all was over. Covent Garden became as ashes in his mouth. He had quarrelled irreparably, over precisely what is not clear, with the embattled directors of the theatre.

Covent Garden nevertheless throve. Would it have thriven without Gruneison's initial impetus and drive? 'Of course not!' he proclaimed. 'The Royal Opera House, Covent Garden,' he vaunted, 'is a child of my own creation.'

Undoubtedly he was exaggerating. In this case I clear Gruneison of braggadocio, however.

29   The Muttonians

From time to time the *Musical World* would carry an advertisement about some antiquarian book which the Editor wanted to sell. Often the ad was printed upside down; and the prices would vary week by week from shillings to hundreds of pounds. When an offer was made the book could not be found. Davison's chuckle over such incidents, wrote Joseph Bennett, was always worth hearing. Davison was, of course, the deviser of these spoof ads – another aspect of that streak in him that delighted in practical jokes. The 'Muttonians' were a further outlet of the same sort. Bennett tells us who or what the Muttonians were. In the main they were 'personal figments of Davison's very quaint and curious intellect – puppets that he used for the expression of ideas and sentiments which, through their plastic individuality, he could represent in the most fantastic forms'.

Each puppet boasted a name on which Davison had expended much ingenuity, usually (Bennett admits) to happy effect. The ruling Muttonian, Owain Ap Mutton – a tall person depicted by Charles Lyall, the *Musical World*'s gifted cartoonist, with a sheep's head and long legs tapering to a point – stood for Davison himself.

Always Ap Mutton was spoken of by the rest of the Muttonian company with deep respect and obeyed with trembling eagerness. As Bennett says, Davison named his Muttonians with ingenious humour. Their names still raise a smile. I therefore list them:

Owain Ap Mutton, Ruler

Dr Chidley Pidding	Admiral Stump (one leg)
Dr Queer	Dr Grief
Thomas Duck	Major Whale
Alderman Doublebody	Dr Beard
Sir Francis Fly	Sir Caper O'Corby
Dr Brandy	Dr Moon
Drinkwater Hard	Lady Fitzbattleaxe
Professor Fourlegs	Dishley Peters
Dr Calm	Septimus Wind
Abraham Sadoke	Lord Blood
Groker Roores	T. Duff Short
Lavender Pitt	Dr Bird
Gruff Lobster	Montagu Shoot
Flamborough Head	Major Tempest
Dr A.S. Silent	Sidey Ham
Dr Samuel Taylor Shoe	Dr Sprat
Shaver Silver	Dr Blidge
Dr Cheese	Purple Pavis
Dr Spider	Thaddeus Egg
Dr Snail	Dr Quince

Of the above, Dishley Peters, Dr Shoe, Abraham Sadoke and Dr Silent were alternative styles used by the leader, Owain Ap Mutton. Thaddeus Egg was Joseph Bennett and Flamborough Head George Grove, another of Davison's young writers, founder of the musical dictionary that later bore his name. The rest were trifles lighter than air, quirks of Davison-Ap Mutton's imagination – 'mouthpieces for odd scraps of knowledge, scrapings and dry tit-bits from literature's out-of-the-way corners'. Such is Henry Davison's judgement. It is on the generous side. Cursorily running through 'Muttoniana', as their dim frolics were sometimes labelled, I feel little but irritation. Virtually all is freakish obscurity, complicated by Gothic type-founts and little alleviated by Lyall's drawings, gifted though he undoubtedly was.

Occasionally Ap Mutton achieves a lucid though laboured pun. He quotes Dr Moon: 'There is no such thing as a foot of one syllable. Every foot must have at least two syllables, just as every man and woman must have at least two feet – and at least four syllables.' In what way was music served by such lumpish levities?

The Muttonians first held sway in the mid-1860s. There were no Lyall drawings then. Joseph Bennett considered them a waste of space. He brought Davison round to his way of thinking. The Muttonians were thrown overboard. Twelve years later Charles Lyall's advent brought the Muttonians to confused and swarming life again. His drawings of Ap Mutton and the thirty-seven members of President Ap Mutton's court were published in *Musical World* 'to the puzzlement, if not amazement, of its readers'. Such was Bennett's comment. He adds: 'The accompanying letterpress was always decidedly cryptic and bewildering – so answering the end of its existence.' Again Bennett unburdened himself to the Editor. This time Davison replied: 'If I can please myself and make fools laugh at what they can't understand, why not?' So the Muttonians survived for a while, fodder for fools – and acknowledged as such.

30   Ah! Now We Understand

Over the politenesses due, as he considered, to his professional pre-eminence Davison stayed watchful to the end. Musical styles and vogues might change, but the big talents went on being deferential to the pundit of *The Times*. It looked to begin with as though a new spellbinder, Hans von Bülow, had made up his mind not to conform. In 1873 von Bülow – who had lost his wife, Cosima (Liszt's daughter), to Richard Wagner – started a series of virtuoso piano recitals in London that crammed concert halls and left the learned and the lumpheads alike breathless. 'It is from von Bülow that the mad worship of the piano virtuoso dates,' judged a later critic, Percy Scholes. Von Bülow conducted, too. The learned and the lumpheads queued and crowded to his

Beethoven's ninth symphony at the Royal Albert Hall. He had a
prodigious memory, invariably conducting or playing for hours
with a blank rostrum or piano desk before him. Occasionally he
would thumb down some modern piece, later retracting. For a
while he found Verdi's *Requiem* a monstrosity. He was clearly a
man after Davison's heart.

Yet in 1873 the weeks went by without sign or word from von
Bülow at Tavistock Place. Then Bennett saw an item in the
Musical World. 'I gather,' he said, 'that you now admire von
Bülow as a pianist.' Davison's reply was to the effect that the artist
had called upon him, that Davison had found him 'an interesting
man', and that von Bülow had taken him to dinner at Verrey's in
Regent Street. Bennett's remark on this was, 'Ah, now I
understand.'

As in the press bar at the Crystal Palace and in his favourite box at
the Albion, Davison ruled genially, not to say uproariously, over
country hotels where he and other pressmen put up for the big
provincial music festivals. These were the Castle Hotel, Norwich;
the Queen's Hotel, Birmingham; the New Inn, Gloucester; the
Greyhound, Hereford; and the Crown, Worcester. About the
last-named we hear from Alexander Campbell Mackenzie, who
was admitted to the 'merry court' presided over by Davison in his
hired sitting room. At that time Davison was administering what
he called his 'Pills for Professionals', or some such title:

> in that crack-brained paper the *Musical World*, in which the
> articles and mysterious allusions were understood only by
> himself and a learned circle of friends . . . I was immediately
> offered one of these pills at one dose, J. W. D. having them ready
> in his waistcoat pocket. The first one . . . was quickly
> answered, though I cannot recall the question. By the second – a
> couple of bars from an early string quartet by Haydn – I was not
> to be beaten. The final question – certain bars of piano music –
> proved troublesome; but, guessing by the style, I made a rapid
> shot at it. 'Dussek, of course!' said I, with the utmost
> confidence. 'Why, he's one of us!' cried the critic, grasping me
> by the hand, and my initiation was completed.

Then Davison would be accosted by a waiter: 'That gentleman what called yesterday is 'ere again, sir. He's waiting in the piano room off the Malvern Suite. What shall I say, sir?' Rolling up his eyes in affected despair, Davison would leave the revels.

It would have been impracticable to bring his dragon-housekeeper from Tavistock Place on the provincial hotel round. She would have kept all at bay. As it was he had little protection against well-intentioned, flattering intruders. These were, for the most part, London professors of music addicted to composition who, knowing that in a hotel aloofness could hardly be preserved, sought to play the mighty, influential *Times* critic their latest albumblatts, bagatelles, variations with fugues and good, plain sonatas. Petitioners often gained audience and were always courteously treated, being often permitted to play on the hotel piano. But always they wished to follow one piece with another. 'Oh!' exclaims Bennett, 'the horror of these to a man weary of listening, a man saturated with music!'

Nobody has written of Davison with greater discernment than Bennett. Six years after Davison's death he wrote a character appreciation that has a surprising nuance or two and is worth quoting:

> Few, perhaps none, of the critics who have arisen since . . . can form any adequate idea of the power exercised by that remarkable man. It was often said that in respect of music he held the London press in the hollow of his hand . . . Over his colleagues [with the exceptions of Gruneison, undependable, and Chorley, independent] Davison's influence was command-ing. Where he led they followed more or less closely . . . submitting to guidance, the secret of which lay not only in superior knowledge and literary skill but also, to a remarkable extent, in personal charm . . . Complex and uncertain as were the manifestations of his nature, the man himself was no riddle. He was the servant of his emotions. These were the determin-ing influence of his life in a degree approaching to that of femininity . . . No man was more devoted to those whom he loved for themselves or admired for their gifts and graces. Against these he would hear nothing; in support of them he

would fight to the bitter end . . . His heart, it is true, was not
open to everybody, and there were many who deemed him
cynical and wanting in sensibility . . . But this was to judge him
mistakenly . . . His friends thought so much of him as a man
that they often hesitated to differ from him as a critic. They
seemed to be shielded from responsibility under the shadow of a
powerful, as well as sympathetic, personality.

To Bennett's credit it is to be said that, a decisive issue having
arisen, he threw off Davison's spell. The issue was Robert
Schumann's music: I give samples of Davison's anti-Schumann
snarls in Part Two. Schumann wasn't original – he *affected*
originality. Schumann's knowledge of the art was superficial.
Schumann paraded an infelicitous disdain of form. Schumann had
had his innings and been bowled out – like Richard Wagner.

From this position Bennett cut clean away, revealing himself in
the *Pall Mall Gazette* (30 November 1868) as an ardent Schuman-
nite. Earlier, (he explains in the memoirs) he had looked to
Davison as teacher and master. Too young to have detailed
opinions of his own, he allowed himself to be influenced against
Schumann's music, distrusting his own opinion in favour of
another's – and being ashamed of himself all the time for doing so.

That his writing in Schumann's praise would grieve Davison
and expose him to the reproaches of his whilom comrade was
certain. 'The article,' he concludes, 'made a certain effect. Davison
was hurt at what he looked on as my defection from a cause to
which he had committed himself.'

31   Criticizing the Critic

As the first professionally trained musician to serve as critic on the
staff of a London daily newspaper – that newspaper being the
pre-eminent and influential *Times* – Davison faced the outer world
with tranquil triumph and, characteristically, with more than a

touch of mischief, a trait which, as we have seen, he could not repress. But what of his mood and performance when, facing the other way, he contemplated Printing House Square and the personalities that were, or strove to be, his masters?

A handful of managerial letters to him have come down to us, with Davison's draft replies. They give the impression of day-to-day differences, managerial rebukes, even snubs. Davison seems often to have stood his ground; but the mood is never of tranquillity, still less of triumph. He was appointed to the paper in the summer of 1846 at the instance of Thomas Massa Alsager who, as well as being part-proprietor of *The Times* and manager of its mercantile and foreign services, could play (as amateur) every instrument in the orchestra: he sponsored the first performance of Beethoven's Mass in D at his house in Queen's Square, and virtually founded the Beethoven Quartet Society. Clearly, a man after Davison's heart. Less than three months after Davison's first 'From Our Own Reporter' byline in *The Times*, Alsager died, however. Most of his duties and many additional ones were taken over by one Mowbray Morris who, installed as Manager, had supervision of all the paper's commercial affairs, nominations of agents and correspondents, the terms of their appointment and control of the advertisement columns. Henceforth, decreed John Walter, its owner, *The Times* was to be controlled by two equals – the Editor and the Manager, independently of one another, linked only by their common subordination to the proprietor-in-chief.

Son of an 'Indian merchant', Mowbray Morris, of English stock, was born in Jamaica and educated at Trinity College, Cambridge, coming down without a degree, 'as the gentlemanly way often was at that time' (see *The Times* official history). Entering the Inner Temple, he was called to the Bar and, at twenty-eight, became manager of *The Times*. Much later on there were marital bonds, too. After the death of Morris's first wife he married a second – the Editor's sister, Emily. As late as 1870 Morris's own sister, Louise, married George Delane, a brother of the Editor, who wasn't at all pleased and didn't conceal his displeasure, saying that George could and should have done better.

Among the roles allotted to Morris when he took over management in 1847, surveillance of music criticisms is not specified. He surveilled all the same. His qualifications were twofold: boundless self-confidence and a stall at the opera, little else. Some of Morris's letters nag at Davison's critiques without specifying which operas he has been 'critiquing' about. Few of the letters are dated, which makes the problem of tracing particular productions or performances harder still. All amount to the same thing, however – they show Davison in a new and unflattering light.

The first is dated 11 February 1850 and deals with the performance of some French piece (unnamed) by a French cast at the St James's Theatre. Morris picks out two singers, M. Nathan and M. Lac, complaining that Davison had treated them much too tenderly. He goes on:

> The former has a powerful voice, but it is quite beyond his control. When I heard him he hardly sang a note in tune. Lac's singing has . . . neither quality, expression nor execution, and his is the most unprepossessing person I ever saw on the stage. Both are unfit for their parts . . . If the opera itself were less charming, the piece would have been damned on the first night.

Morris adds that what the public has a right to expect from *The Times* is not so much instruction as protection:

> The managers of theatres will always be below excellence if they can. The best is always very dear, and their object is to make money. It is our duty to keep them up to the mark in order that play-going people may always be sure of a superior article for their memory. I don't wish you to be violent or ill-natured, but when a thing is decidedly bad . . . the truth should be plainly and temperately stated. With regard to Messrs. Lac and Nathan, had I criticized them myself, I should have pronounced them absolutely unfit for their parts. I must tell you that we are accused of being too partial in all our musical views.

Occasionally Morris contented himself with acidulous snippets: '14 July 1851 [opera not named]. You have praised Alboni (Marietta) too extravagantly. Nothing human can come up to such a description.'

'14 April 1853. My dear Sir, Ronconi [in *Il Barbiere* and *L'Élisir d'Amore*] is no doubt a very accomplished vocalist and a very amusing buffoon, but I do not think he merits the unqualified approbation which you are accustomed to bestow on him.'

Then, by way of change, a sweet snippet: '27 July 1850. My dear Sir, your article on *La Juive* is exactly what I wished it to be, and I think we have on this occasion vindicated our taste and done justice to the public without doing an unnecessary injury to an establishment [Covent Garden] which undoubtedly deserves encouragement.'

Concerning *Le Prophète* there is an undated letter which clearly predates Davison's root-and-branch conversions, around 1855, to Meyerbeer's art and reproves him patronizingly. During the 1854 season *Le Prophète* was put on at Covent Garden. Of Davison's notice Morris wrote:

We don't like your critique, and if you refer to my letter of Monday last you will perceive that what you have written is hardly what I asked for. There is a great diversity of opinion respecting the intrinsic merits of *Le Prophète*. I myself think it a very grand conception and that its beauties are of the highest order of excellence . . . The Covent Garden orchestra is perfect, the *mise-en-scène* has never been surpassed, and the acting of the two principal characters, by Viardot and Mario, has seldom been equalled. Costa is entitled to great praise for having organized so admirable a band, and the managers of the theatre deserve the public's gratitude for [choosing] music which has tended to elevate the public taste and to make us acquainted with a composition that was hardly known except through imperfect performances in drawing rooms. Try your hand again. Avoid the debatable ground of the music except as connected with the execution by the artists; and give due praise to the admirable acting of Viardot and Mario, especially the former.

32   The Albani Wrangle

A forward jump of nearly twenty years brings us to the resounding début of Emma Albani (as distinct from Alboni), who did not resound in Davison's ear quite as compellingly as in Morris's, and Davison's not unreasonable threat to turn in *The Times* appointment if Morris did not leave off his badgerings. For this and remaining *Times* matters we need a further chapter.

Albani was not her real name. She was born, near Montreal, Canada, Marie Louise Cécilie Emma Lajeunesse, which would have looked like a sprawling joke on theatre bills. She switched to Emma Albani on the advice of her Italian vocal teacher, who saw her prosperingly launched on platforms or stages in Milan or Florence, then packed her off to London, where she had been booked by Mapleson for another of his Italian seasons at the Theatre Royal, Drury Lane.

At the London railway station she asked the cabby to take her to the Italian Opera, neglecting to mention Drury Lane. The cabby took her to Covent Garden instead. There she was received by Manager Gye who, not pretending to be Mapleson – he made rather a virtue, indeed, of *not* being Mapleson – extolled his own theatre and its seasons, which were far more splendid than anything Drury Lane could offer. On the strength of her début performances in Italy and her nineteen-year-old charm, without so much as a sample coloratura flight or even a brace of arpeggios, he signed her into his Covent Garden company and put her down for Amina in an imminent *La Sonnambula*. This came off in April 1872. Thus was initiated an English career that went on for nearly forty years, ending with a sumptuous Royal Albert Hall concert under George V.

Of Davison's notice Mowbray Morris wrote that anybody might suppose on reading it that Albani's merits had not been established to Davison's satisfaction and that what sounded like enthusiastic applause might have been *prearranged*. He continued:

Do you mean to doubt that this new singer is a girl of consummate excellence in her art, that her performance was one of the most perfect ever witnessed and that the audience was literally carried away by it . . .? Your faint praise and unusual caution astonish me! I have not observed such qualities before in your critiques of first performances. You did not find them necessary when Marie Marimon came out last May in the same part – you then had no doubt as to the wonderful talent of the performer . . .! Do you wish to persuade the public that of these two women Marimon is superlative and Albani doubtful? It is quite impossible you can think so. Why, then, do you say so, or leave it to be inferred? But if such is your opinion, you must submit to the charge of having lost those qualities of true discernment and just appreciation which distinguished your writings in former times.

I must add one remark of general application. It is not, in my opinion, within the province of a newspaper critic to sit in judgement on the general merit of performers and assign them their respective places in the ranks of fame. It is his business to give a plain and honest judgement of what he sees and hears on each particular occasion, leaving the public to make their own comparisons and draw their own conclusions. If you had been content to follow this humbler and safer course on the present occasion you could have escaped being condemned for an unjust and misleading criticism.

Davison's reply to this was sombre. What he had written about the *Sonnambula* performance, he said, had no pretension to be a detailed account of Albani's qualifications, which he reserved for a future occasion, although the one hearing did not impress him as it seemed to have impressed Morris:

Your letter is very severe, and I am at a loss to understand how I deserved it. As to Mlle Marimon, I have never spoken to her in my life. I do not know her and have not the slightest wish to know her, nor do I recollect ever having bestowed extravagant praise upon her Amina. All I can remember is that she was received with extraordinary enthusiasm on the night of her début in the role, and that I wrote a very few lines to record the event.

With regard to the applause for Mlle Albani having been *prearranged*, such an idea never entered his head, nor could he find anything in his article that insinuated anything of the kind. He went on:

> If you believe that I no longer possess the qualities as a music critic for which you have so many years given me credit, or if you believe that in writing for you I have any other motive than that of doing justice, so far as my abilities permit, to the great journal of which you are the manager, I can only say that a word from you to that effect will suffice. I should leave the old service with intense regret, but also with the conviction that the loss was not yours but mine. I should also leave it with the conviction of having done my duty honestly and zealously to the best of my means during my long connection with the paper.

There is no managerial rejoinder to this in such Davison papers as have come down to us. Perhaps Morris did not offer one. He may have concluded that about Albani's Amina he had been fatuous as well as oversharp. Two months later, at the instance of his wealthier backers, Gye put on *Gelmina*, composed by a Polish amateur, Prince Poniatowski, apparently for no reason at all except that an opera by a prince does not happen every day of the week and is worth putting up with even if the libretto is trashy and the music unoriginal, as was the case here.

'Dear Davison,' wrote Morris, 'your notice of *Gelmina* is a masterpiece. You never did any work showing more ingenuity in escaping from a difficulty or administering censure with a juster or gentler hand. It gives me very great pleasure to write this, and I hope it will make you forget a certain harsh letter I wrote not so long ago.'

Delane's tone as Editor is a touch more human, with jocosity round the corner as often as not. His notes to Davison, most of them undated, are for the most part short as well as pungent:

> My dear Sir,
>   Don't you think you abuse the practice of writing in parentheses? You make of them, as it were, so many asides to your readers, and it gives me the idea that you are perpetually

winking at them. A wink now and then is all very well, but it is an artifice that should only be resorted to sparingly.

Yours faithfully,
John T. Delane

Another note, written on Good Friday, complains: 'It makes my head swim to try to follow your involutions in the enclosed [item], and as I don't want to drive the musical public more mad than they already are, I beg you to simplify it, and oblige – Yours ever faithfully, John T. Delane.'

Then a Boxing Day plaint (again no year given). It has to do with an institution long faded into the mists of fantastic improbability. At the Covent Garden theatre, Gye used to put on a yearly Christmas pantomime, whether with 'dame' and principal boy is not clear, but certainly not an entertainment to consort with the Mozarts or even the Meyerbeers. Yet Davison took it seriously enough to write a yearly critique. Delane commented:

I hear it said by those who have been induced to see the Covent Garden pantomime that a more stupid, witless and altogether disappointing entertainment was never offered to the public. I tried to go there last night but found the audience coming out at 10.45 – rather early for a pantomime – and all of them whom I knew told the same story. I looked therefore for a description of it. In your notice I do not find one word to caution the public against misspending their time and money in going to it, but a very long account apparently all in the interest of the manager. Pray remember in future that we have nothing to do with [theatrical] managers, that all our interest is in the public, and that we justly lose credit and influence with the public when we postpone their interest to that of managers. Real theatrical criticism is capable of great and healthy action upon dramatic literature and upon acting, but mere praise of what is worthless is ruinous to the art and disgraceful to the newspaper.

Believe me, ever faithfully yours,
John T. Delane

From Tavistock Place this brought another resignation threat:

My dear Sir,
Your letter has given me much pain, chiefly on account of the

insinuation it contains about the influence of managers. No
manager since I have been connected with *The Times* has ever
exercised any influence over me – but if you believe the
contrary, give me at once notice to quit. I prefer dismissal to
remaining under suspicion.

With regard to pantomime, Davison goes on, he does not
profess to be any connoisseur. The day he had to write about it
was always the most unpleasant day in the year. He had never
been able to take pantomimes seriously, regarding it as something
exclusively for the entertainment of children. Certainly, the
pantomime then performing at the Covent Garden theatre was
equal to any for years past. That wasn't saying much – but, as well
as he could judge, it was saying the strict truth. It had been his
duty to write about such entertainments in *The Times* for nearly a
quarter of a century . . .

If gorgeous costumes, scenic accessories and so forth count for
anything when young people are to be amused, I cannot think
otherwise than that this year's Covent Garden pantomime is
exceptionally good. I may be wrong, but if so I am wrong in
pure honesty. Nor, believing as I do, can I forget the enormous
power you entrust to me – and that a few [adverse] paragraphs
in *The Times* might throw some hundreds of poor wretches out
of bread for months.

Delane replied:

My dear Sir,
    Please don't be a goose. Pantomimes are absurdities, and I
always grudge every line that is devoted to them. If we are both
playing our respective parts in the pantomime of life next year,
come to me and talk over our way of noticing them, but don't
write nonsense about 'notice to quit' and 'resignation' – or I
should have much need of resignation if you were to resign – a
joke about new enough and good enough for a Covent Garden
pantomime.

                                        Ever faithfully yours,
                                        John T. Delane

33   Bayreuth Bewilderments

The most agreeable of all Delane's notes reached Davison on 4 August 1876. It read: 'My dear Davison, – would you not like a little run in Germany? And would not the Wagner festival at Bayreuth serve you as an excuse? If so you have only to go to Macdonald [presumably the cashier] and tell him you will write pleasant letters upon Wagner and Wagnerism and Wagner-worship and pack your portmanteau.'

Less than a fortnight later he was lodged in Bayreuth, limping to and from the Bühnenfestspielhaus, which had suddenly become a focal point for worldwide hopes, hatreds, puzzlements, yawns and deep musical joys. Davison there threw off, little by little, his Wagner animosities and came to relish much of *Der Ring des Nibelungen*, a phase that lasted him for all of four years. In the eyes of the 'antis' he thus jeopardized his wits, even his soul. Foremost among the Wagner-haters and -revilers stood his old mate, George Alexander Macfarren, secure in his professorship, an unresting teacher and preacher of what he conceived to be the musical purities – and, according to his lights, an endlessly busy composer, despite failing sight that ended in total blindness.

A couple of quotes from the Macfarren dialectic will be helpful. Three days after Davison's 3,000-word introductory piece about the Tetralogy in *The Times* of 9 August 1876, Macfarren wrote this to a young pupil, Charles Hubert Parry, remembered in our own day as composer of 'Jerusalem the Golden', to William Blake's words, regularly sung at the last London Promenade concert of the season: 'I am sorry you are going to Bayreuth, for every presence there gives countenance to the monstrous self-inflation. The principle of the thing is bad, the means for its realization preposterous. An earthquake would be good that would swallow up the spot and everbody on it, so I wish you were away.'

The second quote, from a letter to some West Country

musician, couples Wagner's name with that of Liszt, equally infamous to superstitious ears. He wrote:

> Wagner and Liszt . . . are making a great evil upon music – the first . . . anomalously . . . by reason of the true beauties that are entangled in his vices. To bring them to notice is to applaud their pretensions. Were you to preach temperance at a gin shop door and let your congregation taste the poison sold therein, that they may know its vileness, they would come out drunkards.

Still, Davison set off valiantly. In Paris he had faced the menace of Louis Napoleon's muskets. Metaphorical earthquakes and gin shop poisons were trifles by comparison. Until the last moment it was uncertain whether he was fit enough to travel. He had suffered a leg accident; the leg was inflamed; he found it laborious to get about. At the last moment he decided to make the journey in the company of a colleague, the critic of the *Illustrated Sporting and Dramatic News*, no less. For want of this critic's name, he shall be Mr X.

When the train started from Victoria Station Davison was nowhere to be seen. Mr X concluded that he had called the trip off. At Cologne, however, Davison's face appeared at Mr X's railway carriage window. Davison felt so poorly that he was half inclined to give up and go back to London. An after-dinner drive restored him completely. They found themselves at a fair on the outskirts of the town and began simultaneously humming the *kermesse* music from *Faust* (Gounod's *Faust*, to be sure). They reached Bayreuth the following day. Before he left Bayreuth Davison wrote for *The Times* over 20,000 words, including a snippet or two by telegraph; for the bulk he relied on the postal service. He took the Festspiel's revolutions and revelations at his leisure and with professional calm.

The performance used to end at or around 11p.m. The London mail left at ten in the morning. Having written his couple of columns during the night and mailed them before breakfast, the *Illustrated Sporting and Dramatic News* man would call at Davison's hotel and find him pen in hand, just about to begin – or postpone. A friend's visit at this juncture was the signal for the tabling of hock, of which Davison had a choice supply on hand. Drinking was the solace against all discomfort. The summer of 1876 was a scorcher outside as well as inside the theatre. Between acts Davison and friends would troop on to the sun-beaten Festspielhaus terrace and, beneath sunshades, drink quantities of Bavarian beer.

As was the case with most fashionable people visiting Bayreuth, he had a carriage and pair waiting constantly outside his hotel. Before or after a performance he would obligingly drive anybody anywhere. The truth is, he found it irksome to write about *The Ring*. This was only partly because of his declining facility which, as mentioned earlier, entailed tiresome interlining and revisions. The truth is that, to begin with, *The Ring* bored and evaded him. His 20,000 words for *The Times* left nothing out. Everything is there, externals included: the intolerable heat; a plenitude of water, yet the dust nowhere laid; no shade trees, only dwarf ones, on either side the longish uphill trudge or drive to the new theatre; all hotels jammed; their hire carriages few and dear; at the railway station enormous crowds; railway officials distraught.

Once inside the Festspielhaus one swallowed everything, or as much as one could. Davison's articles narrate the four interlocking librettos with a thoroughness that even after a century and a bit make one sweat and pant for air. There are incidental judgements, some rapt, others dismissive. Here are some of the dismissive judgements, none of them to be found in Henry Davison's official biography, which strives to convey that Davison was the complete addict from start to finish: 'The Tetralogy is no opera at all. It is a play in which the speeches are declaimed rather than sung to orchestral accompaniment which has nearly all the business to itself.' In his development of melodies – 'such as they are' – Wagner cared nothing for the physical stamina of the stage declaimer . . . From the pulling aside of the curtain to the pulling to thereof, tonality shifted from key to key, careless of hitherto recognized laws of modulation . . . The drama's development involved the presentation of objectionable matter that should have been left where Wagner found it, in the mists of Northern mythology. This had reference, of course, to the passionate union between Siegmund and Sieglinde – brother and sister. Their offspring Siegfried wooed and won Brünnhilde, 'the eldest of his half aunts [via God Wotan]. So much for the family tree!'

Now for *Ring* bits or stretches that wormed their way through

Davison's ear and lodged in his heart, making him, for the
moment at least, more Wagnerian than many. Despite its incest
taint the Sieglinde-Siegmund duet (*Walküre* Act 1) enraptured him
musically: 'The music, in which the orchestra plays a tremendous
part, is magnificent from first to last . . . In musical no less than
dramatic merit *Walküre* and *Siegfried* are very nearly equal, the first
act of the former and the second act of the latter standing out with
conspicuous prominence among the finest parts of *Der Ring des
Nibelungen*.' But *Siegfried* was the apogee. If there could have
existed (he wrote), after the two preceding operas of the cycle, any
possible doubt of *The Ring*'s entire success, it was set at rest by
Siegfried, most buoyant and spirited of the series . . . 'The music is
almost everywhere characteristic and expressive, the snatches of
real melody, heard ever and anon, causing regret only in that they
are subsequently shortlived and evanescent. The scene especially
where Siegfried learns the language of the birds is unquestionably
a masterpiece. The performance was keenly enjoyed from the rise
to the fall of the curtain.'

In the Bühnenfestspielhaus Davison sat through two cycles,
bringing away piercing and profound impressions, from the
opening trio of Rhine maidens, 'so charming and airy, as
elementary as themselves', to Siegfried's funeral march, so
'impressive and sublime'.

On those first cycles of *The Ring* Wagner lost money. His
friends rallied round. Gifts intended for his private pocket he
insisted on diverting to the Bühnenfestspielhaus, whittling away
at the deficit. The early summer of the following year, at the
Royal Albert Hall, London, he gave eight concerts, covering his
output from *Rienzi* to *The Ring*, with 169 orchestral players and a
troop of solo singers from the Bayreuth productions. The aim was
to liquidate or reduce further the Bayreuth loss. But the takings
were something of a disappointment. His agents overlooked the
fact that one-third of the Albert Hall's 10,000 seats were private
property, whose owners could occupy them without paying, or
let them for a fee, or just leave them empty. Instead of reducing
Wagner's indebtedness, the eight concerts of May 1877 increased
it. Davison gloried in the performances. About the *Tristan* and
Meistersinger preludes or excerpts he had a reservation or two but
stated these with a newfound civility and reluctance. *The Ring*
excerpts found him open-mouthed and adoring. This man

Wagner, for whom he once had nothing but ridicule and spite, had become a very demi-god of sonority and 'applied' symphonic structure.

On one of those May nights he was conducted by Dannreuther, the German pianist and mutual friend, to a secluded corner of the Albert Hall. There he found himself face to face with Richard Wagner. Exchanging smiles, they talked in French.

'*Vous êtes Monsieur Davison du* Times?'

'*Oui, mon Maître.*'

'*Vous êtes allé à Bayreuth entendre* Les Nibelungen?'

'*Oui mon Maître.*'

'*Et vous allez entendre* Parsifal?'

'*Je l'espère, mon Maître.*'

'*Ah!*'

On *Parsifal*, his last music-drama, Wagner had five years' work before him. The year after its completion he died.

That scrap of conversation in the Albert Hall was not their only encounter. There was a second meeting, engineered by Francis Hueffer who, of German stock and upbringing, early mastered the English language, succeeding Davison (as already indicated) on *The Times* staff. The concerts over, Hueffer resolved to see Wagner off at Victoria Station. He prevailed on Davison to accompany him. They sought out Wagner's railway carriage. A small group of friends were there to bid him goodbye. With most he shook hands. One or two he embraced and kissed, German fashion. As the train steamed out, head out of the carriage window, he said: 'All is lost save honour.' Davison had tears in his eyes.

34 Four Masterworks

The 1870s are ever to be remembered for four masterworks by three composers which then hit London, bringing – instantly or later on – the immense consolation or vital spark that went straight to hearts or straightened backs, or made people smile in wise delight. These four masterworks were the *Deutsches Requiem* of Johannes Brahms (then a newish name in this country), the *Requiem* of Verdi, Verdi's opera *Aida* and the opera *Carmen* by Georges Alexandre César Léopold Bizet – Georges Bizet for short.

How did Davison fare under this triple test? The Brahms piece he brutally blackballed. As with Chopin's recitals in London drawing rooms getting on for thirty years earlier, *The Times* carried not a relevant line. It cannot be that Davison took doctrinal offence at Brahms's text because it departed from the Church's traditional liturgical usage. As we know, Brahms concocted a text of his own, using as his source roughly corresponding scriptural passages from Luther's translation of the Bible.

We must conclude once more that Davison simply missed the musical point.

So, it must be said, did the audience at large. The performance was under Philharmonic Society auspices in St James's Hall on 2 April 1875. The programme contained a long and eloquent commendation of *Eine Deutsches Requiem* by none other than Davison's intimate Macfarren. Notwithstanding this and the devoted efforts of singers and 'band', a feeling of weariness prevailed in the audience, according to the *Musical World*'s rival sheet, the *Musical Times*. Weariness deepened to gloom, inducing the conclusions that the Philharmonic concert room was 'no place for a funeral service'. At the end, a professional friend of Macfarren – it may have been Davison – went up to him and said: 'Well, George, if this is music then I'm no musician.'

In the ensuing decades the emotional surges and strengths of *Eine Deutsches Requiem* were firmly established, prevailing in the generality of musical minds, an enduring item in the musical canon.

There were to have been three performances of the Verdi *Requiem* – the *Manzoni Requiem*, as it is named after the Italian poet and novelist whose memory it perpetuates – Verdi conducting, in the vast arena-auditorium of the Royal Albert Hall, which had opened but five years earlier and still excited all gapers. The first, a dress rehearsal before an invited – but packed – audience, went off so famously that two additional performances were fixed in quick order. Verdi conducted the lot. All drew big audiences. Since the hall will hold 5,600 it is likely that, making allowances for as many as 1,600 empty places a night, some 20,000 persons must have flocked to the *Manzoni Requiem*. Since Verdi stuck as strictly to the traditional liturgical text as the *Requiem* of Mozart himself, many a Protestant ear must have been reflectively, not to say anxiously, scratched. Could these flockings and crowdings denote some popular slide from stout Protestant principles? On second thoughts, no. Clearly, people were piling into the Albert Hall not for the Church doctrines that Verdi was incidentally purveying but for Verdi's superb tunes. And Davison was wholly with them – or pretended to be.

In the *Musical World* issues of 15 and 29 May (1875) he wrote:

> . . . the name of Verdi has long been a household word, and some of his melodies are as familiar and as much in vogue as the most beautiful of our national airs . . . The *Requiem* made an evidently deep impression . . . and closer acquaintance with it can only lead to a conviction that the dramatic genius which has so long distinguished its author as a composer for the stage is likely to serve him in a very different sphere of art . . . The work is not moulded in the shape of certain recognized masterpieces unnecessary to name; but this establishes that Verdi has an original way of looking at [his] themes and treats them in a manner individual to himself . . . The genius of the famous Bussetese is dramatic and elegiac by turns. Severe scholastic forms possess for him little attraction. He is therefore commendably frank in rejecting them whenever he can employ other means to convey and enforce his ideas . . . The beauties of the *Requiem* speak eloquently for themselves, and the intense feeling for which many passages are distinguished cannot but impress all hearers attentively alive to what the composer has to say and willing to accept it in the belief that he is speaking out his mind with earnest sincerity. Thus considered, the latest emanation of the pen of one to whom we are indebted for so much that is intrinsically beautiful can scarcely be regarded otherwise than model in its style.

In short, the Verdi *Requiem* had every reason to rank side by side with the *Stabat Mater* of Rossini – a work of style and merit, yet furlongs removed from the burdens and beauties of the score that Davison was actually writing about. He goes so far as to praise the 'Recordare Jesu' duet as 'melodious and expressive'. He has a kind word also for the octave unison that opens the 'Agnus Dei' – a conception whose startling melancholy called for critical comment by some poet's prose-pen.

So the notice trailed on – seemly, decent, dull.

Verdi's *Aida* was first performed in London at Covent Garden opera house on Thursday 22 June 1876. Four days later Davison came out with a column and two-thirds in *The Times*, something over 3,000 words. He begins by telling the opera's story. It is nothing, he insists, but gloom, gloom from first to last, in the end becoming oppressive 'if only because the heroine's fate and that of her lover, to say nothing of the equally to be pitied Amneris, are destitute of poetic justice and in no way to be accounted for by their actions'. Can it be that Davison's notorious hankerings after lighter operatic pieces, notably those of Rossini, disabled him from taking in – and relishing – tragic themes?

There was one thing he was thankful for, however. There were some who heard in *Aida* a change in Verdi's musical style. With such people, he wrote, he was at a loss to agree. There were some who even traced in *Aida* a leaning towards the revolutionary Richard Wagner. Of this there was absolutely no trace:

> If writing a greater quantity of accompanied recitatives than usual or a smaller number of pieces to be taken out of the score and performed by themselves without regard to the context, or the occasional reappearance of certain phrases or parts of phrases like that with which the orchestral prelude sets out – if [these minor innovations] are like Wagner, why, then, Verdi resembles him; but no further. Verdi knows better than to dive into unfashionable waters. He is still, happily, the Verdi of our long remembrance, our own Verdi, and may he continue to remain so.

Not that *Aida* was immune from an adverse dig or two. He did not greatly care for the man's 'elaborately spun-out finales' (with or without long Egyptian trumpets), much preferring finales of less ambitious texture but of far greater effect that might be cited from his earlier operas, from *Ernani* onwards. He went so far as to prefer the 'Miserere' scene in *Trovatore* to any and every page of 'solemn music' in *Aida* – forgetting that, twenty-one years earlier, he had damned *Il Trovatore* as written in utter contempt of all rules, wanting in refinement, hampered by coarseness of style and persistent disregard for purity of form.

As often happened in his first-night notices, Davison made clear that he declined to speak of Verdi's music in any detail, leaving this for 'another occasion' (not easily traceable). However, he did let slip that audiences were moved by the intense dramatic power of *Aida*'s first-act soliloquy ('Ritorna vincitor') and four duets for her, Amonasro, Radames and Amneris. That the finale of the Triumph scene was very imposing in its way must be 'cheerfully conceded', but it was imposing rather as a combination of strident effects than anything else. To that extent it recalled the finale of *Don Carlos*, which was deficient in primitively fresh ideas.

Times readers were thus left with an impression of good bits and not-so-good bits, the whole gloomed by the story-line and therefore doomed. Not until our own century and Francis Toye's corrective *Verdi, His Life and Works* (1931), did the Musical Establishment, faithful servitors of Davison for the most part, cease turning up noses at a score that, for all its popular following, serves in all ways as a worthy threshold to the Shakespeare settings of the master's old age.

When Bizet's *Carmen* came up at Her Majesty's Theatre (22 June 1878), Davison in *The Times* squandered 1,000 words or more on the story and bade the music take a back seat – the sort of evasion he increasingly practised. He put the evasion thus: 'It is not the intention at present to discuss from a critical point of view the music of Bizet . . . [recently dead]. The subject deserves a notice apart.' Can it be that Davison did not think much of Bizet's incomparable sound-facture and the superb way in which it heightened and fed the story? All that concerned him, apparently, was that Bizet had now wriggled clear of Wagner's 'doctrines' and their exemplification through music which, he insisted, had done much to militate against the success of his earlier operas, *Les Pêcheurs de Perles* and *La Jolie Fille de Perth*. Weeks later, however, he delivered a brief comprehensive judgement in the *Musical World*, proudly heading it with a pen-name from certain of his Bühnenfestspiel articles – 'Our Bayreuth Madman'. It reads thus:

The Musical World.

LONDON, SATURDAY, JULY 27, 1878.

At Carmen.

I no humbug. I say what I think. I like *Carmen*. And that
Minnie Hauk! Per Bacco! She is a *diablesse!* I sorry she go to
America! I no humbug. Per Bacco! I like *Carmen*. That Hauk!
She is a witch. Bring the cloaks!

A wild flower garden of luxuriant growth – pretty, sometimes beautiful, graciously breeding flowers – sometimes weeds – but always pretty – wants trimming, rooting up, watering, setting in order. Later on there can be no question. Georges Bizet would have been his own gardener. Died aged thirty-seven. He should have died hereafter, with at least another *Carmen*, or two, or three, or four, to keep his memory green. He would have been a very excellent gardener. He might even have kept and trimmed an orchard. He was garden and orchard in one. What a loss!

By two modern historian-analysts of opera, Wallace Brockway and Herbert Weinstock (authors of *The World of Opera*), *Carmen* had been defined as *a* (not *the*, be it noted) perfect opera, a judgement shared by thousands the world over, this writer included. In the light of its perfection, the Bayreuth Madman's conclusions have an insufferably patronizing ring. Not surprisingly, the *Musical World* in a later edition slanted *Carmen*'s immense success on to Bizet's principal singer. Mapleson had given the rôle to an American soprano, Minnie Hauk, more than adequate of voice, a lively actress and altogether a young woman of dash and spirit. In the issue of the *Musical World* from which I last quoted, the Bayreuth Madman's paragraph is followed by a Lyall cartoon showing a middle-aged male, foreign, shrewd, untidy, probably a bit drunk. The performance is over. In Her Majesty's foyer he muses: 'I no humbug. I say what I think. I like *Carmen*. And that Minnie Hauk! *Per Bacco!* She is a *diablesse*. I no humbug. *Per Bacco!* I like *Carmen*. That Hauk! She is a witch. Bring the cloaks.'

35   Onslaught by *Truth*

The last chapter but one gave us a glimpse of Davison in the Royal Albert Hall on a Wagner night, in Wagner's presence, with unaccountable tears in his eyes. A few weeks later Davison had occasion for tears of a different kind – tears of exasperation and, perhaps, unease.

In the London weekly which had *Truth* as its venturesome title, a columnist wrote who signed himself Scrutator. In the issues of 5 July 1877, 25 August 1877 and 13 June 1878, Scrutator accused Davison of facilitating, in his function as music critic, blackmail and bribes, the direct beneficiary being his fellow occupant at Tavistock Place, Henry Jarrett (see Chapter 15).

For many years, said the columnist, Davison and Jarrett had lived in the same house 'like two cherries on the same stalk'. As the principal operatic agent in London, Jarrett exacted ten per cent of all fees received by his clients. Among the singers he served was Christine Nilsson, a comely soprano from Sweden, 'whom I espied the other night in a box at Covent Garden with Mr Jarrett and Mr Davison'. The three of them were listening to a now forgotten French piece, *Paul et Virginie*. For each of her operatic performances – and at this period, covering Nilsson's prime, these were many – she was paid £200 (equivalent to £1,500 in our own day), Jarrett pocketing twenty pounds (£150), an inordinate, not to say preposterous percentage, commented Scrutator.

It had not been ever thus. When Mme Nilsson first came to England she declined to have anything to do with Jarrett. As a result, alleged Scrutator, she was attacked by Davison in *The Times* and another sheet with which he had influence. Then she consented to pay Jarrett 'an enormous sum'. Thereafter Davison had nothing but praise for her. Jarrett did not hit it off with all potential clients, as in the case of Estelka Gerster, the newly arrived Hungarian soprano, still in her early twenties. Of her début as Amina in *La Sonnambula* at Her Majesty's Theatre, Davison had, according to Scrutator, written a disobliging notice, damning her with faint praise and her audience with faint sneers for their enthusiastic clamours. The reason, he continued, was obvious. In her case Jarrett had been denied his ten per cent, she having declined his services. Gerster, it was pointed out by Scrutator, had a superb voice and could afford to laugh at Davison's critical coldness: 'There was a time when a word from Mr Davison could make or mar a singer. We are now, however, better educated in musical matters.' Still, the Davison–Jarrett partnership had to be exposed. And extirpated. When it came to pianists, Davison was capable of 'malignant' pertinacity. Scrutator here cited a Czech player of high reputation and ability, Mme Clauss-Szervady, who gave London recitals in 1851 and 1871. He would like to know (he continued) the 'the history of the secret attacks' made by Davison upon Mme Clauss-Szervady, whose performances he wrote down ferociously, while persistently writing up those of Miss Arabella Goddard, 'with whom, as I cannot help remembering, Mr Davison is connected'. Scrutator continued:

> I would respectfully suggest to the Editor of *The Times*, who possibly knows nothing of these wheels within wheels, that he should inform Mr Davison that he would do well not to live in the same house as Mr Jarrett; and that henceforth the criticisms upon Mr Jarrett's clients should be written by someone else. Mr Davison is, I am bound to say, not a man to be influenced by monetary considerations, but friendship is friendship, and neighbours are neighbours . . .
>
> I think it a pity that Davison and Jarrett should have a virtual partnership in their domestic arrangements, if not in other matters, but, in calling attention to the fact, I have simply discharged a public duty. Davison is evidently the dupe of Jarrett, and through him *The Times* has been made the tool of Jarrett. At the same time, weakness, however pardonable in itself, becomes in a critic as culpable as corruption . . . As to Davison, I am willing to believe he is more weak than corrupt and more pitiable than culpable.

At the same time, concluded Scrutator, the process amounted to blackmail, and he did not intend to allow that sort of blackmail to continue, for it was a disgrace to English journalism.

> All foreign artistes who have to complain of the [Jarrett] gang will find in me a friend ready to expose any attempt to levy contributions on them and indifferent to the personalities that the members of the gang lavish on me. I am well aware that these foreigners are afraid of provoking powerful enmities, but they would do well to realize that if they really have talent the public will support them. The proprietors know nothing of the system that has prevailed and would be the first to put it down if brought to their notice.

(Scrutator's references to the Jarrettt 'gang' are explained by support for his and Davison's cause in some theatrical weekly which he dismissively nicknames the 'Penny Gaffe'.)

Scrutator's final volley had a complacent ring. He congratulated himself on having protected Mlle Gerster in particular. Against her there had been a conspiracy – 'and I somewhat congratulate myself on having crushed that conspiracy in the bud. Prima donnas must be judged on their merits and not on the amount of the commission they pay to Mr Jarrett, the friend and cohabitor of Mr Davison.'

36   Davison Denies

Less than two months later, on 1 August 1878, Davison took action against *Truth* in the London Divisional Court for all Common Law Divisions. He had been instructed by the new Editor of *The Times*, Thomas Chenery (Delane having retired in 1877) to place himself in the hands of *The Times*' solicitor. On Davison's behalf application was made for 'a criminal information' against the publishers of *Truth* for libellous articles conveying 'very serious imputations' upon him. Davison did not appear in the witness box, nor did anybody else. The process was conducted entirely by affidavit.

By affidavit, then, Davison gave distinct and explicit denial to Scrutator's charges. It had been alleged by Scrutator that *The Times* had dismissed or displaced him. That was utterly untrue. He had been *The Times*' music critic for thirty-two years and was so still. Jarrett he had known for over forty years but had in no way been connected with him in business. As to their living together, the only truth in it was that many years before, his brother and Jarrett took a house between them, and for domestic reasons Davison had gone to live with his brother. He had never been consulted by Jarrett on matters of business of any kind, nor had he received from him any money or derived from him directly or indirectly any profit, benefit or emolument, pecuniary or other, based on the fees of Mme Nilsson, or anyone else.

As to Jarrett's being employed by particular artistes, this did not affect him or his criticisms either in *The Times* or elsewhere. Mme Nilsson was said by Scrutator to have originally declined Jarrett's services. Of this he knew nothing. Never had she been attacked by him. On the contrary, his first criticism had been highly laudatory. It was equally untrue that he had entered into a conspiracy to crush Mlle Gerster, or that he had levied, attempted, or was party to anyone else's attempt to levy blackmail contributions from her or any other artiste. It was false that he had ever written one up and the other down, as was imputed . . . Whatever he had written expressed his honest convictions.

It was true that in 1853 charges were made against him to the late manager of *The Times*. These charges were fully investigated, the investigation lasting ten days or a fortnight, during which his articles were not published. In the outcome he was told that there was no foundation whatever for the charges, and his articles, being resumed, continued as before. It was untrue that he had been displaced as critic. A gentleman had been named as having succeeded him. Utterly wrong! In truth, the gentleman named had been appointed by *The Times'* management solely as his assistant.

Davison's testimony was rounded off by Jarrett who denied that, in consideration of favourable notices by Davison, he pocketed ten per cent of his clients' salaries.

On the bench were two judges, Justice Mellor and Baron Huddlestone. After a brief retirement they ruled against Davison on quasi-technical grounds. Mr Justice Mellor said it was desirable that music, like every other art or science, should be the subject of fair criticism, and he had no doubt that Davison's criticisms had been written with the utmost fairness and without the least reference to the influences suggested. He quite felt that these articles were libellous. They conveyed, indeed, a very serious libel on Davison. The libel was one which might well warrant an indictment or an action – but it did not follow that it was the fit subject for a 'criminal information'. That was an exercise of the extraordinary jurisdiction of the court which, as a general rule, was reserved for cases of libel upon persons in official or judicial positions and filling some office which made it for the public interest necessary that such jurisdiction should be exercised for the refutation of such libellous charges as were made. This was not so in the present case.

The affidavits filed were, however, sufficient to dispel the imputation that Davison had ever written articles from the motives suggested, the libels being of a most discreditable character. For the reasons stated, however, the present application must be refused.

Baron Huddleston concurred but pointed out that Davison had his remedy by action or indictment, in either of which ways he could vindicate his character before a jury. He had the opportunity, by taking such a course, of publicly asserting on oath that the implications made against him were unfounded.

Davison did not do a thing. The court's ruling and, in particular, Justice Mellor's comments gave him what he seems to have regarded as complete clearance. Some of his friends, in the opinion of Henry Davison, would have been glad had he taken the case further, as the judges suggested, affirming his innocence on oath. Others may have thought *Truth*'s attacks worthy only of indifference. In a letter to Davison his old friend Macfarren made a sharp comment. It had been established, he wrote, that Scrutator told the 'truth' in terms of bitter falsehood.

A general comment by Joseph Bennett written forty years later, is worth quoting here:

> There can be no doubt that Rumour's many tongues were, now and again, busy with Davison as a bribe-taker. But they babbled only lies. It was a matter of course that he should have enemies. *The Times* at this period was a journal of influence now hard to conceive as the possession of a single paper . . . At the height of his power and for many years, every musician, indeed, every man who had a musical log to roll, sought to gain his favour. Of course, all the disappointed ones became more or less his enemies, prepared to believe anything concerning him which was not to his credit. My own conviction is – and I knew him as did very few others and was entirely in his confidence – that, while no less moved by personal sympathy than the rest of us in the discharge of his duties as a critic and in all relations therewith connected, he eminently strove to be just and upright.

But what, one may ask, of the tokens and trinkets, the jewels and precious metals that, according to Henry Davison, came his way from composers, singers and executants? Undoubtedly these, although supposedly covered by the customs and conventions of politeness, refuted Bennett's judgement. But then, Bennett may have known nothing of the diamond scarf pins, the silver snuff boxes and such that were found among Davison's possessions after his death. It will be remembered that Francis Hueffer's widow computed these and other tokens by the cab-load.

37   Burial Pomps

The year 1878 was the one in which Davison was officially superseded by Francis Hueffer, although we do not gather as much from Henry Davison who, on this, as on certain other matters of chronology, is often vague or elusive. He speaks of his father's lapses: important musical events he neglected to cover and lateness of copy concerning those he did. His bosses at Printing House Square told him regretfully that he had lost his old powers and that his services must be dispensed with. They added, however, that his salary (£250 a year) would go on being paid; and so it was, until his death, seven years later.

It has already been said that by this time Davison had lost much of his writing facility and felicity, misapplied though that felicity usually was. According to Joseph Bennett, Davison felt his supersession deeply. Bennett agrees, however, that his work was done by the time he laid down his pen.

In many ways he remained young in spirit, however. His newest professional acquaintance at this time was the eminent fiddler, chamber music leader and small-time composer, Joseph Joachim. He and Joachim used to play a game. Each in turn would whip off his stove-pipe hat and tap the rhythm of some tune on its crown. The other had, of course, to identify the tune, opus number, title and all. Davison is said never to have been caught napping in these contests. Another instance of his sprightliness occurred, probably at the Albion tavern. A dispute sprang up about some thematic turn in the *Marriage of Figaro* overture. Davison, staring his opponent in the eye, hummed correctively; then, to prove his point, undertook to write out the entire score from first bar to last. This he did not do, but made a start and put aside his pen only when he had reached and triumphally included the passage in question.

Occasionally he resorted to places other than the Albion. Whenever a new organ with a hundred or more speaking stops was installed in some great church, he would be invited with other notables to a freak meal in the spacious swell box. There was one organ in which he thus relaxed regularly: the organ of St Paul's Cathedral. Every year thousands of children, styled the Charity Children of London, occupied tier upon tier of seats rising from chancel-level to the top of the great arches, and sang now Mendelssohn, now Handel, now a floridity known as Jones in D with incredible brilliance and beauty of tone. Davison, concealed by the organ curtains, would await a signal from the organist, John Goss (later Sir John), yet another deviser of anthems, glees and psalm settings, who, relinquishing his seat at the manuals to a deputy, led the way through a small door into the roomy organ case where, secure from observation, he would gravely produce a bottle of sherry. On the table glasses and a plate of biscuits waited. Joseph Bennett latterly accompanied Davison to these Charity Children's concerts. 'So,' he writes, 'while the anthems, the multitudinous voices and the thunderous organ tones rang through the cathedral, we refreshed the inner man. This was an annual ceremony, invariable in character . . . Discipline at St Paul's forty years ago was exceedingly lax.'

Now approaching his seventieth year, Davison remained faithful to old friendships. Sterndale Bennett survived till 1875. He had a house in Bayswater. At dinner with him there one night, Davison, poking about in a bookcase, came upon the first movement of a forgotten fourth symphony which Sterndale Bennett had composed in the winter of 1833–34. On leaving the house Davison walked off with the manuscript. At his side was Bennett's son, J.R. Sterndale Bennett, who got him home with the greatest difficulty. In the Bayswater Road, Davison would halt under each lamp post and read a page or two of the score absorbedly. At Tavistock Place he took young Bennett up to his bedroom and showed him a whole collection of his father's unpublished early scores; they were carefully stacked among linen in a small chest of drawers. He told how he read them often for their quality and the memories they aroused. He could not bear the thought of parting with them in his lifetime. After his death they were returned, as he wished, to the Bennett family.

Bennett had predeceased him by ten years, when nearing his fifty-ninth birthday: an untimely end. Because the Royal Academy of Music, with official encouragement, made much of its royal title and status, he was accorded as its Principal a Westminster Abbey burial. The tabulated account of this ceremony in the *Musical World* of 13 February 1875 occupies two pages, full of stately names and titles. From end to end there is an echo of elegiac drums and trumpets.

First came the Requisition to the Very Reverend Dean. Stressing what were held to be Sir William Sterndale Bennett's worth, gifts and genius, the Requisitioners saluted him as the unquestionable head of the musical profession in England, adding that an abbey grave was his undoubted due. Signatures followed of dukes, bishops, conductors, opera singers, pianists, violinists – and Davison. Then came an account of the ornate, endless procession of mourning carriages, including the private carriage of the Queen, with the Prince of Wales in it, and Sir Sterndale's own private carriage conveying the Queen's representative (the Honourable Mortimer Sackville-West) and Colonel the Honourable W.J. Colville. Others who slowly clip-clopped to the west doors were musical bishops, the Duke of Edinburgh, the Earl of Dudley, a university vice-chancellor or two, the master of this university college, the precentor of that, and, in a strictly graded succession of places, the directors and committee of the Royal Academy of Music, plus representatives of the Philharmonic Society and the Royal Society of Musicians. The *Musical World* devotes an 'indented' paragraph to the 'outer coffin' of French polished oak, with projecting lid and plinth, polished silver mountings consisting of 'chaste' handles and corner clasps and a shield-shaped plate with engraved inscription. The sides of the coffin were festooned with white lilac blooms, the lid partly hidden by selected wreaths, including one from the lady students of the RAM, on whom Bennett had lavished (according to some, wasted) courteous but acute piano lessons or singing lessons.

There was a thoroughly drilled choir of twenty-eight boys and
twenty-six men from St Paul's, the Chapel Royal, the Temple
church, the Lincoln's Inn church and the abbey itself. Behind the
coffin hundreds of feet paced and shuffled over black carpeting
that had been laid throughout the abbey. The grave was draped in
black and grey. Former fellow students of Sterndale Bennett led
the way, followed by members of Bennett's family 'and a few of
his intimate friends'. Among the latter Davison is named.

I have detailed the funeral pomps accorded to Bennett by
Monarchy, Church and State because they contrast so markedly
with the condition and prospects of the modestly talented
twenty-year-old whom we first met as Davison's somewhat
deferential companion at the Lower Rhine music festival of 1836.
His death drew from Davison some stately prose that rang with an
orthodoxy he had supposedly renounced in the Marlow woods
forty years earlier. His *Musical World* leader of 6 February 1875
reads in part:

> Sterndale Bennett dead! He is more alive than ever he was. This
> afternoon they will sing over a grave in Westminster Abbey:
> 'His body is buried in peace, but his name liveth for evermore' –
> not his name, merely, let us add, but the man himself in some
> high and grander phase of existence where, with enlarged
> capacities, greater possibilities open before him. To this we do
> not expect assent from all. Never mind. Let those whose
> expectations of human life are bounded by birth and death get
> what comfort a cheerless creed will yield. They are welcome to
> it . . . He lives with us in his works. The music he created
> conquered, in some sense, the power of death . . . We recognize
> this species of immortality when we say 'Beethoven does this',
> 'Mozart does that'. Such men are always in the present tense
> because they ever live. Let us, then, take heart of hope, even
> turning the event to account by changing sympathy for the man
> himself, who does not need it, into zeal for his reputation . . .;
> no longer here as a mark for the jealousies and distractions that
> merit never fails to excite.

Thus did Davison magnify and exalt, evoking venerated names,
Mozart's, Beethoven's, as no whit more illustrious or lasting than
that of his old Marlow mate. Throughout British Music Society

circles, that roundabout of the purblind, his *Musical World* preachments were read, it is to be presumed, with fervent eyes and clasped hands. The fact remained that Sterndale Bennett's music, already sinking, would soon be out of sight and out of mind.

In the following century one of Davison's successors, now styled 'chief music critic' of *The Times*, H.C. Colles, the scholar who edited Grove III, wrote thus: 'Bennett's more serious work as a composer is almost completely neglected now. His . . . refined writing for piano has been obliterated by the rich romanticism and style characteristic of his age . . . Sensitiveness became fastidiousness, his delicate genius contracting to a narrow talent.'

On second thoughts, this hardly goes far enough. The true function of genius is not to reflect his age but to *create* it, a purpose quite alien to Sterndale Bennett's gentle academic dreams. Colles' dismissal of Bennett, I may add, has been upborne in essence by the three later Grove editions.

38   Berlioz, Wagner Reassessed

For the rest Davison held a modified sway, delegating *Musical World* tasks more freely than before – but ever ready to spot newfangled merit, genius even, and stamp on it with inexhaustible zest. Thus it was, more or less, with Berlioz's *Grande Messe des Morts*, a work of beauty and immense power which had to wait forty-six years for its first English performance. This took place in the summer of 1883, under a German conductor, Augustus Manns, at the Crystal Palace, to the discomfort, nay confusion, of Davison and, it must be said, of most other critics. The lot of them were little less than scandalized by the innovations of a work not worthily performed or assessed, in this or other countries, till almost a century later. (What Berliozian does not treasure memories of the requiem as performed under Sir Colin Davis in St Paul's Cathedral, part of the City of London Festival?)

On Berlioz Davison took roughly the line he had been taking for decades. The *Requiem* was patchy: good bits here, bad bits there. This, in part, is what he wrote in the *Musical World* of 25 August 1883:

> What Berlioz wanted to create was a drama of death; and, for its portrayal, the strongest effects, the most glaring contrasts, the most singular orchestral combinations appeared to him permitted, or even commanded. The gigantic always possessed a seductive charm for him; he intoxicated himself with unheard of acoustic effects . . . monster masses of singers and instrumentalists and colossal [venues] . . . We have to do here with an eminently romantic composition and not church music in the traditional and strict sense of the word. Berlioz does not bind himself down even to a strict observance of the text . . . For him the words are, as it were, only slaves whom he commands and tyrannizes over in the service of his musical inspiration . . . Berlioz breaks up and kneads the words to make them fit the rhythms he has selected . . .
>
> He was neither capable nor desirous of writing a requiem in the noble style of Mozart or Cherubini . . . [However] though often eccentric and ugly, Berlioz's score is thoroughly interesting and in some parts thoroughly original and grand. Side by side with passages of strikingly poor invention and technical awkwardness there are brilliant ideas and surprisingly clever combinations, and Berlioz, as far as purely musical work goes, by no means a master in the strict acceptation of the words, reveals himself to us on the whole as an artist of the most glowing fancy, the strongest passion and the most dazzling originality. This last quality is particularly apparent in his treatment of the orchestra.

The honeymoon with Wagner's music was shortlived. It had been preceded, as we have seen, by self-confident incomprehension and derision. In some corner of the Royal Albert Hall he had told Richard Wagner that he hoped to be in Bayreuth for the première of *Parsifal*. When the time came he did not stir. Presumably he had had a look at the score, and that was enough. He pronounced the *Parsifal* music execrable. The outpourings against Wagner which I quote are notable, incidentally, for a bit of literature that will be read with fascination by all who write or propose to write about music and music performances. It did not appear in the *Musical World* until 22 May 1877, nine months after the first Bayreuth *Ring*. Captioned 'Amateur Madman at Bayreuth: Notes on the Spot', it purports to have been written 'at the Asylum opposite the Theatre' and is signed by one of the Muttonian pseudonyms, Thersitis Grunpus Wizzell. Despite these silly trimmings, these are genuine journalistic notes, the sort of thing the *Ring* critic jots down at speed between the acts while sipping his lager on the Bayreuth terrace. As such they have a spontaneity and impressionistic humour that Davison's rewrites and revisions inevitably dispelled. (For Davison's 'Amateur Madman at Bayreuth' notes see Part Two, Chapter 9.)

When Wagner was the assignment, Davison occasionally used other writers – or 'lifted' their work barefacedly. As far back as the 1860s he had covered the *Meistersinger* première in Munich by reprinting, in translation, the Berlin *Echo*'s review of it. For the *Tristan* première he milked the *Presse* of Vienna. This latter review carries no author's name. Usually his Vienna contributions were signed: Eduard Hanslick, like Davison a dissenter from Wagnerism, whom Ernest Newman in his *Life of Richard Wagner* styles (inaccurately, it must be said) one of the 'stupider and baser journalists'. Long before the opening of the Bayreuth theatre, Hanslick had written for the *Musical World* a 2,000-word article about the *Ring*, its story and its philosophy, or pseudo-philosophy.

There was another Wagner piece, however, which Davison affected to prize. This was the early *Flying Dutchman* which, translated into Italian as *L'Olandese Dannato*, had been sung to bored, restive stalls and boxes at the Drury Lane theatre in May 1875, the first Wagner opera ever to be mounted in London. Writing in a quarterly magazine, Francis Hueffer emphasized the deep impression made upon truly receptive minds by a performance that was nevertheless 'cold and uncongenial'. In the *Musical World* Davison picked up the phrase ebulliently: ' "*Cold and uncongenial*" is good! Wagner himself never listened to a warmer or more congenial rendering of his very best opera. – O. Beard (Muttonian).' One cannot avoid the conclusion that the comparison was intended not for its own sake but merely to heighten, by force of contrast, the 'mumbo-jumboish' pretensions of Wagner's later works – *Tannhäuser* and *Lohengrin* no less than *The Ring* and *Tristan*.

About *Lohengrin*, while making allowance for the fewness of its 'good bits', he was, after his fashion, scornful and authoritative. *Lohengrin* was done in July 1875 at Covent Garden, the first Wagner piece ever to reach the Royal Opera House, where it was performed each year thereafter until well into the following century. *Lohengrin* is with us still and it looks like being with us for ever. For that first performance the libretto, too, was done into Italian. Was *bel canto* feasible or bearable in German? The tiaras and gold watch-guards on the whole thought not. In his *Musical World* notice of 24 July, Davison finds Lohengrin's farewell to his trusty swan 'eminently graceful' and has words of praise for a few other passages, including the bridal chorus – 'all of them musical as we understand the term'. But most of *Lohengrin* could only be described as 'sound and fury signifying nothing'. Lumping the *Lohengrin* music undiscriminatingly with 'the Music of the Future', he resented this term and Wagner's use of it as implying that Beethoven was a fumbler in the dark and *Fidelio* alien to the true spirit of dramatic and poetical music; or that Mozart was a mere student of his craft, working on wrong principles; or Meyerbeer an ignorant and misguided concoctor of orchestral effects. Music had been described as 'a heavenly maid', as 'a concord of sweet sounds'. But Wagner drew his inspiration from other sources. Nick Bottom, the immortal Weaver of Athens, had 'a reasonable good ear in music' – which for him meant the tongs and bones. 'And why not?' Herr Wagner would indignantly ask. As the apostle of the 'Music of the Future', Herr Wagner would agree that tongs and bones were inharmonious – but, according to the working of his mind, the requirements of dramatic situations could not be fulfilled without them. So let the tongs and bones be heard respectfully. Let the rest of humanity be derided as Philistines capable of responding to Beauty merely through the sense that Providence had bestowed on them.

For the Covent Garden singers and the producer Davison had praise:

But in opera it is impossible to overlook consideration of the music, if there is any, and of the harmonies and melodies which we have been accustomed to class as music there are few in *Lohengrin*. The work took some four hours and a half in performance, and the score occupies some 383 pages; though it is only fair to the management to admit that two or three dozen pages have been excised. Out of this lengthy book all that is agreeable to the ear could have been played in twenty minutes.

I write this during Richard Wagner's death-centenary year, 1983. In opera houses the world over, in concert halls, on television, in the film studio and recording studio the event has passed not unnoticed but without celebration of an unforgettable kind. This for a simple reason. For more than a hundred years a sustained torrent of Wagner has been sounding in the world's ears. Anniversary emphases are therefore redundant. The world doesn't need reminding of music and gesturings that are for ever in its heart and head.

It may be that towards his end Davison dreamed of killing the Wagner cult stone dead. Among obituary notes in the spring of 1885 was one in the London *Evening Standard* by some writer who esteemed Davison and loathed Wagner in hallucinatory degree. '*It remains to be seen,*' he wrote, '*whether, fifty years hence, the name of Mendelssohn or Wagner will be the more highly esteemed, indeed, whether anything that Wagner has written will be familiar to the twentieth century.*' (My italics.) Could gullibility further go?

39   Margate and . . .

In 1881, Henry Davison tells us, the partnership with Jarrett ended, and Davison found himself 'uprooted' from 36 Tavistock Place. The official biography does not explain the term 'uprooted'. We get the feeling that whatever happened was against Davison's wishes or will. On what had happened to his brother William Duncan Davison, with whom Jarrett and he had shared no. 36, no word is offered. He found a new lodging at the opposite end of Tavistock Place, a 'bare yet grimy dwelling, Bloomsbury noise and Bloomsbury gloom, with cats on a bald patch of black garden giving on to blacker slums'.

With Jarrett he continued on companionable terms and was to

have accompanied him on a musical trip to Hamburg and Wiesbaden. At the last moment, however, he didn't feel up to it. He went to Malvern instead for a change of air and, relaxing in his hotel room, immersed himself in new French writers. Though much taken by *Une Page d'Amour*, he found Zola on further readings loathsome, detestable and 'worthy to be burnt by the common hangman'. Guy de Maupassant's *Une Vie*? A weak imitation of Zola. Théophile Gautier? Cynical filth. Give him Balzac any day. What a solace to go back to *L'Histoire des Treize*! These and other opinions we gather from frisky letters from Malvern to a London friend. Occasionally he touched on music, usually in praise of Mendelssohn, ever his enthroned god. To a *Musical World* subscriber he wrote: 'That *is* a beautiful passage you refer to in [his] A major symphony, but there are others no less so, especially in the slow movement (the series of chords in suspense), as beautiful and touching as anything in music. It always makes me think of another world.'

As usual, loved music reminded him of inferior, ramshackle stuff, meaning (on this occasion) Schumann. 'How you can regard Mendelssohn and Schumann as equals,' he continues, 'is beyond my comprehension.' Yet on one occasion – perhaps as a sequel to Joseph Bennett's revolt in Schumann's favour (see Chapter 30) he took a prudent line and hedged. In one of his *Pall Mall Gazette* pieces Davison admitted that he was beginning to doubt whether Schumann could be properly accused of being a 'dreary and unmelodious mystic' who mistook music for a branch of metaphysics. After all, the domain of music was very wide, affording ample room for any composer who, like Schumann, 'wrote less for beauty than with the intention of faithfully reflecting certain trains of thought'. This is cited in a footnote to Sir George Grove's biography – the sole occasion when Davison, having snapped or sniggered at genius, acknowledged that genius might, just possibly, be right after all.

Back to Bloomsbury and its blackness, its days now ending no longer in the Albion Tavern but usually in one of the large London railway station restaurants, to which Davison would slowly stump his way to eat, drink and talk endlessly, buttonholing strangers if friends didn't happen to be with him. One gets the impression of loud, loquacious loneliness, the words always streaming; of sons (he had two), yet no family circle; of successive dwelling places but no home. Macfarren still kept in touch. Always he had much to tell. Always he was busying himself with concerts. Early in 1883 he was full of his *King David* oratorio. Arthur Sullivan was going to conduct this at the Leeds musical festival. Blind and indomitable, Macfarren outlived Davison by a couple of years. When an amanuensis was not within call, he obstinately wrote himself – or tried to, words and lines getting mixed up indecipherably. 'Sometimes,' narrates Henry Davison, 'the pencil lost its point, but the writer wrote on, leaving no trace on the paper but a blunt, black indenture.' Often he would walk abroad, impetuous to his own cost. He could not bear to rely on his guide-boy but rushed ahead. In Hyde Park he rushed into a tree and broke his nose. The nose healing, he resumed his rushing. He and Davison greatly relished their anti-Wagner exchanges and mutual eggings-on.

Yet Davison felt he had to get away. He pondered and brooded. In the end he decided on Margate, a resort that retained much of the fashionable prestige it had built up during the early Victorian era. On the seafront stood an inn, the York, with comfortable bed-sitting rooms above and, below, a snug jug-and-bottle department for both regulars and 'casuals'. Just the thing.

40 . . . The Last Days

At the York he spent the last eighteen months of his life. He still had writing to do. From Henry Davison we gather that he still turned out copy for the *Musical World*. It is to be taken for granted that he had resigned the editorship. The public telephone had not yet happened. To edit a London weekly from seventy miles' distance was unthinkable. Henry Davison says his father handed over to Joseph Bennett. This Bennett flatly denies. We are not, in short, informed who Davison's successor was.

In any case items from Margate with Davison's signature were always welcome in the old editorial office. To the end he kept the world punctiliously informed about old friends – among them

Joseph Joachim who, worshipped by English quality audiences, was now giving concerts here annually instead of once every two or three years, as had happened hitherto. The following item appeared in the *Musical World* on 14 February 1885, a mere six weeks before Davison's death:

> Joseph Joachim has arrived. Hoch! Hoch! He makes his appearance today on one of the most superb war-horses – the 'spurner of the ground', 'breathing the morning air through his nostrils', 'drinking the wind of his speed', the magnificent '59' of Beethoven. May J.J.'s reception be as enthusiastic and his success as brilliant as on previous occasions. All hail to thee, great master and great friend. – O.B.

'O.B.' stands, of course, for Otto Beard, one of his 'Old Muttonian' pen-names, the '59' of Beethoven for the three string quartets in F major, E minor, and C major. The 'Muttonian' allusion is a reminder that he never tired of his literary quirks and comicalities. The same issue of the *Musical World* carries a note from Joachim himself: 'What about Marlow? If you intend to go on Monday, let me know . . . If you cannot Monday, fix another day next week. Thine, J.J.' To the end, then, he loved and yearned for the Thames-side woods of his youth and the Shelleyite extravagances they had nurtured.

Another chore was analytical programmes for the 'Popular' concerts at St James's Hall. These were given on alternate Saturdays and Mondays down the years. Far from being 'popular' in our late-twentieth-century sense, they maintained a high and consistent classical standard. Davison's analytical notes were brief, almost brusque, on the literary side. His music-type illustrations, on the other hand, spread deep and wide over the page, taking in all salient *motifs* and much else. Between London and Margate there must have been a constant shuttle of music scores by train parcel.

The morning's work over, Davison would shut the inkwell lid, toss aside his pen and descend the stairs for jug-and-bottle delights. By noon most days he was to be found in the public bar of the York, drinking and talking, avidly listened to by both 'locals' and any musician who chanced to be in Margate or had been drawn there by his presence and entertainment-value.

One caller at the York during that last summer was Alexander Campbell Mackenzie, a much younger man – though not more than four years later he succeeded to the principalship of the Royal Academy of Music. There stood Davison before a plate of oysters, radiating comicality. Mackenzie had just had a new oratorio produced. Susan, the waitress, sped by with a laden tray. 'A moment, Susan!' he bade. 'Let me introduce you to the composer of *The Rose of Sharon*. Nothing like it since *Elijah*!' Susan, who had probably never heard of either the prophet or Mendelssohn, grinned and said 'Pleased to meet you, sir.' Davison shoved the oysters towards Mackenzie; and Mackenzie, knowing what he was up to, began to talk about opera. After a moment or two he brought up Wagner's name. Instantly Davison threw up his hands and, eyes dilated with horror, shouted 'Police! Police!' Other drinkers in the bar looked startled. But all the time, adds Mackenzie, there was a twinkle in Davison's blue eyes. Neither was caught by the other's chaff. Chuckles and mutual back-slapping followed.

Until the chills and winds of winter set in, Davison would occasionally take a walk on the pier. One day he saw men in boats shooting seagulls and others looking complacently on. Distressed and impatient, Davison shook his stick at them, exclaiming 'Infernal oafs!' When the weather kept him indoors and there were no callers he contented himself with sitting in his room and looking out on to the sea.

He was spared a long illness. Henry Davison speaks of his being bedridden for 'a few days'. Jaundice seems to have been the trouble. On the morning of 24 March 1885, they found him dead in bed. Six days later he was buried at Brompton Cemetery, London. Among the mourners were Arthur Sullivan, the faithful Joachim, the blind, testy Macfarren and – a surprise for some, perhaps – his widow, Arabella Goddard who, still in her forties, had officially retired after her Paris Exhibition (1878) concerts and was to live on for most of another forty years. Somebody at the funeral is sure to have had a programme of the Saturday Pop concert a couple of days earlier. A girl called Clotilde Kleeberg had played Chopin's F minor fantasia. We know that Davison worked to the end. His analysis of the fantasia was for the most part civil enough. But the last line, referring to a *cantando*-type melody remarked that *cantando* effects were one of Chopin's strongest characteristics – if also, occasionally, one of his feeblest. This equating of Chopin's 'strongest' characteristics with his 'feeblest' implies that his remaining characteristics were, according to the rules of comparative and absolute, feeble or feebler: in other words, that the man's music wasn't worth twopence. That such should have been the tone and turn of Davison's death-bed thoughts, or some of them, induces not resentment but sadness and melancholy.

This ends my biographical section. Now for Part Two, consisting of excerpts from Davison's critical writings.

PART TWO

I

SCHUBERT

An Unpractised, Overrated Man

Musical World, 13 June 1844

This is the issue in which Davison reprints from the Morning Herald *gushing notices of two songs from his pen to words by Shelley, sung by Miss Dolby and Miss Marshall at a concert four weeks earlier in the Princess's Concert Room, Oxford Street. (See Part One.)*

Sixth Philharmonic Concert of the season. The second part of the concert presented no novelty but the overture of Schubert, *Fierrabras*, which is literally beneath criticism. At the rehearsal we took it for an overture by Prince Albert, but on being told that Schubert was the composer we were not greatly surprised. Perhaps a more overrated man never existed than this same Schubert. He has certainly written a few good songs. But what then? Has not every composer that ever composed written a few good songs? And out of the thousand and one with which Schubert deluged the musical world, it would, indeed, be hard if some half-dozen were not tolerable. And when that is said, all is said that can be justly said about Schubert.

Musical World, 9 February 1850

We shall shock the prejudices of many in avowing that Schubert was an overrated man. That he had 'a spark of divine fire' in him is not to be doubted. The concession, wrung with such difficulty from the jealous and contemptuous Beethoven, may be accepted as an epigrammatic expression of the exact truth. 'A spark of divine fire' was what Schubert possessed – not more, not less. He was neither a universal man nor a commanding genius. He was,

moreover, a musician of no great learning. He belonged to that
class of composers and poets, so numerous in Germany, of whom
Carl Maria von Weber, most gifted of them all, may be taken as
the great type and model. These men, from their peculiarity of
temperament and intellect, would have attained a certain degree of
eminence in any pursuit to which circumstances and education
might have conducted them. But their organizations were not, as
those of Handel, Mozart and the great musicians, so happily
attuned to music that it were almost impiety to deny them to be
the instruments selected by Providence to fill the earth with
melody. Morbid and enthusiastic natures, they seem continually
lamenting their incapacity to tell the world their thoughts in plain
and convincing language. Never commonplace or vulgar, they are
for ever in trammels. Such men will always meet with many
ardent worshippers – natures like their own, yearning for the
impossible, disdaining common truths, whose minds are attuned
to their own sympathetic discord. These will proclaim them the
only true prophets; these will assert their pre-eminent superiority
to all others. What is called 'the Romantic School' is really to be
traced to Weber, Schubert and the rest, who in their eager search
for original modes of expression have unconsciously given birth
to a world of mannerisms which have been seized upon by the
vulgar tribe of music-mongers to conceal the emptiness of their
own ideas . . . Schubert was a man of genius, mind and conscience. That he was not a great musician was partly the fault of
his education but chiefly of his organic development. As a painter,
a poet or a novelist – as everything, indeed, but an arithmetician,
logician, mathematician – Schubert would have obtained quite as
much celebrity and quite as great an individuality as that which
awaited him in his career of musical composer.

But, to leave aesthetics, Schubert, in some symphonies,
overtures, quartets, etc., has evinced a great desire to excel in the
sonata form; but he was not entirely successful. He either
disdained or failed to understand thoroughly the indispensable
elements of that form – clearance, consistency and symmetrical
arrangement of themes, keys and episodes. Schubert, though
gifted with an abundant flow of ideas, was greatly wanting in the
power of concentration and arrangement. He accepted all that
came to him and rejected nothing. Thus, while he is never
insipid and almost always interesting, he is diffuse, obscure and

exaggerated. He rarely attempts to develop a principal idea but often conducts an accidental figure, a mere passage of ornament, or a fragment of *remplissage*, through a labyrinth of modulation and progression, until the ear and attention are fatigued and satiety is succeeded by revulsion. In six grand sonatas for the pianoforte *solus*, which, if length and attempt were alone necessary to constitute perfection, would claim a place by the side of the finest Beethoven and Dussek, the tendencies to exuberance of detail, want of connection, superfluous modulation, redundancy of episode, excessive use of strange and unnatural harmonies, are remarkably prominent. They are more diffuse and rambling than those of Weber, to which they are in all other respects inferior . . .

Many of the smaller works of Schubert for the pianoforte – and especially some marches and other characteristic pieces for four hands – are charming from beginning to end; but in these he was not confined to any particular forms; and his ideas are allowed to present themselves in their primitive simplicity, without developments of any kind. In such minor pieces Schubert was quite as successful as in the best of his songs . . . To those who have a tinge of romance in their temperaments, the pianoforte compositions of Schubert . . . must always have a great degree of interest. There is something irresistibly attractive in the melancholy that is never absent from his smallest efforts, while the indisputable originality of his ideas places him far out of the pale of ordinary thinkers and extorts forgiveness for much that is wanting in the form and symmetrical arrangements that have given durability as well as charm to the imperishable models that the great masters have bequeathed to us . . . The peculiarities that have gained him this distinction [that of being placed apart from his contemporaries] have equally prevented his works from exercising any palpable influence on the progress of the pianoforte and on the art of composing for that universal instrument.

THE 'GREAT C MAJOR'

Musical World, 2 April 1859

Franz Schubert's symphony in C was performed at St James's Hall on Wednesday. One important failing, it must be admitted, characterizes all Schubert's instrumental works; this is the evidence of the want of the constructive power which is the one particular quality to give value to the creative faculty. The richness of invention displayed in the symphony before us is [as] profuse as the capacity for order and arrangement is deficient; ideas crowd on one another with never-ending facility, but their purposeless repetition annuls the effect of their beauty and wearies the attention as much as their number and variety exhaust it. A most valuable lesson to the musical student is here presented of the indispensable importance of the rules of form to give coherence and the intelligibility which can be consequent only upon coherence even to the most beautiful imaginings. The ideas throughout the symphony are all of minute character, and the instrumentation is entirely of a piece with the ideas; there is no breadth, there is no grandeur, there is no dignity in either; clearness and contrast and beautiful finish are always apparent, but the orchestra, though often loud, is never massive and sonorous, and the music, though always earnest, is never majestic and imposing. The excessive length of every one of the movements – the fatal characteristic of Schubert as an instrumental writer – induces, on hearing them, a painful impression of squandered beauties, of the effect of which the want of condensation in the work renders an audience almost insusceptible.

Musical World, 9 April 1859

In this issue Carl Klindworth's letter refuting Davison on Schubert's 'Great C Major' symphony is followed by a further Davison assault:

Herr Klindworth defends Schubert's symphony in C major, not so much on the ground of its intrinsic worth as a composition – which he somewhat anomalously and yet, we cannot but think, prudently, leaves an open question – as on account of the very imperfect execution which (if his authority is to be accepted) was awarded it on Wednesday week . . . Had Herr Klindworth simply argued, on behalf of Schubert's symphony against the strictures of our own reporter and other reporters of the London press, our task would, we cannot but believe, have been an easy one – for, if ever there was a positive and irrefutable fact, it is that to Schubert, more than to any other composer – to Schubert's instrumental compositions more than to his vocal works – and to Schubert's one symphony [in C] – the preachers of a modern doctrine which, if successful, would end in subverting music an an art altogether, are indebted for their weapons of defence. Schubert, though a man of undoubted, if not of the highest, genius, was manifestly only a half-educated musician, and the weaknesses around which his ardent imagination threw a brilliant halo have been symbolized by the new prophets – whose ignorance is matched only by their effrontery – as *perfections*, no more to be questioned than the attributes of Jove, no more to be pried into curiously than the Eleusinian mysteries. Herr Klindworth, with innate sagacity, shirks the question of the transcendent merits of Schubert's very laborious but unhappy symphony and gives the new school (of which, we have reason to know, he is a disciple), in some respect, the 'cold shoulder'. He even quotes MENDELSSOHN as an authority – Mendelssohn, the Nemesis of the entire fraternity – and quotes him, too, in conjunction with Schumann, whose musical idiosyncrasy [was] wholly antagonistic to that of Mendelssohn and whose enthusiasm for Schubert was the result of imperfect appreciation while that of Mendelssohn sprang from a certain nobility of nature, which made him look, not merely with sympathy but with a sort of genial tenderness at the amiable efforts of aspiring minds not equal in strength and purity to his own. Schumann, a frail man, bowed before Schubert as an idol; Mendelssohn, an intellectual giant, caressed him as the mailed warrior might caress a fragile maid or grimly fondle an innocent child.

2

CHOPIN

A Morbidly Sensitive Flea

Musical World, 28 October 1841

Under Review: *Souvenirs de Pologne*, Seventh Set of Mazurkas by Frederic Chopin, published by Wessel and Stapleton, London.

Monsieur Frederic Chopin has, by some reason or other which we cannot divine, obtained an enormous reputation but too often refused to composers of ten times his genius. M. Chopin is by no means a putter-down of commonplaces; but he is, what by many would be esteemed worse, a dealer in the most absurd and hyperbolical extravagances. It is a striking satire on the capacity for thought possessed by the musical profession that so very crude and limited a writer should be esteemed, as he is very generally, a profound and classical musician. M. Chopin does not want for ideas, but they never extend beyond eight or sixteen bars at the utmost, and then he is invariably *in nubibus*.

The greatest art in musical composition is that which is deployed in developing or prolonging any thought that may arrive – the thought may be the result of natural ability, but the facility of using it happily – of making it give character to an extended work – or working out of it all of which it is capable – of causing it to be not only the original feature but the prevailing sentiment – this considerable faculty belongs only to the *practised* as well as gifted composer; and this faculty is utterly unexhibited by Chopin – indeed, the works of this author invariably give us the idea of an enthusiastic schoolboy whose parts are by no means on a par with his enthusiasm, who *will* be original, whether he *can* or not. There is a clumsiness about his harmonies in the midst of their affected strangeness, a sickliness about his melodies, despite their evidently forced unlikeness to familiar phrases, an utter

148

ignorance of design everywhere apparent in his lengthened works, a striving and straining after an originality which, when obtained, only appears knotty, crude and ill-digested, which wholly forbid the possibility of Chopin being a skilled or even a moderately proficient artist. It is all very well for a feverish enthusiast like M. Liszt to talk poetical nothings in *La France Musicale* about the philosophical tendency of M. Chopin's music, but, for our parts, we cannot by any manner of means see the connection between philosophy and affectation, between poetry and rodomontade; and we venture to call the ears and the judgement of any unprejudiced person to witness that the entire works of Chopin present a motley surface of ranting hyperbole and excruciating cacophony.

When he is *not* thus singular, he is no better than Strauss or any other waltz compounder; and, being thus singular, he is by many degrees more unbearable, more tiresome and ridiculous. M. Liszt is reported to have said that there was 'an aristocracy of mediocrity in England, at the head of which is Sterndale Bennett'. He might, with a vast deal more of truth, have asserted that there is an aristocracy of hyperbole and nonsense in Paris, of which himself and his philosophic friend Chopin are at the summit. If Messrs Sterndale Bennett and George Macfarren *be* mediocre, most true it is that Messrs Frederic Chopin and Franz Liszt are super-magnificent; no two things can bear a more superlative difference to each other than the opposite schools thus eminently represented; if one be good, the other must perforce be bad – allow this and we are content – let posterity award to each its real desert. There is no excuse at present for Chopin's delinquencies; he is entrammelled in the enthralling bonds of that arch-enchantress Georges [*sic*] Sand, celebrated equally for the number *and excellence* of her romances and her lovers; none the less we wonder how she who once swayed the heart of the sublime and terrible religious democrat, Lammenais, can be content to wanton away her dreamlike existence with an artistical nonenity like Chopin. We have said so much of the man that we have neither the space nor inclination to say much of the music; suffice it – such as admire Chopin, and they are legion, will admire these mazurkas, which are super-eminently Chopinical. That do *not* we.

Musical World, 4 November 1841

This issue carries a letter from Wessel and Stapleton, of Frith Street, Soho, London, holder of copyright in and 'sole proprietors' of all Chopin's compositions. The letter cites thirty-seven composers, eminent musical executants and other celebrities in praise of Chopin's music. The list includes Hector Berlioz, Robert Schumann, Ferdinand Hiller, Sigismund Thalberg, Ignace Moscheles, Clara Wieck, Franz Liszt, Honoré de Balzac, Jules Janin, Mendelssohn-Bartholdy, Henry Field, Jules Benedict and the celebrated George Sand, one of the most brilliant writers in Europe, who considered Chopin anything but a 'nonentity' to trifle her dreams away upon.

The same issue and those of 11 and 18 November carry rejoinders signed 'Ed.M.W.', (George Macfarren, father of Davison's friend G.A. Macfarren). These I ascribe unhesitatingly, on stylistic and technical grounds, to Davison himself.

Though somewhat startled by the formidable array of testimony brought against our opinion – it may be an individual one; but we can vouch that it is an honest one. We cannot recognize Chopin in the rank where fashion has stilted him; but we readily grant him the merit of doing clever eccentric trifles; and whatever the long list of counsellors the spirited publishers have consulted *may* have said to the contrary, we are persuaded they must *think* with us, that such a spirit of ingenuity has no more to do with high art than the contriver of a Dutch toy is entitled to a place beside the inventor of the steam engine, or the fabricator of a Paris caricature to be lauded as a second Raphael. This is not, unhappily, an age for trifling, and the duty of a critic seems to us to be most fully exercised which tends to the correction of a debility in the public taste – to show that adroitness is not genius – that fashion is not intrinsic value – and that extravagant attempt is not poetical achievement – that there is a wide distance between the genuine virtue of those who scatter ingots in our path and those who throw glittering sand in our eyes – and that eminence belongs of right only to the truly great and to the age that fosters greatness. We think Messrs Wessel and Stapleton have misinterpreted their counsellors and have mistaken their author's popularity for his artistical value. If M. Mendelssohn-Bartholdy or Dr Schumann will assert that Chopin is entitled to be considered a great musician

we will endeavour to believe them and succumb accordingly . . .
but we venture to assure them and the publishers that there will be
no difficulty in pointing out a hundred palpable faults and an
infinitude of meretricious uglinesses such as, to real taste and
judgement, are intolerable.

Let not our gallantry be impugned if we presume to differ with
our correspondents and most probably with Chopin in their
estimate of the 'acumen' of Madame Georges [*sic*] Sand –
enjoying, as she deservedly does, a very high and extensive
reputation as a writer of fiction and romanticist, the lady may well
afford that her claims to infallibility as a connoisseur should be
questioned, especially in an art which she treats but superficially
and a science with which she confesses to have very slight
acquaintance. We have wished well to the . . . enterprise of Wessel
and Stapleton . . . in the dissemination of good and salutary
things, and we sincerely hope that such sterling commodities may
substantially compensate them for the bursting of a few air
bubbles.

HORRORS, UGLINESSES

*Further letters in praise of Chopin were printed, including a second from
Wessel and Stapleton and others signed 'Inquirer', 'An Amateur' and 'A
Professor of Music'. Davison retorted in the three following extracts:*

Musical World, 11 November 1841

We have said our say on this subject and we feel no disposition to
gainsay it . . . We still maintain our original assertion to be true –
that M. Chopin is an expert doer of little things; his concerto and
other lengthy works affording no proofs to the contrary; and that
even those little things are sullied by extravagant affectation and a
straining after originality which, uncontrolled by sound knowledge or judgement, lead him into the commission of the most
palpable errors and uglinesses, and one of which we take to be
incompatible with the characteristics of a 'great musician'. If our
readers differ with us on this subject, we will analyse one of M.
Chopin's works and show what we fancy neither amateur nor
professor – no, nor the 'distinguished critics' before alluded to –
will undertake to reconcile with any just notions of art or beauty.

Musical World, 18 November 1841

. . . Our judgement has already been given on M. Chopin's merits, and we see no reason for reversing it. In an early number we shall, at the desire of many correspondents, whose letters we have thought it unnecessary to produce, select one of the works of M. Chopin for analysis, when we hope to maintain, to the entire satisfaction of all impartial readers, the justice of the views we entertain. [The offers (above) to analyse one of Chopin's compositions were never redeemed.]

Musical World, 25 November 1841

We insert Messrs Wessel and Stapleton's second letter out of a feeling of justice . . . but, as we entertain a strong objection to all personalities in discussion, we must decline inserting any more letters on a subject apparently so excitable of mutual ill-feeling.

The passage below, ascribed to Davison, is quoted without provenance by his son in the biography, From Mendelssohn to Wagner *(p. 286).*

Chopin, compared with Berlioz, was a morbidly sentimental flea by the side of a furiously roaring lion. His music was a garden corner full of timid flowers of weakly nerve.

German musicians in Paris addressed a 'memorial of sympathy' to Mendelssohn's widow on the morrow of her husband's death. Owing to what later proved to be a misunderstanding, Chopin declined to add his signature and was rebuked by Davison.

Musical World, 11 December 1847

I have been reproached by some persons for the bitterness which dictated my observations last week apropos of M. Chopin and the late Felix Mendelssohn-Bartholdy. The reproach is unjust; no bitterness gave birth to those remarks but respect to the departed master [Mendelssohn]; in a single person was concentrated the essence of all music; his death is as though from now to a century forward were to be a blank in the progress of the art. The musician who fails in respect where respect is so manifestly due – nay, I will go further, the musician who does not merely respect but revere, worship, idolize the name of Mendelssohn – I do not, I *cannot* consider a worthy follower owing him no respect, I pay him none. Understand well, I speak only of Chopin *the musician*; of Chopin *the man* I know nothing, not enjoying the advantage of his acquaintance. If not to admire the music of M. Chopin be proof of a bitter spirit, let me for ever be called 'bitter'; I like it not, nor can I like it – it sins against all my notions of the proprieties of the art and presents no *ideal* attraction to my fancy. If to think that Chopin forgot himself in not readily paying homage to Mendelssohn – who, in comparison to the Polish pianist, is as the sun to a spark flickering in a tinder box – entitled me to the charge of bitterness, once more I am content to be styled bitter, and, strong in faith, exult in my bitterness. But, gravely, the accusation is absurd; what I said was not bitter but sweet to all rightly constituted minds.

Musical World, 10 November 1849

OBITUARY

This is not the place to criticize the merits of Chopin as a pianist and as a composer. Time will show, when the influence of his presence among us has faded away, whether the high reputation he enjoyed as a composer (of his peculiar merits as a pianist there cannot be a question) was wholly or partially merited, or whether, as some insist, his genius and influence have been greatly overrated by his immediate circle of admirers and only tacitly admitted by the mass who, knowing little or nothing of his writings, were too apathetic or too indifferent to examine them on their own account. At any rate it must be acknowledged that Chopin, by some means or other, was able to acquire the name of a musician at once profound and inventive, and, whatever may be our own opinion, we are not at present inclined to dispute his claims to be considered one of the most original, if not one of the most gifted and accomplished, composers who have contributed to the repertoire of the pianoforte. He produced, in all, sixty-eight works . . . Of these his studies, a capital work, have been unanimously regarded as his most serious effort, and his mazurkas, which are remarkable for a certain air of fantastic melancholy, as the most pleasing and original of his bagatelles.

3
CHOPIN HERO
The 10,000-word Fib

AN ESSAY ON THE WORKS OF
FREDERIC CHOPIN

*London, published by Wessel and Stapleton, Music Sellers to Her
Majesty, H.R.H. the Duchess of Kent, the Court and the Army,
no. 67 Frith Street, corner of Soho Square. Publishers of the
complete works of Chopin.*

*This, the famous 'Yellow Book', so called from the colour of its
covers, was written to oblige the firm that published Chopin's music
– as well as Davison's. His praises are tortuous and perverse.
Their very extravagance serves a secret purpose – to kill Chopin's
reputation stone-dead.*

The appearance of a great light in this age of musical quackery is
an event worthy the attention of all reflecting followers of art – an
incident not to be passed over by those whose task it may be to
chronicle important matters ere they merge into oblivion. The
prevailing tone of the most important pianoforte music of the
present is unhealthy and vicious in the extreme. Morbid
sentimentality has usurped the prerogatives of passion, while
passages of mere finger-dexterity preside over what was once the
dwelling place of pure melody and ingenious contrivance. The
love of beautiful and unaffected harmony seems wholly dead in
the bosoms of modern composers, who, influenced by the clever
trickery developed in the music of MM. Thalberg, Czerny, Herz,
Dohler and a host of others (the bare mention of whom is, to us, a
matter of infinite distaste), think of nothing but showing how an
idea, in itself absolutely phantasmal, shall be presented in new
forms of clap-trap and arpeggioed into fresh showers of triviality.
With the exception of Felix Mendelssohn-Bartholdy, Henri

Reber, Stephen Heller, Adolph Henselt, Charles Mayer, William Sterndale Bennett and the subject of the present essay, there is scarcely an existing pianoforte composer who does not repeatedly mistake and substitute inflation for energy – maudlin mock sentiment for true feeling – vapid roulades for natural brilliancy. The above are, indeed, honourable exceptions, and, hereafter, we propose to analyse their several compositions – to dilate upon their styles – to explore the metaphysical tendency of their writings – and to measure how far they influence the age which they so eminently adorn.

To begin, then, with Frederic Chopin, an illustrious example of pure and unwordly genius, of true and artistic intelligence – unbending to the polyhedric wand of motley fashion – despising the hollow popularity awarded by an ill-judging and unreflecting mob – laughing at the sneers of shallow critics who, unable to comprehend 'the subtle-souled psycholograms' of real genius, lay bare to the public their plenary ignorance and, ill-fitted to appreciate the unvitiated motives of exalted merit, expose the dullness of their feeble capacity to the contempt of the ill-natured and the pity of the wise. On surveying the entire works of Chopin, we find their grand characteristics to be a profoundly poetic feeling, which involves a large degree of the transcendental and mystic but is essentially and invariably of passionate tendency, of melancholy impression and metaphysical colouring. Chopin does not carry off your feelings by storm and leave you in mingled maze of wonder and dismay; he lulls your senses in the most delicious repose, intoxicates them with bewitching and unceasing melody, clad in the richest and most exquisite harmony – a harmony which abounds in striking and original features, in new and unexpected combinations. The first works which Chopin presented to the world though, of course, not endowed with the decisive and individual character of his now perfected style, clearly pronounced themselves the offspring of a vigorous intellect, of energetic, organitive genius, untrammelled by conventionalities, unfettered by pedantry. As he has progressed his style has grown up and expanded like some goodly tree which casts the shadow of an exuberant foliage over a labyrinth of untrodden paths; a refuge for all beautiful and fantastic shapes – children of his ethereal fancy, of his plastic and glowing imagination. The extent and variety of his works, which are almost wholly devoted to the pianoforte, plainly indicate the unequalled fertility – the overflow-ing luxuriance of his invention – the endless diversity – the unprecedented abundance of his resources.

His concertos – only surpassed, if, indeed, they be surpassed, by those of the great Beethoven – are vast in their conception, bold in their outline, rich in their motives, minutely and dexterously finished in their details. The first, in E minor, op. 11, combines all the passion and intense excitement of the *great* modern schools, with the distinct plan and clear development of the old masters; the learning of a Sebastian Bach is joined to the ideality of a Mendelssohn, the untiring melody of a Rossini, the mystic grandeur of a Weber, the dreamy restlessness of a Sterndale Bennett – the whole coloured with the delicious peculiarities of Chopin's own piquant and charming manner, seasoned with the infinite and captivating graces which distinguish and place him apart from, and beyond, the reach of all other modern composers. This concerto has been made known to the amateurs of music in England by the artist-like performances of [several] distinguished members of the Royal Academy, where it is a stock-piece, a complete *cheval de bataille*, a last test of perfect execution and elaborate expression. The second concerto in F minor, in addition to the above-named enviable characteristics, has an originality so marked as to place it beyond the pale of all ordinary compositions of the kind. The difficulties, though enormous, are amply compensated by the fascination of its melody, the richness of its harmonies and the ingenious management of its orchestral accompaniments.

Next in importance to the concertos must be ranked those inimitable studies, which have effected more for the rapid advancement of pianoforte playing to the uttermost limits of perfection than any elementary works that are extant. The universal reception of these at all the great musical schools throughout Europe is an irrefutable argument in favour of their intrinsic excellence. They comprehend every modification of style necessary for the attainment of a thorough mastery over the pianoforte, from the grand to the playful – from the grave to the gay – from the elaborate to the simple – from the simple to the beautiful – every shadow of sentiment is deputed – every mood of passion – every diversity of phrase – is not merely touched upon but thoroughly and effectively accomplished. To obtain an entire command over these splendid studies (which command involves an undoubted mastership over every difficulty that modern or ancient pianoforte music presents) it is advisable to commence with a careful practice of the twenty-four preludes, through all the keys (op. 21) which are evidently intended by the composer as a preface to his more elaborate work. These charming sketches might be easily mistaken for some of the lighter effusions of Sebastian Bach from the remarkable adherence to the severe diatonic schools of progressions (smacking so strongly of the manner of the old masters), for which they are distinguished – suggesting one proof among a hundred of the large range of Chopin's musical reading, which has evidently been directed to the works of every composer whose labours are worth knowing. One thing is certain, viz., – to play with proper feeling and correct execution the preludes and studies of Chopin is to be neither more nor less than a *finished pianist* – and, moreover – to comprehend them thoroughly, to give life and tongue to their infinite and most eloquent subtleties and expression – involves the necessity of being in no less degree a poet than a pianist – a philosophical *thinker* than a musician. Commonplace is instinctively avoided in all the works of Chopin – a stale cadence or a trite progression – a humdrum subject or a worn-out passage – a vulgar twist of the melody or a hackneyed sequence – a meagre harmony or an unskilled counterpoint – may in vain be looked for throughout the entire range of his compositions – the prevailing characteristics of which are – a feeling uncommon as beautiful – a treatment as original as felicitous – a melody and a humming as new, fresh, vigorous and striking as they are rare, utterly unexpected and out of the ordinary track.

In taking up the works of Chopin you are entering, as it were, a fairy-land untrodden by human footsteps – a path hitherto unfrequented but by the great composer himself; and a faith and a devotion – *a desire to appreciate and a determination to understand* – are absolutely necessary to do it anything like adequate justice. As Coleridge remarks, in reference to the inspired truths of Holy Writ, 'There are beautiful things that find us (rather than are *found by us*), more great ideas that *come to us* (rather than we *go to them*)' in the compositions of Chopin than in those of almost any other author existing or dead, if we except, possibly, Bach, Beethoven and Mendelssohn-Bartholdy.

THE GUILELESS HEART

Among the longer compositions of Chopin the mazurkas – those
'cabinet pictures', as Liszt has happily designated them – those
green spots in the desert – those quaint snatches of melancholy
song – those outpourings of an unworldly and trustful soul – those
exquisite embodiments of fugitive thoughts – those musical floods
of tears and gushes of pure joyfulness – those sweet complaints of
unacknowledged genius – stand alone and unrivalled. These are
wholly and individually creations of Chopin, which none has
dared to imitate (for who, indeed, would aspire to imitate that
which is inimitable?), portraying in vivid colours the patriotism of
home-feeling of the great Polish composer (we need hardly
remind our readers that Poland boasts the honour of having given
birth to Chopin), affording vent in passionate eloquence to the
beautiful and secret thoughts of his guileless heart. Of these there
are eight sets, all of the rarest loveliness – sparkling with genius –
redolent with fragrant thought – very nosegays of sweet and
balmy melody. If we have a preference, where all is beauty
unsurpassed, it is for the first and sixth sets, which for quaint and
happy melody, rich and delicious harmony, ingenious and novel
treatment, are unrivalled since music was an art. How often have
we turned our laughter into tears – our tears into laughter (for
some are merry, some are sad), – by the aid of these delicate
idealisms, these sweet glimpses of a world far from our own, –
'where music and moonlight and beauty are one' – these dear
confessions of a bashful mind, retiring within the mantle of its
own loveliness from very modesty of its own deserts! How often
have we soothed an anxious hour – healed a mental grief – *flattered*
a despairing love – aroused dreams of a loved one and all that is
most heaven-ful – transported ourselves to a distant realm of
happiness – lost sight of this world and all that it contains – by the
simple administration to the desire of one of these loveliest
effusions – gentle – consolatory – melancholy – caressing –
blooming and fragrant, buds of mingled joy and sadness which,
on the ear, – 'sing like the melody of early days' and act as
reposeful opiates to the embittered mind – as balm to the wounded
heart – as sweet ointment to the suffering spirit – as delicate
reproval to excess of grief or merriment; – little rivulets which
sport unseen amidst the mountains and deserts – laughing or

weeping as they flow along – innocent as childhood – tranquil as unborn desire! If death were to summon us tomorrow to our last house, we should be happy in its embrace, could our soul but be soothed into eternity by the balmy breath of these breezelike melodies, 'as far as the fabulous Asphodels', touching as the complaint of a love-lorn maiden – thrilling as reciprocated epipsychosis of heart-gushings, bewitching as the smile of Eugénie!!! These charming bagatelles have been made widely known in England through the instrumentality of [several] eminent pianists, who enthusiastically admire and universally recommend them to their people.

Another interesting feature among the miscellaneous works of Chopin is comprised in the nocturnes, a species of composition which he has carried out to a greater degree of perfection than any other author. On these elegant sketches, all the finesse, all the coquetry, all the infinitesimal delicacies, all the minute and barely perceptible graces which, conglomerated into a whole, form what is termed STYLE, must be lavished in order to interpret fairly their infinite meaning – to develop completely their manifold beauties. They are triumphant answers to the aspersers of Chopin, who, from inability to seize his intentions, by reason of their intense subtlety – who, from incapability of *bringing out* his phrases, owing to a lack of *legato* quality in their playing, are bold enough to accuse him of a deficiency in melody – a requisite which, needless to say, he possesses in a more remarkable degree than any other living composer for the piano. To hear one of these eloquent streams of pure loveliness delivered by such pianists as Edmund Pirkhert, William Holmes or Henry Field, a pleasure we have frequently enjoyed, is the very transcendency of musical delight. Every and each of them is a perfect gem – we would not disparage the rest by giving a preference to any one of them – they are, without an exception veritable *chef-d'oeuvres* of their kind, and would have placed Chopin in the first rank of modern composers had he indited nothing else. There are fourteen of them, and were we to be three days deprived of any one of them, we should be absolutely melancholy, feeling towards them the sort of affection that we are apt to attach to such objects as are familiar and necessary to our well-being and happiness.

In his polonaises, too, of which he has written seven, of various lengths and forms, Chopin has marched many strides beyond the vulgar track of the generality of such things. These are remarkable for a boldness of phraseology, a decision of character, a masterly continuousness of purpose, and a sparkling brilliancy of passage which are entirely out of the reach of second-rate thinkers – as is amply manifested by the failure of one and all the attempts to ape their peculiarities which are daily issuing from the hands of the engravers and die as soon as they are born, causing the shelves of the publishers to groan under excess of corruption and decay. Chopin, in his polonaises, and in his mazurkas, aimed at those characteristics which distinguish the national music of his country so markedly from that of all others – the quaint idiosyncrasy – the identical wildness and fantasticality – that delicious mingling of the sad and the cheerful, which invariably and forcibly individualize the music of those northern countries whose language delights in combinations of consonants, *nvcdf-hlzwrbms*-wise, such as the Russian and the Polish. As mere pieces of display they are equal, if not superior, to those noted compositions of the same class which have proceeded from the inspired pen of Weber – and [for the marked effect which they always produce on a mixed auditory, are admirably calculated for drawing room display and would most beneficially occupy the place too often usurped] by the contemptible puerilities, blasphemed into importance by reason of their enormous assumption, with which . . . such harmonic knife-swallowers – such crotchety turners of somersaults as Messrs Thalberg, Dohler and their detestable tribe of empty followers* belabour the ears and dull the understandings of the votaries of music.

The waltzes of Chopin are distinct from those of any other composer by reason of their fluent melody – their greater length – their superior elaboration – their ampler resources of harmony – and other characteristics of an elegant and cultivated mind. Of these there are five, all of extreme beauty and singular originality – and far superior to anything else of the class extant. If we may be

---

*These charlatans would never be tolerated in this country, were it not for the support afforded them in the press by such inflative spouters of hyperbole and rank nonsense as the musical critic of the *Athenaeum* who, 'ever returning to his vomit' monotonously mouths it, as though Cloacina vouchsafed him her special and distinctive favour (*Dunciad*, b.2) and even recollected his bygone begettings from their nearest goal –

'Renewed by ordure's sympathetic force . . .'

allowed to entertain a preference we could select the exquisitely
plaintive *morceau* in A minor (no. 2 of the *Trois Grandes Valses*,
op. 34) which, for contrived and energetic brilliancy, for fresh,
invigorating melody, has scarcely a parallel.

Beside these there are the ballades (three of them), a species of
song without words, equal in their way to those of the celebrated
Mendelssohn, though in no way whatever, be it understood, an
imitation of them. They require an infinitude of varied expression
in their performance – and a *singing* tone, of which only
intellectual pianists can boast but which [is] stringently imperative
in order to ensure their entire appreciation. They will not endure a
slovenly, scrambling, uncertain mode of playing; the performer
must think as a poet and possess the power of giving a reality to
his impulse through the medium of remarkable manual dexterity.
We have frequently met with instances of very remarkable
musicians who have been excluded from the comprehension of
Chopin's music simply from inability to render it exactly
according to the intentions of the composer, by reason of a want
of those finger-requisites which are at least half the battle in the
formation of a perfect pianist; labouring under this deficiency,
they have rashly denied Chopin the rare distinction with which
the first authorities in Europe have endowed him, until, chance
favouring them to the hearing of one of his compositions,
correctly and thoroughly mastered by some *pianiste de premier
force*, they have immediately and with the ready frankness and
liberality only appertaining to *real talent*, owned the error of the
impression under which they had been labouring and ranked
themselves henceforward among the crowd of his most enthusiastic admirers. We mention this especially because the ballades,
more so almost than any other works of Chopin, absolutely insist
upon a finish of performance only attainable by severe study and a
strong desire to 'read, mark, learn and inwardly digest'. 'He that
hath ears to hear, let him hear.' He who enters upon the study of
Chopin's poetical music with the heartlessness of an infidel or the
indifference of a sceptic will be at a discount for his trouble; let
him cease his endeavours to attain what, to him, FROM LACK
OF FAITH, is unattainable; let him descend from the loftiest
clouds of ideal sublimity and grovel amid the mire of the mindless
mummery of the *popular* composers and the unmythical in art –
Chopin is beyond him. He, on the other hand, who approaches

him with veneration and a faith and a love pre-created by the
coupling of anticipation and desire will find to his delight his most
extravagant preconceptions realized and will at once declare that
Chopin is by far the most poetical, by many degrees the most
purely intellectual, of modern pianoforte writers.

WILD, GLOOMY

Perhaps one of the most extraordinary of all the works of Chopin
both on account of its exceeding originality and its strangely
fantastic structure is the grand sonata, in the sullen and moody key
of B flat minor. This wild and gloomy rhapsody is precisely fitted
for a certain class of enthusiast who would absolutely revel in its
phantasmagorical kaleidoscope. At its first setting off, it hurries
you irresistibly into regions mountainous and dreary where no
presence but that of the vulture reigns – where storms are asleep,
wrapped in the embraces of the clouds and terrible even in
slumber – where the torrents, tormented into a thousand courses
by the jutting and jagging and twisting and twirling and rising and
falling and smiling and frowning of the rocks – rush here and there
with a gushing sound of despair as of unburied spirits or fretful
maniacs in their cells, submitting to fatality with a groaning and a
gnashing that sickens the heart and – 'Make men tremble who
never weep' – so awful is the influence of this eternal plaint. As
you proceed the scene becomes darker and more terrible – the
ravines are peopled with distorted and grim-visaged figures –
embodied frights – personified vices – crimes made manifest in
shape; the storms awake – the clouds unlock their clasp and let
them loose – the fretful waters are lashed into million-fold fury –
the rocks cry out in a hollow sound of inward pain – fires peep
from out the mouths of the volcanoes and make grimaces at the
warring elements – the thunder rolls down in a lazy but vociferous
bellowing, pursuing with hopeless precipitation the swift lightning, whose course is felt, not seen, its presence in all space being
immediate – the scene one of mingled sublimity and horror; and
just as the imagination is to the highest pitch excited, a silence
sudden and deep – 'A pool of treacherous and tremendous calm' –
comes over you as a dream and envelops you in its soft embrace; –
anon the silence is killed – new storms arise and wage a boisterous
warfare, and the scene closes in elemental turmoil. Such are the

impressions to which we are subject under the influence of this wonderful work — a very triumph of musical picturing — a conquest over what would seem to be unconquerable — viz, the mingling of the physical and the metaphysical in music — the sonata representing a dual picture — the battle of actual elements and the conflict of human passions — the first for the multitude, the last for the initiated.

In his trio for pianoforte, violin and violoncello, Chopin has had to contend against the popularity of the lighter effusions of Reissiger which are almost the life and soul of the great body of amateurs and — a harder task still — against the gorgeous imagination of a Beethoven, the earnest intensity of a Mendelssohn and the flowing facility of a Hummel; — yet we feel bound to say, he has succeeded in producing a work which steers clear of the peculiarities of each of the schools — the flimsy, the poetical or the strictly classical, as above eminently represented — a work of a mixed kind, that, were it more generally known, would be hailed with delight by the lovers of this most interesting and thoroughly domestic species of chamber music. Its superior attraction to the trios of Reissiger depends mainly on the higher beauty of the materials with which it is composed — since, as a matter of mere execution, it is perfectly within the reach of the great mass of trio-players. Its profound thoughtfulness will conduce to the elevation of the common feeling for music of so grave and lofty a character — while, on the other hand, it will facilitate his powers of execution by the novelty of its forms and passage and the freshness of its combinations, which place it wholly apart from any work of the kind hitherto produced. It is by no means so abstruse as the Beethovens (the great ones), still less does it emulate the deeper intricacy of those of Mendelssohn, and further off than ever is it from the enormous complexities of the trio in E minor of Spohr — the only work of the kind which has proceeded from the pen of that great master. A tolerable pianist — a good second-rate violinist — and a moderately skilful violoncellist — may easily master this trio with satisfaction to themselves and pleasure to the hearers; and its excessive beauty cannot fail of conducing to its extended popularity when once it shall become known. In regard to style it resembles neither Mozart nor Beethoven nor Hummel nor Weber nor Mendelssohn, nor Spohr nor Reissiger — but simply it is *Chopin* — to the lovers of his delicious captivations of style, — his arch playfulness – his healthy naiveté – his happy melancholy – his tender passion – his brilliant passage writing – his quaint harmonization – his ingenious contrivance – and his fresh, flower-like, balmy, inspiring, delicate, subtle, passionate and soulful melody – an ever-flowing stream which falls into some far ocean of sound, where all the divinest strains are floating like naiads on the bosom of the waters – to these it will be a draft of veritable nectar – a heart's feast of passion and beauty, with which the sails will be filled as with an atmosphere of luscious breezes – refreshing – fragrant – bracing – exhilarating and contentful – to these it will be a real love-gift.

We must next speak of the scherzos of Chopin, of which there are three, each deserving individual notice both on account of rare merit and distinct character. The first, in B minor, known in England as *Le Banquet Infernal*, has a wildness and a grotesquerie about it which, in addition to the immediate difficulties, will prevent its *immediate* appreciation by any but thorough musicians. A careful investigation, however, of the materials of which it is composed cannot fail of inducing a comprehension of what, at first, might have appeared almost incomprehensible, and *that* once obtained, the path is open to the hearty admiration which must invariably follow. With Chopin's music, it is often that the intellect must be satisfied before the heart can be touched; but once obtain the sanction of the intelligence – once render clear the artful labyrinth which the philosophical composer has imagined – once catch a sight of his design and encompass his meaning – and enthusiasm at once usurps the place of frigid analysis – the heart sits on the throne but now occupied by judgement. We know no better instance of what we have often asserted to our musical friends, viz, that in Chopin's music what frequently appears dryest and most uninviting on a first and superficial acquaintance, becomes on closer intimacy, matter of such evident and undeni-able beauty that you are astonished how you could ever have presumed to question its supremacy or doubt of its transcendent excellence. And so, this scherzo in B minor, which at first appears crude and obscure, in process of time comes out as clear as the noon, without a speck or flaw, without, in fact, a blemish of any kind; and we venture to predict that those who at first will hardly be persuaded to look into it, terrified by its seeming vagueness and complexity, will, in the end, make it a stock-piece for performance either at home or abroad. The second scherzo in B flat, though not a whit less mystical and abstruse, is infinitely less sombre than its predecessors, and it is likely to encounter a larger number of admirers, both on a first acquaintance and after a longer intimacy. It is in the *brilliant* style, and, for pure effect, is equal to any of the most popular pieces of Thalberg, besides being immeasurably superior in a musical point of view, to anything which that overrated composer has ever produced. The third scherzo in C sharp minor is the most *recherché* of the three and altogether one of the most extraordinary of the works of Chopin. For wild and unearthly grandeur it may vie with the best movements of the same kind that have proceeded from the pen of Beethoven, and, though extravagantly rhapsodical and almost catachrestical in the strangeness and rude texture of its motives, it lacks none of the essentials of classical and fine music, being symmetrical in its wandering, appropriate in its oddity (for it will be admitted that a grotesque subject will require grotesque handling – and here both subject and handling are grotesque), continuous in its mysticism; exemplifying, in short, most admirably the golden precept of Homer – SIBI CONSTET, which invaluable and eternal maxim, the very super-quintessence of all artistic truth, permits men of real genius to roam about in [remote] regions with safety and consistency where the less gifted must inevitably flounder and become sport for the laughter of the scornful and the pity of the philosophic few. There are, here and there, scattered throughout the scherzo, uncouthnesses of harmony and false relationships which hypercritical ferreters-out of blemishes might perhaps carp at but which we pass by respectfully as the idiosyncrasies of a great man. Pulling in old Horace once more to our aid with one of his oracular and immortal sayings,

> *Ubi plura nitent in carmine, non ego paucis*
> *Offendur maculus.'*⋆

BENDABLE, TARANTELLISH

Who shall say that the sun is less bright, forsooth? There have

---

⋆Let there be inner harmony. When there are several brilliant things in the tale, I shall not be offended by a few blemishes.

been spots discovered on its surface by some molelike philosophers, who (to use the satirical observation of Voltaire on his 'Micromegas' levelled at poor Fontenelle) *ont pris la nature sur le fait*. Do any of these spot-seekers comprehend the significance of the spots any more than of the light itself? We can safely answer, NO. Let them cease, then, to imitate Vaninus (who, because he comprehended not and railed, was burned as an atheist by the wicked doctors of the Sorbonne, though literally no infidel but a *simple sceptic*) – let them eschew their pryings into the *effigies rerum* and keep their eyes steadily directed to the omnipresent light, and they will find that, as the sun's brightness can be seen through the bodies of the dark spots on its surface (which, though dark, are transparent), so the inspiration of Chopin oozes through and covers with glory the few specks that float upon its vast expanses of light.

We now come to the tarantella op. 43 which, for sparkling animation and deliciously characteristic gaiety, has no competition among the smaller works of Chopin. We can liken this characteristic sketch to nothing so appropriately as to one of the pictures in our English Unwins, by whose pencil the tarantella has been so often rendered poetical in the purest sense. As we proceed with the tarantella of Chopin we are gazing all the while, mentally, on the canvases of Unwin, and our doubt is solely with whom to adjudge the preference – a doubt which merges into certainty of the absolute and entire equality of painter and musician, a greater compliment than which could scarcely be paid to either. This piece is in the key of A flat major, of itself a new feature – for, till now, we never heard of a tarantella in other than a *minor* key. However, Chopin shows us that he can render the major mode as supple and bendable as the minor – as tarantellish and twist-about-able – as mournfully gay and sparklingly melancholy – the true subject of this singular national dance. The time is *presto* and the theme, in melody as simple as the first axiom in mathematics, is rendered piquant and apician by the assistance of the most tasteful, savoury and palate-tickling harmonies conceivable. The course of this simple motive lies through a world of evolving progressions – among the intricacies of which it is conducted on the supple shoulders of a rolling accompaniment of light-footed triplets, which bear away their delicious burden with all the delight of a lover carrying his mistress to the world's end – anon carrying it and kissing it tenderly – anon coqueting with it and leaving it to its own guidance – anon rushing back to it as rapidly 'as comets to the sun' – anon embracing it and hugging it with close amplitude, exemplifying mystically the arcana of pyschical anastomosis – the synarthics of intellectual comprehension – till joyfully and fleetly they bear it to the end of the journey on the wings of an irresistible and inflammable pedal passage which is enough to lift you off your feet with bare excitement. We could play this tarantella for ever, and yet – ought we not to be ashamed to confess it? – until we heard it interpreted by the master fingers of Mr Henry Field, of Bath – we distrusted and miscomprehended it! All hail to thee, Henry Field! If thou hadst effected nothing else to win our regard, the commentary which thou hast given us on this vivid flash of lightning-like genius would have sufficed to waken all our sympathies in thy favour!

The impromptus of Chopin, of which there are two, are remarkable for the *laisser-aller*, which should inevitably characterize compositions partaking in a great measure of the *essential* of improvisation. They also present in an eminent degree another feature, no less necessary in the structure of such pieces, viz, a continuity of feeling, distinguished from monotony by the skilful manner in which the artist develops his resources. Thus, a certain subject is given out and is diversified, transmogrified, modified, beautified, abstrusified, simplified, etc, etc, *ad infinitum* – not through the medium of fugal treatment but simply by the artful management of its progressions and the varied contrivance of its harmonies. Nothing can be more delicately playful than the first impromptu in A flat, with its graceful episode in F minor, wherein Chopin, by the happy usage of the *ornamental*, shows himself a perfect master of this, as of all other modifications of style – and nothing more glowing and impressive than the second, in F sharp major, an unusual key but rendered wonderfully effective in the hands of Chopin.

Of the rondos and lighter effusions of Chopin in the purely brilliant style, we shall merely state that they possess all the requisites for effective display which are the prepossessing charm of the great majority of the writings of Herz and his school, in addition to those more solid qualities that appeal to the understanding and afford that improvement to the mind which in such music is ordinarily confined to the fingers. The rondo in C minor op. I (known to us in England as the *Adieu à Varsovie*) is an admirable specimen of the brilliant and solid styles most felicitously combined, and, in the hands of a tolerably skilful pianist, can hardly fail of producing a powerful effect; since, in addition to the brilliant flow of its passages, it pervades the entire composition – directly in the motives – indirectly (but not the less apparently) in the passages. The rondo *à la Mazurka* in F major op. 5 (known in England as *La Posiana*) is remarkable for the most picturesque and striking character – and the *Krakowiak* or *Grand Rondeau de Concert* in the same key, op. 14, is one of those surprising feats of digital agility which, in the hands of Chopin, are rendered so piquant and enticing as to induce the most scrutinizing critic to lay aside his cynicism and listen with unfeigned delight. The bolero in A minor, which has been somewhat aptly christened *Souvenir de l'Andalusia*, is a delicious specimen of the *melée* of the sad and cheerful in which none have so frequently and happily indulged as the subject of this notice. The subject is rife, with the peculiar feeling of that quaint national dance, and in its treatment the thoughtful composer never once loses sight of the character which is indicated by the first eight bars of the work, continuing it to the close with masterly ingenuity and untiring fancy. How few there are happy enough to possess the enviable power of *continuity* those who *do* possess it best know; and those who do but know, provided they also know the works of Chopin, must admit, without hesitation, his supremacy in this, the highest attribute of the musician.

Among the miscellaneous pieces of Chopin which we have not individualized in detail none has afforded us more gratification than the grand fantasia in A flat major, op. 49. The philosophical and poetical tendency of the writings of Chopin is so manifest and its consideration on passing judgement on them critically is so enticing, that we are apt to forget what to the multitude is of infinitely more importance – viz, their usefulness in the development of the hand and in the finished execution necessary for the formation of a perfect pianist. First, then, it is an admitted fact, even by such as dispute his supremacy as an intellectual composer, that the works of Chopin effect more for the enhancement of pure dexterity – do more towards producing equality of touch – lend more substance to the attainment of flexibility of the wrist, if studied with undiminished assiduity – than those of any other master whatsoever. Thus, they are eminently serviceable even by inexperienced performers; while to the finished and well-read pianist, from the startling novelty of their progressions and the original *tournure* of their passages, they present a totally new field for practice – an altogether unexpected channel for the development of powers hitherto latent and unexercised. It is quite certain that anyone who possesses sufficient command over the instrument to enable him to execute the works of Chopin properly and with the feeling intended by their composer, has it in his power to play whatever else, of whatever difficulty, of any other author that may chance to be placed before him. The compositions of Chopin have no species of difficulty unprovided for – no peculiar figure of passage unexplored – no cunning twisting of an antique cadence untried – so that in matter of execution their utility is universal, and a careful practice of the execution of them is of consummate importance. To show how various is their tendency and how general their applicability to the purpose of attaining universality of style and infinite diversity of executive power, we will merely, for the convenience of our readers, endeavour to throw them into classes and sections so that those wedded to peculiar species of music may all know where to find something to their taste – and that something of the highest order of merit.

INTELLECTUAL REPAST

Davison here inserts tables which classify Chopin's compositions, as published thus far, according to their relative difficulty of execution and also according to characteristics and style. His classes and sections are devised for pianists of 'first force', 'second force', 'third force' and 'ordinary force'. He also distinguishes between 'difficult' and 'moderately difficult' works, and further breaks down Chopin's oeuvre into the 'brilliant and bravura' style, 'metaphysical and poetical' style, the 'expressive and legato' style, the 'characteristic and dramatic' style, and the 'light, amusing' style. He adds that many of the best works of Chopin 'have been ably adapted for two performers on one pianoforte by himself [Chopin] and others, and in this form the greater part of them are easily accomplishable by pianists of moderate pretensions'. In one of the 'moderately difficult' categories, comprising three sets of mazurkas, four nocturnes and three grandes valses, Davison advertises Davison as follows:

Fifth set of mazurkas, arranged by J. W. Davison,	op. 3
Seventh set of mazurkas, arranged by J. W. Davison,	op. 41
Eighth set of mazurkas, arranged by J. W. Davison,	op. 50
Two notturnos (*sic*), 6th set, arranged by J. W. Davison,	op. 37
Notturno in C minor, arranged by J. W. Davison,	op. 48
Notturno in F sharp minor, arranged by J. W. Davison,	op. 48
Grande valse, A flat major, arranged by J. W. Davison,	op. 34
Grande valse in A minor, arranged by J. W. Davison,	op. 34
Grande valse in F major, arranged by J. W. Davison,	op. 34
Grande valse in A flat major, arranged by J. W. Davison,	op. 42

Davison goes on:
Of the extraordinary merit of these compositions we have already spoken so profusely that it is unnecessary here to add another word; simply we must premise that they lose not a particle of their effect or an atom of their interest in their present form of piano duets and, to a couple of intellectual executants, will be a delicate and intellectual repast.

The brilliant polonaise in C major (known in England as *La Gaîté*) is so popular that arrangements of every description have been eagerly demanded by the public. Among the most attractive we may mention that for pianoforte and flute by M. Sedlatzek, a most able and judicious adaptation, in which the powers of both instruments are employed to ample advantage, that for pianoforte and violoncello not less deserving praise; and last but not least an admirable arrangement for pianoforte and violin which is played with enthusiasm and delight by almost every amateur of the violin who has the merest particle of discriminative appreciation of the beautiful in music and the humblest qualities of execution to gratify his mental yearnings.

Moreover, Chopin, ever anxious to bestow pleasure on all, even the humblest partisans of art, has condescended to compose, with the assistance of M. Franchomme, the eminent violinist, a popular duet for piano and viola on themes from the *Robert* of Meyerbeer, which is also arranged for piano and violoncello and is very generally admired.

The estimation in which Chopin is held on the Continent may be tested – firstly by the enormous demand for his works (especially in Germany) – secondly by the unanimous and enthusiastic testimony in his favour of the most celebrated living

musicians, *literati* and men of general learning, including among
them artists of such various opinions and opposite characteristics
as the fantastic and headstrong Berlioz, the despiser of all systems,
past, present and to come; – the wealthy Meyerbeer, whose
celebrity is a paradox; – the *ignis fatuus*, jack-a-lantern, salaman-
der, *feu-follet*-like Liszt; – the respectable John Cramer, whom all
musicians consent to admit 'as a light to lighten the Gentiles',
provided they be not obligated to become acquainted with his
compositions, unnumbered and unknown; – the mystical Robert
Schumann (the well-known 'Eusebius', critic and composer of
triune celebrity) with his charming and talented wife (late the
beautiful, admired and universally wooed Clara Wieck); – the
careful Moscheles, who is ever on the right side; – the abundantly
prolific Czerny; – the ephemeric Herz – whose path is the
lightning's! – and whose fame is as a shooting star; – the laborious
Onslow, prurient of quintets; the animated and sparkling Auber,
the prince of music 'light and airy'; – the Amalekitisch Halévy; –
the gorgeous and lazy Rossini, who, in the oily fatness of his gross
maturity – 'lulled with the sweet nepenthe of a court', has taken to
the composition of sleek anthems and adipose 'Stabat Maters'; –
the classical Henri Reber, in whom unclassicality is a virtue; – the
lengthy Fétis, a mountain in labour; – the studious Stephen Heller;
– the vivacious Schlesinger, whose gift is ubiquity; – the showy
Henselt; – the well-known Kalkbrenner, who has flung a stone at
the bull's eye of two opposite schools, the 'sterling' and the
'flimsy' and has gone over the one and under the other; – the
useful Bertini; – the bombastic Wolff; – the solid and sensible
Mayer; – the ponderous Thalberg, whose *musical* position is a
riddle for an Oedipus to solve; – the industrious Hiller; – the quiet
Dreyshock, whose very soul is an octave; – the Liszt-like Litolff; –
the Thalberg-like Dohler; – the self-opinionated Guhr, who
ejaculates: 'I am Guhr!' and is satisfied that to be Guhr is all that to
be is worth; – the imaginative and gifted Mendelssohn; – the
practical and melodious Sterndale Bennett, a disciple whose light
burns with scarcely less brilliancy than that of his master; – the
modest Rosenhain; the Dutch Verhulst; – the mighty and
metaphysical Spohr; and a host of others we could mention,
without alluding to the *literati*, including the wordy Jules Janin –
the philosopher de Balzac – the fiery Victor Hugo, whose motto is
– '*Le laid – c'est le beau!*' – the paradox-supporting Gustave

Planché; – the devilish Soulié, at whose expense his moral countrymen have made this epigram – Frederick Soulié SOUILLE *tout ses livres* – the double-dramatic Dumas the pseudo-sophical Chorley, whose lucubrations are of parenthetical importance; – the Janus-visaged Sue, of whom it was wittily said – *'Eugene Sue, sang et eau'* – the heady Jules Maurel; – and the passionate George Sand, at their head – all of whom, a daedal throng with opposedly discordant principles – with various and opposite feelings – with diverse and multiplex degrees of merit – with complex and irreconcilable opinions on most points of art – all of whom unite, we say, in the unmodified, decided, reiterated, unmitigated and unanimous opinion of the musical supremacy of FREDERIC CHOPIN. When, then, men of such high celebrity, such vast attainments and such various principles, *co-think* entirely with regard to the transcendent merits of our composer – and, moreover, when, as we know, they all of them are fully cognisant of every note that he has published and much that, unfortunately for art, he preserves yet unpublished in his portfolio – which cognisance, combined with their own undoubted merits, render them judges fit and competent – and, more, moreover, when we are told that gifted men consider the works of Chopin as a Koran for true believers, as a Talmud to enlighten the dullness and opacity of infidels in art, – all this considered, what argument that prejudice, or ignorance, or carelessness, or interest . . . or ENVY, or all of them mingled and jumbled together into a paradoxical pot-pourri of art-prejudicing malignity – stirred up in the tureen of folly with the ladle of obstinacy – poured out into the dish of fatuity – and thence down the throat of incredulity – what argument thus created, what abortion from such a weed-producing womb, can have sufficient preponderance with the unprejudiced and calm observer to shake the firm basis of *our* confident assertion that Frederic Chopin is one of the greatest living composers, and, Beethoven and Mendelssohn excepted, THE MOST ACCOMPLISHED PIANOFORTE COMPOSER THAT EVER EXISTED?

Musical World, 27 December 1876

The ravings of some transatlantic papers about Chopin are becoming absolutely nauseous. He was Mendelssohn's

'Chopinetto' (Chopinettino?) and no more. The attempt to magnify a sentimental drawing room composer into a colossus is simply absurd. Chopin was Chopin – which said, all is said that can be said.

4

BERLIOZ

Vulgarian and Lunatic

Musical Examiner, 18 March 1843

The immense celebrity which this singular composer has acquired in France and Germany imperatively demands that he should have a fair hearing in England. He has not yet been given a chance of making himself known to our musicians. His overtures to *Les Francs Juges*, *Benvenuto Cellini*, *King Lear* and *Waverley* [the only Berlioz pieces heard, as of that date, in England] are certainly by no means calculated to place him, in our estimation, in the ranks of the great living composers. To judge from these we should rather be inclined to class him a daring lunatic than as a sound, healthy musician. Their sole merit lies in the great command of orchestral effect, which they certainly display to an eminent degree. In melody they are particularly deficient – so much so, indeed, that we feel inclined to believe M. Berlioz incapable of producing a complete phrase of any kind. When, on rare occasions, some glimpse of a tune makes its appearance, it is cut off at the edges and twisted about in so unmusical and unnatural a fashion as to give one the idea of a mangled and mutilated body rather than a thing of fair proportions. Moreover, the little *tune* that seems to exist in M. Berlioz is of so decidedly vulgar a character, as to exclude the possibility of our supposing him possessed of a shadow of feeling for pure melody. As regards harmony and counterpoint . . . we are not at all prepared to award him any capacity beyond the merest commonplace. To be ugly and original at the same time is very possible, as M. Berlioz plainly shows – but the kind of originality which depends on ugliness can claim no consideration from a rightly thinking mind. To produce disagreeable sensations can never be the province of music.

Musical World, 26 December 1846

MUSIC IN PARIS

From Our Own Correspondent

The long expected 'legend' of Hector Berlioz, *La Damnation de Faust* has at length been produced at the theatre of the Opéra Comique. The equivocal reception of his first and only opera, *Benvenuto Cellini*, about which his *collaborateur* Jules Janin wrote such a pathetic dithyrambic in the *Journal des Débats*, disgusted Berlioz with the theatre and induced him to follow the example of Beethoven and abandon opera altogether. But *Fidelio* and *Benvenuto* are very different matters, and it is well known that what determined Beethoven never to write another opera was the trouble he had with the singers. Beethoven was a proud man to be turned aside from a path that he might have chalked out for himself, by the coldness of a first-night audience. He knew that his works were destined for immortality, but his sensitive and impetuous temperament revolted at the commonplaces of the *coulisses*, and the squabbles and discontents of his vocalists irritated him to such a degree that he vowed never to expose himself to similar vexations, and he kept his vow. The one opera of Beethoven, however, the superb *Fidelio*, has increased in popularity ever since, and the united judgements of the artists and the laity have long since placed it among the imperishable masterpieces of dramatic music.

How different a man is Hector Berlioz! Endowed with mental qualities of a high order, with an inquiring spirit, an acute observation and a correct judgement, he has won for himself the position of the first musical critic in France. His *feuilletons* in the *Journal des Débats* are the most enlightened and intelligent criticisms of the day. Their habitual severity is tempered by justice, and their style – albeit occasionally fantastic and smacking of . . . modern French romanticism, whereof the motto is '*Le beau c'est le laid*' – is so pointed and vivacious that they find as many readers among the crowd as among those to whose consideration they are specially directed. But Berlioz is a striking example of the possibility of being able to criticize with intelligence, and yet, in the exercise of art, to produce monstrous absurdities that will not bear the test of scrutiny. The music of Berlioz sets at defiance all the wise rules he has been at so much pains to enforce by his literary eloquence. The symmetry of form which he has so frequently recommended as a model in Mozart, the stern simplicity he advocates in Gluck, the power of development he apostrophizes in Beethoven – where are they in *his* works? Despising these absolute essentials of his art – which in hs criticisms he explains and insists upon in terms so glowing, in argument so overpowering – Berlioz, once with pen in hand and music paper before him, treats them as obsolete conventionalities, as remnants of the antique *régime*, unworthy of the consideration

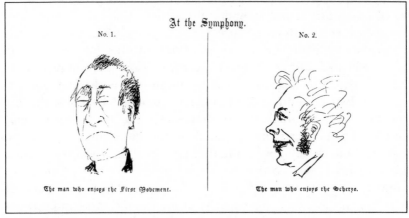

'At the Symphony', *Musical World*, 1 Jan. 1876. Left: No. 1. The man who enjoys the First Movement; right: No. 2. The man who enjoys the Scherzo

of a follower of the modern school, of which he proudly considers himself the chief exponent. Alas!, for this school, so falsely termed romantic, disregards the true mission of romance! What is it but a grand mistake? The ravings of impotence unable to give a form to its conceptions, whose ideas are wild – wild, incongruous and misshapen as the images that delirium paints on darkness. And shall this, the very worst of paradoxes, with its blue and red fire, its garish tinsel and its frantic mummery, put out the eyes of art and lead that divine mistress blindfolded to annihilation? No! While the song of the mighty dead shall vibrate in our halls from the hundred voices of the orchestra, while our theatres are yet open to their immortal inspirations, while our churches echo with their divine harmonies, so long shall their example hold its empire over the hearts of musicians, so long shall the crowd be delighted and purified by their influence. The oppositions of a small knot of egoists, false enthusiasts, self-styled prophets shall not prevail against the long tried principles of truth eternal.

The new work of Berlioz is in manner and construction like all he has previously made known: void of form, as in the earth before creation, confused in colour as the paint-bedaubed pallet of a limner, vague, inflated and unnatural. The golden precept of Horace, *sibi constet*, is violated in every part of it. An indomitable will, and patience worthy of a better object, have doubtless been exercised in its composition, but it can serve no purpose, since it has neither the natural conditions of art nor the poetical expression of the sentiments and situations it pretends to illustrate. M. Berlioz plays no musical instrument – unless the guitar be considered worthy of the name – and holds in avowed contempt the rules of counterpoint and the necessities of rhythm. But without counterpoint there cannot be harmony, and without harmony and melody there cannot be music, properly speaking. M. Berlioz, therefore, writes something under the name, which has none of the conditions of music. How, then, can the position he holds be accounted for? The forced admiration of artists who live in fear of that *pen* which he wields with such unbending sternness in the first journal of the French empire may be readily imagined, and perhaps it is to their tolerance and the liberal indulgence of his brother critics in the other journals that he owes his celebrity, which is, however, as baseless and fantastic as his music.

Perhaps no one of the works of M. Berlioz bears stronger evidence of his peculiar defects than *La Damnation de Faust*, his latest. Were it the production of an ordinary man like Felicien David, I should feel inclined to dismiss it with one word of decided condemnation, for it is at best but an elaborate mistake. But it is the work of a fierce innovator – of a man whose obstinacy in the promulgation of his insane creed has won him, like the martyrs of old, an army of disciples who worship him as a genius unappreciated, as a victim of coldness and envy. Thus, as *Le Critique Musicale* has truly stated, he has propitiated the suffrages of all the paradox-lovers of the day, men who aim at effect by the strangeness and inconsistency of their opinions; he has won the formidable advocacy of the majority of the press – protection, aid, support, honours and sinecures, in short, the tenth part of which, distributed with discernment, might have sufficed for the revelation of ten artists of real genius . . .

Faust? Pah!

The Times, 23 December 1846

Paris. The new 'legend' of Hector Berlioz, *La Damnation de Faust*, has produced the usual effect of this composer's works. It was performed at the theatre of the Opéra Comique by an immense band and chorus, under the direction of M. Berlioz himself, and attracted almost all the musicians of Paris. The *Faust* of Goethe has furnished the subject for M. Berlioz's 'legend', which is nothing more than an opera without action. Many parts of the work were extolled to the skies by the composer's admirers; but, on the whole, it was found lengthy, tedious and incoherent by the general audience. The music of M. Berlioz depends for effect almost entirely upon the massive orchestral combinations he employs and the vast number of his instrumental performers and choristers. Deprived of these adventitious helps, it has little to distinguish it, having scarcely any melody and no decided rhythm. Beethoven thought sixty instrumental performers a force sufficiently powerful for the effective execution of his great symphonies. At least double that number is considered requisite by M. Berlioz, and how insignificant is the result in comparison!

Musical World, 20 June 1863

Well, then – what is *Faust*? Musicians will tell you that, as a work, it is not very remarkable; amateurs insist that it does not to any great extent reveal the faculty of inventing *tune*; purists will add that its style of harmony and modulation is based upon that of Richard Wagner, that it contains not a single ingeniously constructed *morceau d'ensemble* (grave objection to a *grand* opera), that dramatic or melodramatic colouring of the whole is now from Weber, now from Meyerbeer, now from Verdi, now from Halevy.

Musical World, 13 March 1869

Another great musical thinker has gone . . . A more earnest man, a musician more thoroughly persuaded of the absolute truth and rectitude of his own adopted convictions, never existed. It is not now the time to criticize the claims of Berlioz as a composer; but . . . a nature more guileless and honest, an enthusiasm more ardent for all that was great and good, a more staunch and unquenchable hatred of everything that was not genuine than his could not be cited . . . With regard to the man, wholly apart from the musician, to know him was to love him – and this was not [so much] because he was socially attractive and fascinating as because he was good and right-hearted to the core, and, above all, eminently sincere.

Berlioz, whatever views may be entertained about his compositions, was a truly wonderful composer; he had this enviable privilege – that even those who have have conscientiously objected to his general notions of music . . . could not do otherwise than respect him. Among the dissenters from very much that he took infinite pains to promulgate by example was the writer of this valedictory sentence: [The] world is poorer by an honest, upright man and an artist of splendid natural endowments.

5
VERDI
Maker of Wretched Music for Mobs

Musical World, 18 May 1850

Ronconi has arrived and is announced to appear in Verdi's *Nabucodonosor*. Signor Ronconi has no greater admirer than ourselves, but if we must needs admire him through the spectacles of Verdi our admiration will be strongly neutralized. Highly as we esteem Signor Ronconi's dramatic and lyric genius, we have no desire to witness their exposition through the medium of young Verdi's music. No vocalist has a larger and more varied repertoire than Signor Ronconi and why he should be driven to select the worst piece of the worst composer in Italy we cannot comprehend. The subscribers of Her Majesty's Theatre who fostered the rising genius of young Italy and upheld him through good and ill-report – having been gorged with him *usque ad nauseam* – are beginning to repudiate him and pant for healthier strains; it is not, therefore, to be imagined that the subscribers to the Royal Italian Opera, who are feasted with Mozart, Rossini, Weber, Auber and Meyerbeer would put up with Sir Unison and the Knight of Pou-Crash. Verily, no; Verdi will get his quietus in one night, as he did two seasons ago; he will hide his diminished head, and for ever hide it. Let not Signor Ronconi imagine that even his magnificent talents can render the music of Verdi acceptable to the frequenters of Covent Garden. Twenty Ronconis could not make the composer of *Ernani* popular at the Royal Opera House. The directors have taught the public better than that. But surely Ronconi has characters enough in his repertoire which belong to the works of the 'Masters' without having recourse to the *Nabucodonosor* of 'Maestro' Verdi. We grant that his performance of the part is one big *chef-d'oeuvre*; but is that sufficient for a whole night's affliction of listening to wretched music? We trust that

Signor Ronconi, in considering his own reputation will also consult the public ears with a little less selfishness. If he persist in Verdi – why, then, we see no possible use to be derived from his accession to the Covent Garden company. We set our face entirely against the introduction of Young Italy to this theatre.

Musical World, 1 June 1850

Saturday was a sad and joyful night for the Royal Italian Opera. Sad because it brought us the prince of musical mountebanks, Verdi, the Jew-Peter *tonans*; and joyful inasmuch as it restored to our longing eyes and wishful ears one of the greatest masters of song that ever adorned the lyric stage [Ronconi] . . . When Verdi wrote the *Nabucco* he had evidently *Semiramide* in one eye and *Mose in Egito* in the other . . . Had he kept the music in his hearing as well as he seems to have kept the stories in his sight it might have been all the better for his reputation. Young, uneducated, imprudent and fatuous, he determined to pluck the dramatic crown from Rossini and to place it on his own head. His own drama should have read him a severe lesson. The impious Nabucco insisted on his godship and was struck blind for his temerity. Verdi undoubtedly imitated or attempted to imitate Rossini in his so-called grand operas, but it is the imitation of a schoolboy who piles up a two-foot wooden house and fancies he is building a St Paul's. Never was writer of operas so destitute of real invention, so destitute in power or so wanting in the musician's skill. His sole art consists in weaving ballad tunes – we never find any tune in his songs – into choruses, which, sung in unison make an immense noise; or in working up a finale by means of a tremendous crash of the brass instruments, drum and cymbals and voices screaming at the top of their register. Strip his finales of their noise and nothing remains – absolutely nothing. His instrumentation is thin, insipid and pointless; the colouring overcharged; the construction feeble, the developments puerile. He has not a notion of real effect.

Musical World, 14 May 1853

Royal Italian Opera. Tonight the much talked of *Rigoletto*, by young Verdi – who is no longer young – will be produced. From

all the papers and from all rumours, we are authorized in believing
that *Rigoletto* is one of Verdi's masterpieces. Be that as it may, the
subject is a fine and interesting one, as those who have read Victor
Hugo's celebrated tragedy must be aware. Besides, Ronconi plays
Rigoletto . . . and Mario also has an important acting and singing
part . . . Mario and Ronconi together would render less interesting music than that of Verdi more than tolerable . . . The cast
could hardly be stronger.

HOW VERDI COMPOSES

When Verdi has an opera to compose, he waits patiently until the
midnight bell has tolled. He then enters his study, in which there
is a piano placed between a big drum and cymbals, and seating
himself at the piano, he first bangs the drum on the right hand,
then clashes the cymbals on the left hand, then thumps the piano
in the midst, and while the air is reverberating with the mingled
sounds he commences the first chorus. This is the way Verdi
composes. Can anybody have a doubt on the subject?

Musical World, 21 May 1853

Verdi's semi-serious, or rather, melodramatic opera, *Rigoletto*,
was produced for the first time in this country on Saturday. The
reputation this work has gained on the Continent is considerable.
Perhaps not one of the composer's operas – if we except *Ernani* –
has had such a decided success. In all the principal Italian theatres it
has now become one of the stock pieces and is being played at the
moment in twenty or thirty different houses. In some of the
German states, too, it has been produced with great applause, and
last year, at St Petersburg, in the Imperial Theatre, may be said to
have achieved a *furore*. The success has not been all owing to the
music. The drama, though highly objectionable in its principal
features, is interesting and absorbing, and the chief characteristics
are drawn with wonderful art . . . If the new opera on Saturday
night did not achieve an eminent success it must be attributed
solely to the want of any great interest in the music.

POVERTY AND SWAGGER

There is little offensive music in *Rigoletto*; the ears are seldomer stunned than in most of the composer's other works, and there is, we fancy, little pretence in the writing. Nevertheless, Verdi's sins are apparent in every scene. Poverty of ideas, an eternal effort at originality – never accomplished – strange and odd phrases, lack of colouring, and a perpetual swagger in the dramatic effects, are unmistakably true Verdi. Most of all the composer is deficient in the serious parts, and poor Ronconi, with all the fire and power of his genius, could not lend interest to his music. Yet, there are airs – melodies if you will – in *Rigoletto* which are sure to find favour with the barrel-organs. First of all is the *ballata* in the last act, '*La donna e mobile*', as enchantingly sung by Mario, a very pleasing and catching tune, if not new, and worked out with effect. There is an agreeable tune, too, in the duet between Ronconi and Madame Bosio in the second scene; and another in the aria of Gilda in the same scene. Mario's first song, also, we feel will find many admirers. A quartet in the last act, skilfully managed and well voiced is the best piece in the opera. In the theatres of Italy it creates a *furore* . . . With all that has been accomplished for *Rigoletto* by the directors of the Royal Italian Opera, it cannot live. It may flicker and flare up for a few nights, fed by the oil of Ronconi's genius and blown into momentary vitality by the soft breathings of Mario's voice; but it will go out like an ill-wicked rushlight and leave not a spark behind. Such is our prophecy for *Rigoletto*!

Musical World, 5 May 1855

Our clever contemporary the *Leader*, whose musical contributor is a staunch adherent of Herr Wagner and Signor Verdi, has the following ingenious apology for the last-named in its number of the 28th ult.:

> We confess to a weakness for the absurd operas of Verdi who, whatever be the verdict of those severer critics whose purism denounces equally the 'music of the future' and the music of the day, has at least this rare merit – his operas beat with the pulses of Italy. It is well enough for a public sunk in indifference, apathy and lassitude and, invoking despotism as a cure for the difficulties of freedom, to ask for more enervating strains. For the Italy of our day, Art itself is an inspiration after

independence, a menace to tyrants, a call to arms. And such is the music of Verdi.

If the heart of Italy beats to the strains of Verdi there is danger of convulsions. So far so good. But to be told that the inefficiency of certain musicians to master the rules of counterpoint is like to the longing for freedom, which is the right, and should be the happiness, of every people on the face of the earth – this is really too much. Because Verdi is a bad harmonist his music is a menace to tyrants! – because his unisons are boisterous and shrill, [they are] a call to arms! What next! Cannot the *Leader* perceive a difference between those wholesome laws which regulate the science of harmony and the edicts of despotism? To offend the first is to be illiterate, nothing more; to set the last at defiance the mission of a patriot. Is there a shadow of resemblance? No. To oppose unjust governments is one thing; to make war against art is another. The *Leader* does the first, and we admire it. Herr Wagner and Signor Verdi, whose weapons bear no resemblance to each other, do the second, and we oppose them . . . Be assured that the mission of composers who writhe under good rules because they *cannot learn* how to obey them, is not to set the art of music at liberty but to degrade it.

Musical World, 19 May 1855

Second Leader. If not precisely the best, *Il Trovatore* is one of the longest operas of Verdi and in some respects the one in which he has attempted most. We cannot perceive in any part of the music, however, that thorough transformation of style which some of the Continental critics have announced. On the contrary, we find the composer of *Ernani* and *Nabucco* as plainly declared as in either of these works, with the same forms of melody, the same disregard of construction, the same straining of voices, the same choruses in unison, the same violent contrasts and the same poverty of instrumentation . . . *Il Trovatore* is written in contempt of all rules; no *ad captandum* qualities, no contemporary success, however imposing, can atone for the want of refinement, the coarseness of style, the habitual contempt for pure form, which are as apparent as in any of the previous attempts of the composer and are to be regretted, since even with such evidence of dramatic feeling, individuality of manner and fluency of execution, they render it impossible to hope for any newly-awakened desire on the part of Signor Verdi to become essentially an artist. The question of art is distinct, however, from the question of popularity. Signor Verdi, had he known more, would, there is no doubt, have done better. As it is, he may rest satisfied with the applause of the mob and affect to despise the educated few. When *Oberon* failed to obtain the success anticipated and someone told the composer that 'It was too abstruse for John Bull', 'Hang John Bull!' cried Weber. 'I wrote *Oberon* for the world!' He may have written with a view

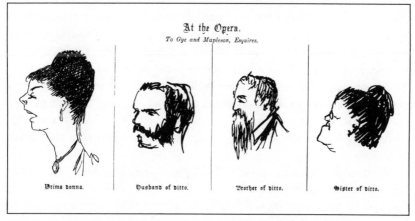

'At the Opera', *Musical World*, 22 Jan. 1876. Left to right: Prima donna; Husband of ditto; Brother of ditto; Sister of ditto

to immortality, but he did his best, for all that, to please John Bull. John Bull was exhausted by *Der Freischütz*, and why not with *Oberon*? Here is matter for speculation. Signor Verdi also writes for 'de world' in which he lives and is heedless about 'the future'. Applause is to him the breath of his nostrils. To gain applause he must conciliate mobs and ignore 'ears polite'. From mobs he takes his cue, having studied their tastes, feelings, sympathies and prejudices. He writes exclusively for mobs and is accepted and worshipped as their idol. His aim is less to be a musician than a popular composer. He has revolutionized the musical stage in his native country; for his operas all others are forgotten. In time he made himself a name on the other side of the Alps. Other mobs caught up the enthusiasm, which spread from kingdom to kingdom until new countries were invaded and conquered, and the mob idol of one land became the mob idol of all. Is this, or is it not, the secret of Verdi's career? Would this have been effected without talent, and is Verdi the nonentity that musicians would make him out? We say nothing. It is amusing to compare the opinions of 'judges' with the emotions of the public. Meanwhile grumblers are in a minority. *Il Trovatore* is applauded; and the directors of the Royal Italian Opera put money in their pockets every night it is performed.

From another point of view, those partisans who are for ever bawling and bawling about 'Young Italy' and its middle-aged musical representative and rate all who differ from them as blockheads, pedants or men without principle, are not worth an argument. They are for the most part if not *ignorami*, simply worldlings who date everything from success, which they worship with a sort of obstreperous and presuming flunkeyism. They are not a bit less vain, foolish, blustering and empty than a certain class of mundane speculators of the school ironically termed 'fast' who, incessantly presuming to detect the 'weak side' of humanity, are intellectually blind to distinguish one side from the other . . .

Verdi should communicate with Richard Wagner – the other red republican of music, who wants to revolutionize the art after a fashion of his own. Richard Wagner could whisper something in his ear by which Joseph (Giuseppe) might benefit. The firm of Wagner and Verdi would then be able to export their musical views to all parts.

A word to the Brothers Escudier. Has Verdi ever heard *Lohengrin*? If not let him hear *Tannhäuser*.

ITALY 'FINISHED'

The decay of the Italian school of singing is traceable to several causes, the chief of which is, unhappily, the death of composers, which has made the last quarter of a century the most barren in the history of Italian opera. The last great genius, the last great composer of Italy was Rossini. Bellini was a plaintive echo of his [Rossini's] strains; Donizetti a vigorous imitator in whom everything was found but the divine fire. Rossini, disgusted at the growing apathy for his works in the land of his birth, went to Paris and composed French operas. He altered his style entirely and gave the death blow to the true Italian school. This was his revenge for the neglect of those who should have cherished him as their only hope. To Rossini, Bellini and Donizetti succeeded Verdi.

Verdi exhibits all the worst faults of his predecessors exaggerated one hundredfold, with none of the genius of Rossini, little of the tenderness of Bellini and less of the facility and *savoir faire* of Donizetti. Nevertheless, Verdi has his merits! – viz, occasional facility of tune, considerable energy and a dramatic fire that cannot be denied. But these are not enough to sustain a tottering edifice, rapidly crumbling into dust. The Italian school has seen its best days; its decline is near at hand; and it is doubtful whether anything can restore it. *C'en est fini.* There are now no composers, no orchestra, no choruses, no librettists in Italy.

The Times, 26 May 1856

On Saturday night [at Her Majesty's Theatre] one of those important experiments was made that are generally preceded by a vast amount of conjecture and . . . trepidation among the patrons of the lyrical drama. We do not, of course, allude to the production of a new opera by Verdi, since it is one virtue of the prolific composer that he does not much disturb the equanimity of the public either by rousing expectation or weighing on the memory. We allude to the début of Mademoiselle Piccolomini . . . whose performance of the principal character in *La Traviata* had been declared one of the most perfect witnessed . . . The book of *La Traviata* is founded on *La Dame aux Camélias* by Alexander Dumas *fils* . . . Whereas the play is supposed to represent modern French life, the Italian libretto changes the period to the year 1700. [*Lengthy summary follows of Piave's libretto.*]

We have been thus minute about the plot because the book is of more importance than the music which, except so far as it affords a vehicle for the utterance of the dialogue, is of no value whatever . . . Perhaps on some occasion we may return to the consideration of Signor Verdi's part in the performance, apart from the libretto. For the present it will be sufficient to treat *La Traviata* as a play set to music. To M. Dumas *fils* and Mademoiselle Piccolomini belong the honours of a triumph in which the composer has as little to do as possible . . . Mr Calzolani, who played Alfredo, sang exceedingly well, but no art could have rendered his songs fascinating; and '*Di Provenza il mar, il suol*', which was sung by M. Beneventano, in the character of Germont and which, according to tradition, was the great song of the piece, produced hardly any effect whatever.

The Times, 12 June 1867

From Davison's account of the Swedish soprano Christine Nilsson's début as Violetta at Her Majesty's Theatre.

The opera selected for an occasion of such interest to the fortunes of [this theatre] was the by no means edifying *Traviata*, notwithstanding which the success of the newcomer was never for one moment doubtful . . . Her mock sentimental duet with the elder Germont – among all 'heavy stage fathers' the most intolerable bore – and the final scene, where Violetta gradually sinks under the repeated insults of her lover, in all respects more vile and contemptible than herself, brought down the curtain with renewed applause. The last act, with all its revolting details, into which we have no inclination again to enter, was for Mademoiselle Nilsson a renewal of the success of the first . . .

The unexpected interview with Alfredo who, having expedited the end by his heartless cruelty, returns, one might imagine, with a morbid curiosity to witness her last lingering moments and to cheat her with hopes he knows cannot be realized; the maudlin duet, '*Parigi o cara*' . . . in which the model youth of M. Dumas the younger once more gives fervent expression to his unhealthy passion; and the dying scene, which is horrible and, under the circumstances, utterly unedifying – each and all [it must be owned] created a lively impression . . . Meanwhile, dismissing the *Traviata*, to which it is to be hoped there may be no future occasion of returning, we state in postscriptum that . . . [*The sentence and paragraph end with further purely personal compliments to Mlle Nilsson.*] Mr Santley, whose Old Germont is about the most endurable on the stage, was, as a matter of course, compelled to sing twice the lachrymose and monotonous '*Di Provenza il mar*' . . .

6

WAGNER, I

Patchy, Puerile, Poisonous

Musical World, 6 May 1854

The overture to Tannhäuser *was played by the orchestra of the New Philharmonic Society (London) on 26 April at the end of a six-piece programme conducted by Herr Lindpaintner.*

After all the talk there has been, at home and abroad, about Herr Wagner's overture to *Tannhäuser*, we were certainly led to expect something better than we heard. It is enormously difficult to play and taxed the powers of the magnificent band . . . to the utmost. With regard to the music, it is such queer stuff that criticism would be thrown away upon it. We never listened to an overture at once so loud and empty. And Richard Wagner, according to Franz Liszt, is entrusted with no less important a mission than the regeneration of the musical art.

Musical World, 22 July 1854

Reviews. March from *Tannhäuser* by Richard Wagner. J.J. Ewer and Co.

As, according to some transcendentalists it is the mission of Richard Wagner to announce to the world 'the music of the future', he merits attention. But for that we should have dismissed the present composition with a line, which is as much as it is really worth. A more commonplace, lumbering and awkward thing of its kind we never perused. That, however, our readers may not accuse us of prejudice, we shall present them with a specimen. Here, for example, is a lofty specimen of 'the music of the future' which no one but Dr Liszt is profound enough to understand.

[*There follows a music-type 'quote' of incidental passage-work from the overture.*]

Towards the end this puerile, Frenchified, patchy tune is resumed with all the pomp and stridency of the Wagnerian full orchestra (by which we mean one much noisier and much thinner than the legitimate full orchestra). The rest of the march is quite worthy of the above; and, at the end, the violins are screaming up to B flat in *alt* . . . as is Mr Wagner's frequent and disagreeable custom. *There* is a 'future' for you, O musicians!

Musical World, 24 March 1855

Wagner owes Liszt his fame, his position and *even his 'FUTURE'.* Without Liszt and the Jesuits he would never have emerged from the oblivion into which he had fallen before the Revolution of 1848. It is attributable to Liszt and the leading journal of his party that the public began to be excited by a desire to see and hear something of the man 'of the future'. Wagner was not slow to profit by the opportunity . . . [The third book of] Richard Wagner's *Opera and Drama* contained the poems of *Die Fliegende Holländer, Tannhäuser* and *Lohengrin,* with addresses to the men he professes to love; for love and friendship with Wagner are synonymous . . .

While this was going on Liszt at Weimar *forced* three of the operas upon the stage. The public, allowed for a time to listen to nothing else, at least endured them patiently. But Weimar has no influence; a more important arena was necessary – Leipzig, for example. *Tannhäuser* was put on the stage at Leipzig and . . . endured patiently. What is *Tannhäuser?* [There] is nothing new in its ideas or construction. The instrumentation is always heavy; but it is not new. The orchestration is often so 'thick' that the sense of the words is lost; but that is not new. There *is* nothing new in *Tannhäuser* except certain abrupt modulations and very clumsy harmonies.

There were great hopes in Leipzig of this 'best piece', as Wagner calls it. But alas! in spite of friends, press, decorations and favourable circumstances, the public would not endure four hours of *uninterrupted recitative*; and *Lohengrin* made an unequivocal fiasco. There is no cessation, no rest for the instrumentalists, singers or public; the action moves on continually, accompanied

To the strains of his Valhalla music, Richard Wagner
sits in the Royal Albert Hall, London, where he
conducted eight concerts of excerpts ranging from
Rienzi to *The Ring*. He had hoped his takings would
cancel out his Bayreuth Festival deficit. Actually they
increased it – *Musical World*, 26 May 1877

by music, except one or two short phases where the orchestra stops with a somewhat melodramatic effect. The whole is a long, tiresome recitative.

Musical World, 31 March 1855

The selection on Monday night at the second concert of the Philharmonic Society from the 'drama' of *Lohengrin*, Wagner's last completed work, the one in which his particular theories are most thoroughly developed and which in consequence he avowedly esteems the most – was both interesting and strange. It was interesting as the anticipated solution of a problem which had previously been looked upon in this country as very hard to solve but not as insoluble; and strange because it went far to upset all preconceived notions of the system of 'the future', as derived from 'the books' . . .

[The] heroes of Wagner's operas – we beg his pardon, dramas – are myths. *Tannhäuser* is a myth. *Lohengrin* is a myth. Tannhäuser is a wandering minstrel with whom we have nothing to do just now. Lohengrin is an enchanted hero, a knight of the Holy Graal, who appears in a skiff drawn by a swan, rescues a persecuted lady at a critical moment, and marries her on the condition that she will not ask who and what he is; and when, of course, she does, [precisely that] is off again in the skiff drawn by the swan, leaving the persecuted lady to her fate. This, briefly, is *Lohengrin* – the whole of *Lohengrin*, the drama, from which to divide the music, or any part of the music, would be 'complete annihilation'.

Musical World, 30 June 1855

Let us not lose sight for a moment of who Richard Wagner is and what are his pretensions. He is a poet, musician, dramatist, philosopher, essayist, revolutionist (political) as well as artistic, and the assumptive leader of a new musical sect which publicly threatens its determination to overrun and convert the whole of Europe. He must needs have unbounded confidence in himself; for, throughout his writings on art, we find either expressed or implied an unwavering current of assertion that all other musicians are in error, here venially, there flagrantly; and this not on points of technical detail but technically as to first principles.

He alone has discovered the key to their faults; he alone in his own creations can exhibit their remedy. Throughout we perceive the stubborn resolution to cast down the idols of this world and build himself a shrine from their ruins. It was, then, wise, right and due to the progress of art that the Philharmonic Society should bring this man to England. All the great kinds of music are intimately known in this country; and, if his mission be really one of truth and power to convince us of yet greater things, he could scarcely have a richer field for his labour.

FAILURE, SHAME

Well, then, Richard Wagner came to London, an object of deeper curiosity, we venture to say, than was any foreign musician who ever visited us, and, having had full scope, both as composer and orchestral conductor, for the vindication of his pretensions, he leaves it, we also venture to say, convicted of making one of the profoundest failures on record. Of his compositions we can only repeat what we have said in other words, namely, that they are the clever and dashing *shame* of a well-read and ambitious man, wholly ungifted with the faculty of developing beauty – having, in plain phrase, not a particle of music in his *nature* – who would fain persuade the world to mistake his idea-less and amorphous ravings for the utterances of a Heaven-descended originality and thought too profound for ordinary penetration.

As a conductor, it is a matter of notoriety that, with a band containing some of the finest existing elements and against which, though it may suit him to arraign it, he will never obtain a European verdict, he has merely succeeded in producing a series of performances much inferior in general view, on the whole, to those with which the society was chargeable even in its early days of the square pianoforte at which the conductor was seated . . . We say this generally of the eight concerts of the present season, and we say it with tenfold speciality of the last on Monday evening.

In those gloriously mistaken old days of the 'leader' and 'conductor', when the band had not attained the half of its present force, either mental or material, did one ever hear so many slips, messes, perversities – so much bad performance, in short, on a single evening? Could we, by [remote] possibility, hear anything worse? In those olden times aforesaid we often heard much that was not perfection. The performances were occasionally rough and incorrect, very generally not remarkable for any refined distinctions in the grades of *forte* and *piano*; and precision in the simultaneous actions of the machine had not attained that advanced stage of development it has since reached under the strict military rule of Mr Costa. Yet the instruments went tolerably well together, they expressed the composer's intention, on the one hand, with not perhaps the last delicacy of style, on the other hand, without affectation or ridiculous mock sentimentality. Even in the most novel and complex music attempted, it was but rarely indeed that we were annoyed by absolute discord or put into a state of nervous tension by some hairsbreadth escape from a total breakdown.

How comes it, then, that in 1855, since the band must have improved greatly at all points, since the knowledge of all the great music habitually performed must be deepened and strengthened, in spite of three years' drilling by Sig. Costa – who, however his opinions may differ from our own, is wholly unexceptionable as a disciplinarian – how comes it that the performances of this season have been so markedly worse than usual? How comes it especially that all the music of the last concert . . . sounded little better than if the band were rehearsing it for the first time? How comes it that Mendelssohn's *Midsummer Night's Dream* overture was all at sixes and sevens throughout? – that poor Herr Pauer [solo pianist in Hummel's piano concerto in A flat] was accompanied so wildly in that very simple score? – that Mlle Krall, with all her energy of voice, could not urge forward that lazy orchestra to anything like the [*tempi*] she must have known and felt Wagner intended for various movements of his scena? – that Beethoven's B flat symphony was played so generally ill and that where the *scherzo* enters after the trio a catastrophe fatal to the renown of the orchestra – to say nothing of the feelings of the audience – was only just averted by the decision of the performers themselves? – that in the overture to *Oberon* the giant stringed-band of the Philharmonic Society became, for the first time, all but voiceless for the utterance of [salient] passages . . . and sank murmuring among the general roar of the mass?

There can be but one answer, and that answer points to the incompetence of the conductor. The Pundit-Praeger may say what pleases him, may hurl all 'the books' and as many more as he sees fitting at our heads; . . . but facts are too potent to be overturned by mere talk. Last season the performances were generally admirable; this season they have been generally the reverse. Nothing has been changed except the conductor, and to what, then, except this change can the falling off be attributable?

There needs no inferential evidence to prove the unfitness of Wagner to conduct a great orchestra. His manner, his attitude, his mere action in the indication of [*tempo*] are sufficient in themselves. Though square, hard and abrupt in the last degree, his 'beat' is always wanting in the decision necessary to fix and carry with him the attention of the orchestra. There is a well-known toy, the delight of babyhood – a wooden figure from the nether part of whose person depends a string which, being pulled, the arms and legs are suddenly thrown into contortions of a very amusing and certainly inelegant character. To this and to nothing else can we compare Herr Wagner when in the heat of conducting an *allegro*. He gesticulates with much energy and the least possible degree of grace but yet fails to indicate the divisions of a bar with anything like intelligible point. Of his new 'readings', as they are termed, we have but two observations to make: first, that in all music whereof to assist our judgement we have only English tradition and our own taste, we notice that he applies the same description of alteration to similar parts of every composition, no matter what its style or intention, and this is, therefore, merely a mechanical artifice and not a suggestion of intelligence; and, second, that in all the music we have heard directed by its composer, we notice that Herr Wagner's direction differs essentially from the author's, and therefore that Wagner's must certainly be wrong. *The Times* has said, 'One more such season will destroy the Philharmonic Society,' and we may add: one more such conductor will annihilate the reputation of the society's orchestra. It is to be hoped that in future no experiment will be made likely to imperil either one or the other, for the Philharmonic, with all its faults, is far too important an institution to be sacrificed – at least for the present.

Musical World, 30 June 1855

Leading Article. Richard Wagner has departed. On Tuesday, 5

o'clock a.m., the morning after the last Philharmonic concert, the representative of the 'Future Art Works' bade adieu to this commercial metropolis, the inhabitants of which have been hitherto insensible to his preaching. What he may think of musical London we are unable to guess; but if there may be any truth in physiognomy, the 'small man with the intellectual forehead', as [someone] has playfully designated him, must regard us as a community of idiots.

We hold that Herr Wagner is not a musician at all but a simple theorist who has conceived the unhappy idea of aiming a blow at the very existence of music through melody, that element which has won for music the epithet of 'divine'. This excommunication of pure melody, this utter contempt of tune and rhythmic definition . . . so notorious in Herr Wagner's compositions (we were about to say Herr Wagner's music) are also one of the most important points of his system. Let us turn to some of the promised fruits . . . in the shape of Wagnerian 'Art-Drama'. What do we find there? So far as music is concerned, nothing better than chaos – absolute chaos; consistency of keys and their relations overthrown, condemned, demolished; the charm of rhythmic measure . . . destroyed; symmetry of form ignored or else abandoned; the true basis of harmony cast away for a reckless, wild, extravagant and demagogic cacophony, the symbol of profligate libertinage.

Lohengrin . . . is poison, rank poison. This man, this Wagner, this author of *Tannhäuser*, of *Lohengrin* and so many other hideous things – and above all the overture to *Die Fliegende Holländer*, the most hideous and detestable of the whole – this preacher of the 'Future' was born to feed spiders with flies, not to make happy the heart of man with music, with beautiful melody and harmony. What is music to him, or he to music? His rude attacks on melody may be symbolized as matricide. Who are the men who go about as his apostles? Men like Liszt – madmen, enemies of music to the knife who, not born for music and conscious of their impotence, revenge themselves by endeavouring to annihilate it. We are becoming as hyperbolical as Richard Wagner himself; but really the indignation we feel at the revelation of his impious theories is so great that to give tongue to it in ordinary language is beyond our means. No words can be strong enough to condemn them; no arraignment before the judgement seat of truth too stern and summary; no verdict of condemnation too sweeping and severe. To compromise with such false preachers is a sin. To parley with them mildly would be sheer heathenism. *Lohengrin* is an incoherent mass of rubbish, with no more pretensions to be called music than the jangling and clashing of gongs and other uneuphonious instruments with which the Chinamen, based on the brow of a hill, fondly thought to scare the British bluejackets. Wagner cannot write music himself, and for that reason arraigns it . . . We would grant him forty years to produce one melodious phrase like any of those so profusely scattered about in Rossini, Auber and Meyerbeer.

These musicians of young Germany are maggots that quicken for corruption. They have nor bone nor flesh nor blood nor marrow. The end of their being is to prey on the ailing trunk until it becomes putrid and rotten. Instead of life they would present us with dust, instead of bread with a stone. There is as much difference between *Guillaume Tell* and *Lohengrin* as between the sun and ashes.

7
WAGNER, II
Rant, Fustian, Bombast

Musical World, 1 June 1861

Review of WAGNER'S CELEBRATED OPERA TANNHÄUSER,
edited for the pianoforte (Boosey and Sons)

This arrangement is faithful and moderately difficult. Not a piece,
not even a recitative, is omitted. Every pianist, amateur or
professional, who would like to know something of a man so
unmercifully abused by one set of people and so unmercifully
praised by another, will here find a sort of epitome of Wagnerian
inventive powers as a composer. What melody he can make is
almost absorbed by *Tannhäuser*; for assuredly there is little in
Lohengrin, none in *Tristan* and less than *none* in *Rheingold* . . . If
Tannhäuser possessed no other recommendation, it can boast of
being the best abused opera (*en attendant* its successors) of the
present or any other century. This alone must stimulate curiosity.
Here, moreover, it is in the power of a moderately skilled pianist
to do in a couple of hours what it took [the Paris Opéra], under the
immediate supervision of Wagner himself, six months to accom-
plish – and even this by no means to the composer's satisfaction.

Musical World, 25 September 1869

A BACHE TO THE RESCUE

Leader. Herr Richard Wagner's friends, from the Majesty of
Bavaria downward, must be well-nigh in despair about him. Such
is the sure fate of all worshippers of eccentricity. The man who,
like Herr Wagner, is chiefly remarkable for doing odd things and

advocating odd notions, becomes the slave of a law which finally ruins him. A similar law shapes the ends of all workers of 'sensation'. It drives on the acrobat to break his neck; leads the speculator into a dilemma from which only a pistol can extricate him; and gives to monarchs choice of humiliation or revolution. Nothing is so soon forgotten as 'striking' achievements, and he who would keep in favour with the world must go on achieving that which is more striking, otherwise he will drop out of sight; or, which is worse, remain a thing for laughter and derision. This

'At the Opera', *Musical World*, 5 Feb. 1876. Above, left to right: *Tenore*: C above the lines; *Basso*: E flat below the lines; *Mezzo-Soprano*: Con sentimento within the lines. Below: In the orchestra

necessity tyrannizes over Herr Wagner. Apart from eccentricity, Herr Wagner is no more than the Giant Chang, [presumably an entertainer, from the Far East, of exceptional stature] apart from inches. Rid the first of the craze, and – which is, perhaps more possible – the latter of his superfluous height and both would assume the form of very ordinary men. Chang, by no amount of thought-taking, could add one inch to his stature, and the memory of him therefore is fast fading out. Herr Wagner, on the other hand, can more and more develop his craze, the result making him more and more notorious. Such a development must be, if the Prophet would not follow the Giant into the lumber room of used-up curiosities. What would it avail Wagner now if

he were to produce another *Lohengrin*? Simply nothing. The
public stands at the open door of the lumber room aforesaid and
cries to Herr Wagner – 'Be more ridiculous than ever, or in you
go.' So Wagner is more ridiculous than ever and staves off his fate
for a while. To this supreme necessity we owe *Rheingold*, the
impossible prelude to an inconceivable trilogy – the work at which
sane men do not know yet whether to laugh or weep. Beyond the
absurdity and cacophony of *Rheingold* it is hardly possible to go; if
we may credit the evidence of witnesses, so much the better,
because the sooner will its composer be used up. There are,
however, some people who really admire Herr Wagner, who
believe him a true prophet and follow him as one who leads to a
musical Paradise. These are 'the faithful', whose faith is now being
tried as by fire. They could not have anticipated the antics of their
Prophets, and must now look upon them as Michael looked upon
David's unseemly dancing before the Ark. The fiasco of *Rheingold*
doubtless carried dismay into the Wagnerian ranks; but so did the
delivery of Joanna Southcote into the congregation of her
followers, who, 'rallying in nooks and corners', continue to
believe in Richard.

Yet, as there are Southcotians still, so, also, are there Wagner-
ians. One has even had the boldness to rush into print, there to
defend his master. We admire the courage of Mr Walter Bache
[Walter Bache, b. Birmingham, 1842 (d. London, 1888), piano
recitalist, pupil and upholder of Liszt]. His letter to the *Athenaeum*,
in reply to that of Mr H.F. Chorley, shows him to be of the stuff
that builds up faiths. There is about it a disregard of consequence
and a readiness of self-sacrifice we are compelled to admire.
Whether Herr Wagner will thank Mr Bache for his advocacy we
do not know; at all events the master should be proud of a disciple
who chooses the moment of greatest humiliation for that of the
loudest profession.

The thoughtful reader will at once discern the fallacy upon
which Mr Bache rests his vindication of Herr Wagner's music. He
contends that it forms only one part of several which go to make a
whole; and that to judge it by itself is absurdly unfair. This is
equivalent to a declaration of rank heresy, never likely to be
accepted, and against which, therefore, it is bootless to argue. We
hold that the province of music in opera is supreme; that the work
is essentially musical and that to the forms of art all the demands of

realism must give way. This is the general belief and, because it is general, Herr Wagner's compositions are everywhere, out of a limited circle, scouted as formless and void. It is of little avail for Mr Bache to urge the argument we have stated. He must first convert the majority to a belief in the premises on which it is based.

Mr Bache's assertion that Wagner's music must be heard, and cannot be read, is puerile. Mr Bache, we are sure, does not say so from experience; he is too good a musician not to be able to read anything. Can he not understand the possession by others of a like gift? As to his fling at the critics, we will not take him to task about it. He naturally feels sore because an unbelieving press abjures Wagner and all the Wagnerian works. If it comforts Mr Bache in the slightest degree to hurl stones at the critics, nobody is likely to complain, least of all those most concerned. We are, nevertheless, sorry that Mr Bache has come forward at an unlucky moment – sorry even while we admire his pluck. He has averted nothing from the head of the Prophet, and he has drawn down something on his own.

WEARIED, DINNED

Musical World, 18 March 1876

Leader. The principle adopted by actors and singers for last appearances has been reversed by Richard Wagner, who has applied it to first performances. How long have we not had to wait for the first performance of the Tetralogical Trilogy at the Grand-National-Stage-Play-Theatre of Bayreuth? How often have our hopes of that exciting event been raised only to be crushed, as skittles are set up merely that they may be ruthlessly knocked down an instant afterwards? But we will not be so incredulous as the rustics who turned a deaf ear to the cry of 'Wolf!' when the wolf really came. Richard Wagner has at last promised definitely that the Model Performances shall taken place next August, and we are only too glad to believe him. We want to think he will be able to carry out what he says. The wish is father to the thought. We are tired of the rant, the fustian, the bombast which we have so long heard concerning the wonders in store for the fortunate possessors of Patrons' Tickets; we feel wearied and dinned by the noise of the very loud trumpet which Wagner has blown so perseveringly and vigorously for many years that we have had more than enough of the pretensions of this Musical Claimant, and we would give him all the rope he can possibly require to perform what we shall designate a graceful and laudable act. To quote the words of Banquo to Macbeth: 'The earth hath bubbles as the water has.'

Of these bubbles the so-called Music of the Future is, in our eyes or ears, one of the greatest. When Father Time shall touch it with his finger we feel convinced that it will burst and be forgotten. Richard Wagner has made a name and achieved triumphs. What of that? He is not the first false prophet who has boasted of many disciples. He has been more than equalled in this respect by Joanna Southcote and Mahomet; not to mention scores of others who have devoted their talents to the same line of business . . . There is no superstition so gross, no theory so exaggerated that it will not be eagerly received by thousands. Wagner has been wonderfully successful. He is indebted for this, however, not to his music but to his literally unbounded power of self-praise. *La musique, c'est moi*, says this would-be Louis XIV of Art – and a host of feeble-minded people take the assertion on trust . . .

The Times, 19 August 1876

From Our Special Correspondent, Bayreuth.
The orchestra must for ever be doing something – like a wind that is always blowing or a stream that is always flowing, or trees that are always bending in obedience to the swaying of the breeze; but what that something shall be, the poet [Wagner] can alone decide . . . Apart from the drama to which it is allied the orchestral music of *The Ring* would signify little more at the best than a succession of chords, scales (not infrequently chromatic), figures and snatches of tunes, distributed capriciously among the instruments, *tremolandos (ad infinitum)*, strange and unheard of combinations, perpetual changes of key, – a chaos of sound, short, now more or less agreeable, now more or less the opposite and, deprived of the weird and singular fascination that obviously attends it when obviously explained by what is being said and done upon the stage, almost unmeaning. Wagner's symphony may be likened to

an omni-coloured kaleidoscope, where the same bits of painted glass instantly appear and disappear, yielding prominence to others that have been seen before and puzzling the eye of the examiner, as the Wagner orchestra puzzles, while it frequently enchants the ear. Without being distinguished by anything affording evidence of uncommon contrapuntal skill, it is crowded with details, many of which, till after repeated hearings, would elude detection, however closely scrutinized.

With each separate personage of the drama Wagner connects a certain musical phrase which, identically or modified according to circumstances, recurs whenever the personage comes back to us or is even passingly alluded to by others . . . With the working out of this theory the orchestra has much more to do than the singers on the stage, for it is the orchestra rather than the voices which chiefly stamps each special identity. As not seldom, too, in the course of a single scene, more than one personage, incident or emotion is brought back to the mind, at times almost simultaneously; the themes, or such fragments of them as may be suitable, are ingeniously interwoven. This is accomplished by the poet-musician with consummate artistic propriety and often produces an indescribably beautiful effect.

The funeral march that accompanies the body of Siegfried is, as we have already hinted, impressive and sublime. The melody sung by the Rhinemaidens . . . in seven-bar rhythm is charming; and, indeed, all the music that characterizes the presence of these charming beings is as airy and elementary as themselves, a most refreshing impression being created by their trio – in harmony, for a wonder – when Siegfried encounters them on the bank of the river . . . In *Die Walküre* the characters of Siegmund and Sieglinde provide the opportunity for melody of a more impassioned character; and a particular phrase of which ample use is made in the magnificent duet at the end of Act 1 becomes conspicuous as an example. Here, too, the first apparition of the heroic Brünnhilde and her wild Valkyrie sisters introduce quite a new element which Wagner has turned to admirable purpose. In *Siegfried* we have more fresh, inspiriting and appropriate phrases . . .; the introduction of the delightfully tuneful strains of the wood-birds, in one of the most perfectly idyllic scenes imaginable, and another grand duet in which Brünnhilde, now endowed with human, womanly impulse . . . shows that she can be more

impassioned than Sieglinde herself, and with far more healthy and
legitimate cause . . . In *Götterdämmerung* . . . Wagner . . . has
taxed poor Brünnhilde with screaming high notes and climax after
climax out of all measure and proportion – a prevalent fault with
him, as it would seem, when situations occur which lay strong
hold on his imaginative sympathies.

The Times, 23 August 1876

From Our Special Correspondent, Bayreuth.

Franz Betz, upon whom devolves the not too grateful task of
impersonating the god Wotan, is held in great esteem by his
compatriots, and deservedly. This gentleman is a Wagnerian
singer (synonymous with declaimer) of the genuine stamp. He
has, moreover, a fine voice, a dignified presence and keen
histrionic intelligence, all of which serve him to admirable
purpose in relieving from dreariness some of the dreariest and
lengthiest accompanied recitatives imaginable. In *Rheingold*, *Die
Walküre* and *Siegfried*, Wotan is ever a conspicuous personage, so
eloquently prosy, so sententiously lackadaisical (for a god, be it
understood), so perversely addicted to talking about himself that,
when his once-omnipotent spear is shivered to pieces by Siegfried's sword, Nothung, and we are thus rid of it, not many are
likely to complain – although upon Wotan's original error and its
consequences the whole story turns. The actor however, must not
be blamed for this; and it is exclusively the fault of the
poet-musician who, in his anxiety to place 'the word' and the
music on terms of equality, prevents each from exerting its
influence.

The Times, 26 August 1876

In his anxious desire to exhibit the musician as the poet's humble
slave, Wagner not only prevents him from soaring to the highest
regions of fancy but, by crushing the buds of melody as they
spring up, buds that might blossom into seemly flowers, cramps
the manifold resources of expression which are the golden heritage
of art. True, the serene arch-dramatist in the *Ring des Nibelungen*,
with becoming self-abnegation, practises this to his own detri-
ment, for he, too, possesses abundant melody, if not Orphean,

like Mozart's, or coming directly from the innermost sources of his being, like the endless melody of Beethoven, is at least sufficiently frank, independent and alluring not to submit gracefully to the treatment it receives at his hands. Wagner allows his melody to awaken expectation by an opening phrase but seldom or never rounds off and finishes that phrase so as at once to delight and satisfy the ear. His principal charm, in fact, is the unexampled, almost magical colouring of his orchestra, which keeps us enthralled and spellbound to the last – though speculating rather than understanding, disposed to marvel rather than to sympathize.

8

WAGNER, III

U-turn: *The Ring?* Gorgeous! Magnificent!

Musical World, 12 May 1877

Davison reprints as under his radiant Times *notice of 9 May* re *the opening concerts of the London Wagner Festival.*

Herr Richard Wagner had little reason to be otherwise than satisified with the welcome accorded to him on Monday night in the Royal Albert Hall, when the first of his series of projected concerts was given. A very large audience greeted him with a cordiality not to be mistaken. Everybody, in fact, was glad to see the man about whom all musical Europe had been talking; and who, by talking on his own account, has incited all musical Europe to talk for more than a quarter of a century.

The particular theories of Herr Wagner with regard to art, however, have been sufficiently discussed and, just now, had we the inclination, we have not the space at command to discuss them again. Enough that in August of last year he persuaded curious speculators from almost every part of the civilized world to visit an effete town situated in the midst of the Franconian hills for the purpose of testing the ultimate result of his labours, as exhibited in a cycle of four dramas, or 'Stage Plays', performed at a new theatre but entirely through his own indefatigable exertions. Such an unexampled assemblage of noted personages belonging to so many different spheres of thought and action was in itself a thing to remember; and if the Tetralogy of the *Ring des Nibelungen*, while generally admitted to be an artistic success, turned out a pecuniary failure, is not the less to be regarded as a significant sign of the times, inviting consideration of a new tendency which, as things progress, may lead art into other channels and cause it to assume other forms than those to which we have hitherto been accustomed. That Herr Wagner, whatever diverse opinions may be entertained about him as a man of controversy or a working representative of art, has caused earnest people to think a good deal is undeniable. It is not so much his poetic ideal as his mode of setting it forth that has provoked, and still provokes, and is likely to provoke, antagonism. But enough of this for the present.

The programme of Monday night was more immediately interesting on account of the excerpts from *Das Rheingold* than for the miscellaneous selection preceding them [the *Kaisermarsch* and excerpts from *Rienzi* and *Tannhäuser*]. Best of all – worth the rest, indeed, put together – were the excerpts from *Das Rheingold*, consisting of the opening and closing scenes – the stealing of the gold from the Rhine-daughters by Alberich and the entry of the gods and goddesses over the rainbow bridge into the giant-built Walhalla. How much of its effect the music with which Herr Wagner has almost magically illustrated these passages must lose by separation from the dramatic context and stage accessories it is easy to understand. Nevertheless, enough remains to excite interest, and this in spite of the by no means clear exposition of varied and minute orchestral details under any circumstances obtainable in a building so constituted with regard to acoustic properties as the Albert Hall. The immense orchestra, however, directed by Herr Wagner himself . . . worked zealously from beginning to end. . . . With [the singers] no fault could be found. At the end there were loud calls for Herr Wagner, who came forward and was enthusiastically applauded.

The conspicuous feature in the programme of the second concert (Wednesday) was the superlatively magnificent opening scene of the *Walküre*, in which the music attains its very highest flight as poetical illustrator of human emotion. Here . . . we are 'convincingly convinced' that Wagner is no musician, no poet, no painter, no sculptor, no architect, no anything except the 'all' combined, as Dramatist. In the *Ring des Nibelungen* the characters we pity and therefore *love* the most are Siegmund and (darling!) Sieglinde. For a look at Sieglinde we would draw one hundred swords out of as many ash trees – provided only that she sang as Richard Wagner makes her sing. – Dishley Peter [a pen-name of Davison's]

Musical World, 19 May 1877

We again quote *The Times* (of 4 May) with reference to the Wagner Festival which today (unhappily) comes to an end:–

The second concert of the series on Wednesday evening began with a selection from *The Flying Dutchman* with which Mr Carl Rosa, through his admirable performance at the Lyceum, has made us so well acquainted. This was followed by the first act of *Die Walküre*, the second drama of the *Ring des Nibelungen* – about which more hereafter. The third concert, on Saturday afternoon, drew together an audience which might have outnumbered the audiences attracted by its precursors put together. The occasion of this is not far to seek. There was distinguished patronage; and, this being generally expected, many – how many we dare not guess – setting the weather, which could have been less favourable – at nought, proceeded to the Royal Albert Hall, uncertain as to how they should arrive and all the more uncertain as to how they should get away.

The programme was materially altered 'by desire', and those who had been satisfied with one hearing of the *Tannhäuser* 'Processional March' had the unexpected satisfaction of hearing it again. The first part was devoted to a selection from *Tannhäuser*, consisting generally of pieces such as the overture, the march, the song addressed by Wolfram to the evening star, etc, – which have been heard over and over and over again. These were listened to with the usual equanimity and applauded, from time to time, with the accustomed warmth by an audience whose curiosity would have been more gratified if the programme had consisted entirely of excerpts from Wagner's last and, by very many degrees, greatest work – the *Ring des Nibelungen*. It was a mistake, at any rate, to place the Bayreuth music, which, as Herr Eduard Hanslick says, is, compared with any preceding composition by Wagner, like the Falls of Niagara to a glass of water, at the end instead of at the beginning of the programme. After the first part of a concert the attention flags; and, while the most extraordinary things go on, the audience are leisurely departing.

Thus, many lost one of the most magnificent performances ever listened to of a truly magnificent piece of orchestral music. Under the splendid conducting of Herr Richter, the 'Ride of the Valkyries', which began the second part, was more than worth all that preceded it, while the exquisite singing of Mlle Materna, no less irreproachable in a dramatic than in a musical sense, imparted special interest to this part of the tetralogy. Admirable at the second concert as Sieglinde, she was still more admirable at the third as Brünnhilde. Beyond saying that the 'Ride' was encored in a storm of applause and in defiance of Wagner's known objection to repetition of any passages, however striking, from his dramas . . . we shall add nothing more just now, believing a general comment upon the series of performances will be more to the purpose than a detailed account of each. . . . Herr Wagner, who directed a great part of the *Siegfried* performance on Saturday, was received with the same cordiality as before.

M.W.'s concluding comment: The programmes of the fourth and fifth concerts, owing to circumstances which neither Herr Wagner nor the managers of the undertaking could have foreseen, were considerably modified. Nevertheless, each contained enough from the gorgeous and magnificent *Ring* to delight all present. More in our next. – Theosophilus Queer [a Davison pen-name]

BACK-GLANCE

Musical World, 26 May 1877

For a retrospect of the Wagner Festival we have again recourse to *The Times*:–

. . . The Wagner Festival came virtually to an end on Saturday afternoon with what, if we may judge by the audience thronging the Albert Hall and the indiscriminate applause bestowed upon piece after piece, was the most successful concert of the series. The programme contained a selection from *Die Meistersinger*, another from *Tristan und Isolde* and yet another from *Götterdämmerung*. The most interesting part of Saturday's programme was the selection from the second act of *Tristan*, which the large majority of Herr Wagner's disciples, encouraged, as is generally believed, by the opinion of the master, regard as his superlative effort, the *ultima thule* of his operas. Some, nevertheless, who have carefully studied the work may not exactly be of that persuasion; and we cannot accuse them fairly of misappreciation when they insist that any one of the four parts which comprise the tetralogy of *The Ring of the Nibelungen* is, for boldness of conception and originality of treatment, superior to either *Tristan* or *Die Meistersinger*. That, be it said with deference, is our . . . own impression. To accept Wagner, under any circumstances, as a comic writer would demand an unlimited degree of faith in the 'absolute'. Take for example those passages in the overture to the *Meistersinger* which represent a 'clandestine declaration' and the chattering of the Mastersingers' apprentices as proofs of his idiosyncratic deficiency in this respect. The first aims at a quasi-sentimental humour, the second at humour unrestrained. Neither hits the mark, and the reason is not far to seek. When Wagner attempts this sort of thing it is against the grain, or, as some old French writer would express it – '*il caresse son chat à rebrousse poils*' (allowing *chat* to stand for Muse). That Herr Wagner can be *grimly* humorous his powerfully characteristic delineation of Mime, the ill-treated brother of Alberich . . . whether in *Das Rheingold* or *Siegfried*, emphatically shows; but he cannot be comic like Rossini in one style, Auber in another and even Mozart in another (witness *Die Zauberflöte*) – to say nothing of Haydn in his rondos or of Beethoven and Mendelssohn in many of their scherzos, etc. The humour exhibited in *Die Meistersinger* is laboured, not spontaneous. On the other hand, while we cannot but feel that in *Tristan und Isolde*, absorbed in his subject, Herr Wagner has, in his enthusiasm, striven to make too much of it, he soars high into regions of poetry and both as lyrist and dramatist prefers claims that are undeniable . . . The talk about the relative positions of music and poetry in Wagner and Sophocles is pure moonshine, for nobody knows or ever can know what position music held with regard to tragedy among the Greeks. Leave Wagner to himself; take Wagner for what he is; and enough remains entitling him to be regarded as a man of wonderful intellectual power – a man who, having a great deal to tell us, tells it in such a way as to enforce serious consideration. A more convincing illustration of this, apart from passages in the *Ring des Nibelungen*, could not be cited than the marvellous duet which, on Saturday, was the chief feature of the selection from *Tristan und Isolde*, wherein the lovers echo one another, phrase after phrase, as if what one said was precisely what the other would have said if their positions had been reversed. Here the melody never ceases, the orchestra playing a most eloquent part throughout – involved, it may be, but always in perfect keeping with the sentiment to be expressed . . . The singing of Mlle Materna was so touchingly expressive and artistically faultless that the duet, long spun out as it unquestionably is, created an extraordinary sensation, the 'encore' being too unanimous even for Herr Wagner to resist. As the last few bars died away *pianissimo*, little doubt could have remained that, not only many scenes in the operas of Herr Wagner, despite his own reiterated protests, may be separated from the dramatic context without material loss but that in this particular instance the absence of scenic accessories is rather a gain than otherwise. As occurring in the opera, the situation is scarcely to be tolerated on the boards of an English theatre, but as presented at the Albert Hall by Tristan and Isolde, book in hand (the watchful Brangäne might as well be omitted) the supreme beauty of the music was appreciated on its own account. In the selection from *Götterdämmerung*, which brought the concert to an end, there was no Siegfried, but the grandly impressive funeral march, with its splendid singing and declamation of Mlle Materna, offered sufficient compensation.

Extra concerts are announced for Monday afternoon and Tuesday evening – at one if not at both of which it is hoped that the promised selection from *Siegfried*, including the fresh and charming music of the forest scene, where the hero of the *Nibelungen* is instructed in the language of birds and taught the way to the dormant Brünnhilde's fire-encircled prison, will be introduced . . .

9
WAGNER, IV

U-turn Reversed: *The Ring*? Restless, Rambling,
Mumbo-Jumbo

Mumbo   *Musical World, 12 May 1877*   Jumbo★

AMATEUR MADMAN AT BAYREUTH

Diary. Notes on the Spot.
August 1876. – Dear Mortimer Collins, t. Hood, f.c. Burnand[†],
Tom Taylor, etc – E flat, Rhine bottom –.fifths ensuing – restless
modulation, keys everywhere and nowhere, fifths, diminished
sevenths!!! – orchestra (under) wonderful effect – of hearing music
somewhere – now near, now far – now loud, now soft – now 'twixt
the two. In, to and on Wagner's own – let no one attempt to
follow or inspect it for fear of danger (kaleidoscopic) – never a true
burst of *ff* without the aid of brass – strings restless and rambling
about – basses queerly used – combinations of wind often queer –
anvils – too many – heard before (Verdi) – form none, proportion,
completion (ending or beginning) none – more than rainbow
colours – switches of melody always streaming about reminding
of *Tempest* and *A Midsummer Night's Dream* – all a dream – in fact,
every melody belongs to somebody and comes in somehow or
other unexpectedly whenever that somebody is alluded to – two
or three notes [only] sometimes constitute the reminder. This all
through the four dramas to the end (cite the Rhinemaids, by the
way) – compare *Götterdämmerung* with *Rheingold* for that. Pity no

★For years Davison used these engravings in the *Musical World* to drive home the
vileness of what he regarded as inferior music and poor arguments.
†In using lower-case initials Davison here anticipated a humorist of our own day,
the American e.e. cummings.

continued music – no chorus. Gods' ensemble? – *never*! Giants *a due*? – NEVER! – Nibelungs, although all under the same tyranny, *never* in chorus – (good characteristic chance lost), chorus being against Wagner system. (In *Götterdämmerung* retainers of Hagen and Gunther an exception.) Even no duets – each says what he has to say in his own manner – never mingled voices, only dialogue (few soliloquies) – orchestra mingles up themes *ad lib* – but no *free* bass, no counterpoint, etc.

August 1877 (resumed). Stage management *unparalleled* – all *act*, down to the smallest Nibelung, and with significant meaning. Name the character. Wagner stamps each indelibly with his melodic – beautiful or queenish, unmistakable – figures (return in snatches or fragments). The unexpected appearance of fixed melodies, or fragments of ditto, at times perplexes. All the parts well played – though the voices! Machinery, painting, decorations (name authors). Conductor Richter (Bülow's successor). When themes come together one above another, etc – the *tremolando* shift occurs – this in *oppressive excess*, and one gets tired of the [anvil motif]. Orchestra superb – nevertheless should like to hear it once above the ground. Wilhelmj's solos *ravishing* – W. condescends occasionally to that means of effect happily. But all sounds wonderful! Are there no angels or something of the sort in Walhalla and thereabouts to welcome Wotan and [lead them], followed by the discarded Loge, to the huge, battlemented castle? Opportunity [here] for grand chorus of invisibles lost. Duet in form for Alberich and Mime would have been welcome – surely they may respect [repeat?] their sentiments. Wagner always goes on, spinning out, referring and re-referring to same figure for his gathering intensity . . . Nowhere independent bass for orchestra . . .

Ah! poor Mozart, poor Beethoven, whom Wagner is said to have said never had such homage!

Asylum opposite Theatre, Thersitis Grumpus Wizzell

Musical World, 19 June 1880

Davison prints letters from the Rev. H.R. Haweis, an endlessly busy writer on music, and from an anonymous musical professor who respectively lamented and rejoiced in the relative absence of Wagner pieces from the orchestral programmes that season at St James's Hall, London,

of Herr Hans Richter, conductor of the first Bayreuth Ring cycles. Mr
Haweis spoke respectfully, among other works, of Wagner's Kaisermarsch. *Davison's comment:–*

The whole of this is utter delusion. Wagner, merely as Wagner,
has ceased to draw at both London opera houses [which were
playing *Tannhäuser* and *Lohengrin*]. Only amateurs who talk of
what they know less than nothing can be deceived on this point.
The real fact of the success of Richter's concerts this time is the
comparatively small share in the programmes devoted to Wagner
and the substitution of Beethoven for that oracular mumbo-
jumbo . . . Herr Richter is a much shrewder man than Mr Haweis
suspects. The reverend gentleman must be a very cormorant to
want Wagner's *Kaisermarsch* twice within a month. Only the other

The *Parsifal* Sickness
Sir Stephen   Dr Mildew

night the *Kaisermarsch*, with the assistance of Liszt's infernal *Battle of the Huns*, went far towards taking off the roof of St James's Hall and endangering the lives of all present. Herr Richter knows well enough and will rather listen to the sensible professor, whom we all know and respect.

From a letter dated 16 January 1883 by Davison to an unidentified correspondent. See From Mendelssohn to Wagner, *p. 340.*

The music of *Parsifal* is simply execrable. I have entirely changed my opinion about the book. Gurnemanz is an absolute bore and Parsifal an insipid donkey – not the Parsifal of genuine romance. Kundry alone redeems the thing from hopeless inanity.

OH, FOR *IOLANTHE*!

Musical World, 18 August 1883

The dialogue below is between two members of Davison's 'Muttonian' fellowship. It is accompanied by a Charles Lyall cartoon of a savage-looking doctor giving an injection to a prostrate, thin-beared balloon of a man.

THE PARSIFAL SICKNESS

At the King and Beard

DR MILDEW (*feeling pulse*). What's the matter with you?

SIR STEPHEN ROUND I feel very ill. I've travelled all the way from Bayreuth without stopping.

DR MILDEW What took you there?

SIR STEPHEN *Parsifal*. I heard it six times.

DR MILDEW That explains your case. No physic is of any use, because no physic can minister to a mind diseased.

SIR STEPHEN (*gasping*) Is there then no remedy?

DR MILDEW None that I can think of – unless you go to Monsalvat and have a dip or two in the matutinal bath of Amfortas.

SIR STEPHEN That can hardly be. Besides, I –

DR MILDEW I know Kundry has favoured you as of yore; she

compelled Amfortas to her wish and Klingsor into the bargain. Fie! At your age! You ought to be ashamed.

SIR STEPHEN I am not ashamed. Kundry is so beautiful in the scene of the enchanted garden that I fain would have –

DR MILDEW No doubt; but you didn't.

SIR STEPHEN Oh! I feel so ill. That Parsifal got plenty of kisses before he assumed the impeccable-defiant, and I –

DR MILDEW Yes, yes, I see – you would not have submitted to one of them?

SIR STEPHEN (*feverishly*) I certainly would not have assumed the impeccable-defiant.

DR MILDEW And chase away poor Kundry? Of course not! But now, if you don't want a raging fever, get at once to your bed. I'll set you to right in a day or two, and then we can go and hear *Iolanthe*.

SIR STEPHEN Will that cure me?

DR MILDEW In a trice. Hear but one tune of it, and if you want to dream o'night, listen to the dream of Lord Chancellor Grossmith. I suppose you never heard an *opéra comique*?

SIR STEPHEN Oh yes, I heard one at Drury Lane in a foreign language. Augustus Harris [Mr (later Sir) Augustus Harris, at this time manager of opera at Her Majesty's Theatre, Drury Lane] played the leading part. I never laughed so heartily. It was capital.

DR MILDEW Name?

SIR STEPHEN *Tristan* and something.

DR MILDEW And *Isolde*?

SIR STEPHEN Yes, that's it. When A. Harris was stretched on a couch, groaning as if he had been wounded to the death it was excruciating. It *was* funny. I shall never forget it. The same lady in the previous act had been groaning in company with him upon another couch for half an hour or more; but then he was not wounded.

DR MILDEW I say, old boy, you are getting better. How did the music impress you?

SIR STEPHEN Why, except for something sung by seafaring people up a mast, which was queer, and something else sung by people on shore, which was queerer, I heard nothing but one tune from beginning to end. This was the queerest and seemed to go inner and inner as it went on.

DR MILDEW Poor fellow, he means – [Here a music-type quote

of the four opening bars of the *Tristan* prelude.] And the orchestra?

SIR STEPHEN Why, the gentlemen in the band seemed to be poking fun at it, now and then kicking up such a row that it couldn't be heard for the life of it.

DR MILDEW Well, that's enough for the present. Let's feel the pulse again. (*Feels pulse.*) Oh! Twenty degrees better. Take this pill at bed-time. In three days you'll be all right. I dine with you, mind, and you shall have two stalls for *Iolanthe*. That is the best antidote for Wagnerian fever. Bring Lady Round, of course. If, through relapse, you go to sleep, I can entertain her, sustain her with flagons and comfort her with apples. Goodbye!
(*Exit Dr Mildew*)

SIR STEPHEN I'll be blowed! (*Throws pill into grate*) Shan't take that – but shall go to *Iolanthe*!

IO

SCHUMANN

Chamber Music Bad, Symphonies Worse

Musical World, 9 April 1853

Philharmonic Concert, second of the season, Monday 2 March. *Overture, Scherzo and Finale*, Robert Schumann. Robert Schumann and Richard Wagner are representatives of what is styled the 'aesthetic' school in Germany. The latter has written chiefly for the theatre, the former for the orchestra and chamber. Of Wagner we hope to have [further] opportunity of speaking; of Schumann we have been compelled to speak frequently; and, as it has happened, never in terms of praise. So much has been said of this gentleman, and so highly has he been extolled by his admirers, that we who, born in England, are not necessarily acquainted with his genius, have been led to expect a new Beethoven, or, to say the least, a new Mendelssohn. Up to the present time, however, the trios, quintets, quartets, etc, which have been introduced by Mr Ella at the Musical Union and by other adventurous explorers for other societies, have turned out to be the very opposite of good.

An affectation of originality, a superficial knowledge of the art, an absence of true expression and an infelicitous disdain of form have characterized every work of Robert Schumann hitherto introduced in this country. The affected originality had not enough of feeling to be accepted, while the defects by which it was accompanied gave its emptiness and false pretensions a still smaller chance of taking hold of public favour. The statement of these objections, however, has always been met by the answer: 'Oh! you have not heard Schumann's best works; you should know his orchestral compositions, his symphony in B flat and, above all, his *Overture, Scherzo and Finale*.'

This was performed on Monday, and admirably performed,

under the direction of Mr Costa, at the second concert of the Philharmonic Society, and, we regret to say, bad as we consider the chamber compositions of this author, we are forced to pronounce the present orchestral work still worse. Throughout the three movements, so unusually designated, we failed to recognize one musical idea. The *Overture* is the weak first movement of a symphony; the movement in C sharp a weaker *Scherzo*, and the last movement a [peculiarly] weak *Finale*. The general style betrays the patchiness and want of fluency of a tyro; while the forced and unnatural turns of cadence and progression

'At the Symphony', *Musical World*, 15 Jan. 1876. Left to right: No. 3. The man who enjoys the Slow Movement; No. 4 The man who enjoys the Finale; No. 5. The man who don't see it

disclose neither more nor less than the convulsive efforts of one who has never properly studied his art to hide the deficiencies of early education under a mist of pompous swagger. The whole work is unworthy of analysis, since it has no merit whatsoever; and our own task is completed when we state that everything that could possibly be done for it was done by Mr Costa and his splendid orchestra; and that, in spite of all this, there was scarcely a hand of applause for any one of the three movements, while, at the conclusion, several of the subscribers expressed their dissatisfaction in an unequivocal manner.

And yet, Robert Schumann, according to some, is the composer who in combination with Richard Wagner (Brother Wagner, be it understood) is to raise a new school of art, to extinguish Mendelssohn and to teach the worshippers of Bach,

Handel, Mozart and Beethoven many important secrets which the scores of those great masters have never yet disclosed. Oh, that a musical Pope would start up and write a musical *Dunciad*! Thus, and only thus, would the so-called aesthetic school be exposed to the world in its proper light.

As if to spite Schumann, whenever one of his works has been played in England, something by Mendelssohn has been given on the same occasion. On Monday night the magnificent finale to the unfinished opera of *Lorely* was the most interesting feature of the evening . . . This remarkable composition . . . created an impression on the audience so deep and so unanimous as fully to justify its repetition at a future concert during the present season. The musician whom Schumann is to extinguish extinguished Schumann on the present occasion (by no means the first); and the *Overture, Scherzo and Finale* were forgotten in the beauty and variety of the spirit-chorus and the passionate adjurations of Leonora.

Musical World, 10 June 1854

Philharmonic Concert, seventh of the season, Monday 3 June. Queen Victoria, Prince Albert, the King of Portugal [and two Royal children] were present.

The only novelty was Herr Schumann's symphony in B flat, which made a dead failure and deserved it. Few symphonies of the 'Society of British Musicians' were more incoherent and thoroughly uninteresting than this. If this music is all that Germany can send us of new, we should feel grateful to Messrs Ewer and Wessel if they would desist from importing it. The performance was spirited but coarse and unfinished.

Musical World, 28 June 1856

The Philharmonic Society's last concert of the season was devoted entirely to *Paradise and the Peri*, a cantata for solo violin, chorus and orchestra by Dr Robert Schumann. The poetry is from Moore's *Lalla Rookh*, translated and adapted to the music by William Bartholomew. First time of performance. Conductor, Professor Sterndale Bennett.

HARDLY MUSIC AT ALL

[Jenny Lind's] singing was entirely thrown away, the music of *Paradise and the Peri* being everywhere unvocal and scarcely anywhere interesting. Indeed, many who heard Jenny Lind for the first time went away disappointed, having expected something very different from a singer of such colossal reputation. In short, a more dreary concert was never listened to at the Philharmonic.

Of the music of *Paradise and the Peri* it is not easy to speak. If judged by the standard of the great writers it can hardly be considered music at all. It has nothing akin to Handel, Bach, Haydn, Mozart, Beethoven, Spohr, Mendelssohn, Weber, Cherubini, Rossini, or any of those whom we have been taught to regard as the masters of the art. There is no melody, no form – nothing that 'appeals' to the ear – nothing that touches the heart. Even the effects to which the disciples of the new school point so triumphantly are produced by means anything but legitimate. Dr Schumann, in short, is not possessed of that musical organization without which all the talent and ingenuity in the world avail nothing. He has mind – but his mind is not musical. He has power – but he lacks the instinct for music. He produces by some mysterious rule of his own; but nothing he does springs naturally from the heart. For years Schumann reigned a high authority in musical matters, but in an evil hour he fancied he could compose, and began, as he imagined, to exemplify his doctrines of taste by music of his own. Finding that he could not follow in the path of the really great masters, he determined to strike out a new one for himself, which he effected accordingly in a totally opposite direction. The world will never be wanting in those who think that whatever is new *must be* good and that what is unintelligible must surely be profound. Dr Schumann was hailed as an apostle of a new school and became the prophet of a certain clique.

The new preacher nevertheless did not boast of many disciples and was soon compelled to abdicate in favour of another apostle, who brought with him greater eloquence, subtlety and daring, with an equal contempt for precedents. The old was deserted for the new; Schumann was dethroned and Richard Wagner set in his place. Such is a brief outline of Schumann's music. The asylum at Düsseldorf can tell the sequel . . .

The orchestra and chorus were as zealous as if they had to play

Walpurgis Nacht or [Mozart's] Requiem. The singers did their utmost, and Professor Sterndale Bennett took immense pains and never more earnestly strove for a success, but all would not do. There was no success – even the shadow of a success. The applause at the end was faint until the Queen arose [*sic*] to depart, when loyalty gave vent to that enthusiasm which the music itself failed to excite . . .

Same issue, leading article:
Robert Schumann has had his innings and has been bowled out – like Richard Wagner. *Paradise and the Peri* has gone to the tomb of *Lohengrin*.

   When, to drop the metaphor, is all this trifling to cease? How many more times shall we have to insist that the new school – the school of 'the Future' – will never do in England?

   If the Germans choose to muddle themselves with beer, smoke and metaphysics till all things appear to them through a distorted medium or dimly suggested through a cloud of mist, there is no reason why some sane and sober Britons should follow their example. The moon-struck zealots of Weimar, Halle and Leipzig have their Liszt to (mis)guide them; but without a Liszt . . . it is impossible for ordinary thinkers to apprehend the meaning, if meaning there be, of such strange fish as Wagner, Schumann, Brahms, Franz and Co . . . Unhappily, or happily, we are unprovided with a jack-o-lantern. Thus, when listening to the music of such men we are compelled to wander at random in a dark and unpenetrable forest without even the cheat of a will o'the wisp to deceive us for a moment into the notion that we are going somewhere, that we are really about to light upon an unseen path conducting us to an outlet from the labyrinth of trees and undergrowth. We are lost, like the babes in the wood when night approaches – seeing nothing but shadowy phantoms, hearing nothing but the howling of furious wolves and the roaring of pitiless pards. Why, then, we repeat in the absence of Liszt – who will not travel from Weimar to London to enlighten us but sends us books which we cannot understand – why, then, helplessly afflict us with Wagner and Schumann? We put it to Professor Bennett, who took such care to introduce the *Peri* in her best attire, that, but for her moral deformity, she might have passed for something decent and becoming – we put it to Professor

Bennett, who has redeemed the Philharmonic sins by good works and saved those who, justly, should have done penance in a winding sheet – we put it to Professor Bennett, a musician and composer of genius and attainments who knew Mendelssohn intimately and worships John Sebastian Bach with all his soul – to Professor Bennett, the champion of English instrumental music among foreigners and the spoiled child of his own country – Professor Bennett, who was nurtured in harmony and brought up in the path which all sincere musicians should tread – we put it to Bennett whether such a tuneless rhapsody as *Paradise and the Peri* was fit for those delicate ears which, during half a century, more or less, have been nurtured with the pure and sweet and healthy strains of Haydn, Mozart, Beethoven, Spohr and Mendelssohn? We anticipate his answer – 'No!'

After the disastrous failure of Richard Wagner and his music last season there was no excuse for devoting *a whole concert* to another composer of 'the Future'. Since these gentlemen have written for 'the Future', let 'the Future' enjoy the exclusive benefit of their inspirations. Why disturb and vex the present to no purpose? The Present – as the most enthusiastic partisans of Schumann and Wagner admit, nay insist – is incapable of fathoming the depths of their philosophy; all the length of time which it can throw out is insufficient to get half way down to the bottom. To abandon it as hopeless, then, and rest satisfied with Mozart and his successors would surely be the wiser course.

Such an experiment as that of Monday evening must not, on any account, be repeated . . . Imagine, oh uninitiated reader! – three uninterrupted hours of Schumann, three uninterrupted hours of music 'without form and void', three hours of organized sound *without a single tune*! We are not exaggerating but stating a simple fact. Seriously, this passes the limits of toleration. It was sad to listen to the efforts of [Jenny Lind] and her associates – so clever, intelligent and zealous – to give life to music which has no more spark of vitality than a corpse . . . Last year Richard Wagner very nearly annihilated the Philharmonic. Luckily he did not *quite*. But now that Wagner has returned to Zurich, never again to be summoned 'to the rescue', if Robert Schumann be allowed to represent the school of 'the Future' (not as conductor, of course, but as composer), a still greater peril will be incurred – for, though Richard is more subtle, uncompromising, arrogant and fearless,

Robert is more specious. *His* music, at times, more nearly resembles music than the monstrous combination of *Tannhäuser* and *Lohengrin*, yet, inasmuch as, in principle, it is just as vicious and bad, for that reason it is all the more dangerous.

II

LISZT

Music? Hateful Fungi, Rather

Musical World, 30 June 1855

Turn your eyes, reader, to any one composition that bears the name of Liszt if you are unlucky enough to have such a thing on your pianoforte and answer frankly, when you have examined it, if it contains one bar of genuine music. Composition indeed! – decomposition is the proper word for such hateful *fungi* which choke up and poison the fertile plains of harmony, threatening the world with drowth – the world that pants for 'the music which is divine' and can only slake its burning thirst at the 'silver fountains' of genuine, flowing melody – *melody*, yes, melody, *absolute* melody.

Musical World, 25 October 1856

Liszt has been ordered to Zurich by his master, Richard Wagner. The *Nibelungen* is rapidly progressing, and the unhappy piano-king (who has recently been perpetuating some orchestral symphonies and a festival Mass, in humble emulation of the Zukunft) is obliged to be present at the parturition. Where are the other wise men?

Musical World, 18 April 1869

Leader. In another page we reprint an article from the Viennese correspondent of the *Daily Telegraph*. It is a description of the Abbé Liszt's 'oratorio cantata' or 'cantata oratorio' *Die Heilige Elisabeth*. The author evidently writes in great anguish of body and spirit after the endurance of a lengthy and tremendous bore. Nevertheless, his article contains, here and there, certain observations which so plainly show him to be a mere amateur that we have very little sympathy for the sufferings he has undergone. If he knew anything about Liszt's music before and still voluntarily underwent a three hours' probation of it, we have no pity for him. Clearly he is neither musician nor connoisseur, or he would not have referred to Liszt's antecedents in such terms as these:

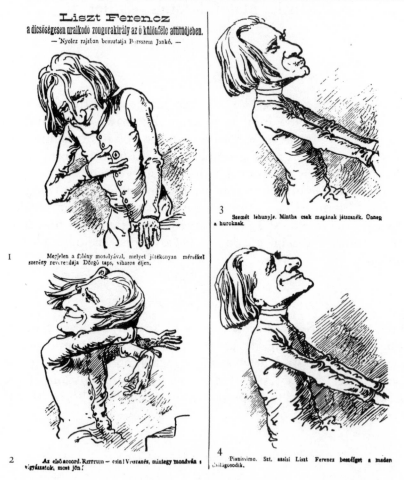

These eight drawings of Franz Liszt are by a noted Hungarian caricaturist whose pseudonym, Borszem Jankó, means 'peppery-eyed dwarf'. They appeared in a Hungarian periodical, *New World*, and on 1 January 1876, in Davison's *Musical World*. The captions read: 1. With practised smile and rather shabby clothes, Liszt makes his bow to a tumult of applause. 2. Opening chord. Pause. He looks over his shoulder, as if to say: 'Watch out! It's coming!' 3. With closed eyes, he forgets

No one could recognize the genial author of the *Transcriptions*. There is little more of common between the Liszt of former days and the Reverend Fr Francis than there is between Ariel and a hooded familiar of the Holy Inquisition. Where is all the airy lightness of manner, the dainty fretwork of ornamentation, *delight of the ear* and despair of the fingers, *the magical modulation*

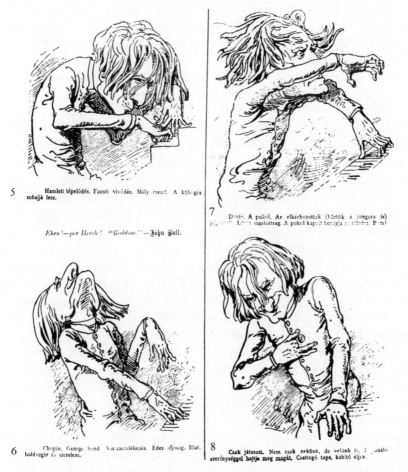

5 Hamleti tépelődés. Fausti vivódás. Mély csend. A köh-gés sohajjá lesz.

*Eheu!—per Hercle! "Goddam!"—*John Bull.

7 Dante. A pokol. Az elkárhozottak (törtük a zongora is) ... Lá--- izgatottsag. A pokol kapu-t bevágja a zrléré. Eml!

6 Chopin. George Sand. Visszaemlékezés. Édes ifjuság. Illat, holdvugár é szerelem.

8 Csak játszott. Nem csak nekünk, de velünk is. i gnaló szerénységgel hajtja meg magát. Csattogó taps, káb tó éljen.

his audience and plays to and for himself. 4. Radiant pianissimo. Donning the mantle of Saint Francis of Assisi, he preaches to the birds. 5. He wrestles like Hamlet, struggles like Faust. 6. Chopin brings memories of sweet youth, fragrances, moonlight and love. 7. In Dante's Hell. Storms of sound that slam Hell's gates. Even the piano is penitent. 8. Concert ends with rowdy acclaim. Liszt bows modestly, conveying that he has been playing not only for us but with us.

that glowed like an aurora borealis of sound over his exuberant effusions, where the elfish and yet touching fragments of melody that were ever shown with no stinting hand over the wildest wastes of his musical dreamland?

Where, indeed? Just as previously – nowhere. He who imagines that, at any time within the last half century Franz Liszt was a musical composer must entertain either very odd notions of art or must be, *qua* music, an absolute ignoramus. The 'transcriptions' to which the *Daily Telegraph* correspondent refers are at the best but empty rodomontade. In fact Liszt was by nature intended for nothing more than a 'virtuoso' and – thanks to his unlimited technical resources – he carried the theory and practice of virtuosity to such a point that he became, in the end, a mere polyhedric pantomanipulator. At length the world had enough of Liszt and, so to speak, grew out of him. Hence, out of simple egotistical self-assertion, the 'creation' by Liszt of Richard Wagner, who to music would be, if he could, what Satan would have been, only he couldn't, to Heaven – the Arch-Destroyer. Where Satan went – to speak in myth – so will go Richard Wagner, and let us hope that (despite his ceremonials) Abbé Liszt – next to Wagner the greatest enemy of music and, therefore, to Wagner, most sympathetic of beings – may accompany him as Prime Minister of the cacophonous Frebus. If music be, as it is described by certain poets, 'the art divine', both Wagner and Liszt are inevitably condemned. There is just now such a hot-bed of confusion about music as it ought to be and music as it ought not to be, that it is as well that a line should be drawn somewhere. There are certain blasphemous folk who – judging from the sneaking kindness shown by Robert Schumann to such men as Wagner and Liszt (by 'sneaking kindness', let us, *en parenthèse*, say yearning sympathy) – would include the said Robert among the fraternity of demoniac cacophonites. But Schumann was not really of the craft, and those who are striving hard to place him above Mendelssohn and by the side of Beethoven should do their utmost to prove how from time to time (in spite of occasional misgivings and misleadings) Schumann thanked Heaven that he was not like those 'publicans'.

Du reste, they who run may read. We have unfolded to the gaze of our readers the *Daily Telegraph* correspondent's letter on Abbé

Liszt's *Heilige Elisabeth*. For our own part, phrases here and there considered, we don't value his criticism at a straw's worth. He has at last, by reason of length, found out that Liszt's music is an infliction – *voilà tout*. Others had discovered that long before.

Musical World, 2 June 1877

Review, by Otto Beard [a Davison pen-name] of *The Life of Chopin*, by Franz Liszt, translated from the French by H. Walker-Cook, London:

Liszt gives a fearfully long and prolix description of Polish dances – he enters into their quasi-philosophical aspect. We find a 'religious robe' associated with the national dance of the polonaise; he mingles prelates and priests in these national displays and customs. To find all that Liszt finds in the national expression of Chopin's music is to need *no* history. Tradition and custom are therein more indelibly imprinted than can otherwise be portrayed. Language, painting, Moabite stones, even the tablets of Esarhaddon fail to give man that psychological insight into ages and feelings which a few bars of Chopin's music are capable of doing. Wonderful metempsychosis! Grotesque hyperbole! When a musician writes of music, we expect a musical work; but here we have a semi-philosophical work by one who has learned in the cloister the parrot phrases and current *patois* of psychological science, and, by the abuse of language, terms and idioms, makes the subject of his sketch fit into all the apertures and orifices of a foregone set of ideas.

WEIMAR IDYLL

The Boston newspaper account which follows of Liszt in his Weimar drawing room playing to girls from America errs, perhaps, on the side of fulsomeness. The piece Liszt chose may have been the first section of the incomparable Bénédiction de Dieu dans la Solitude. *Davison's concluding comment (below) that the proceedings betrayed Liszt as music's 'enemy' is less malign than laughable.*

Musical World, 22 December 1877

If any reader is desirous of knowing how far the charming young ladies of America can be influenced by Weimarian sham, let them read what follows – transposed from the columns of the *Boston (U.S.) Transcript*:–

AN HOUR PASSED WITH LISZT

How much more some of us get than we deserve! A pleasure has come to us unsought. It came knocking at our door, seeking entrance, and we simply did not turn it away. It happened in this fashion. A friend had been visiting Liszt in Weimar and happened to mention us to the great Master, who promised us a gracious reception should we ever appear there. To Weimar, then, we came, and the gracious reception we certainly had to our satisfaction and lasting remembrance. After sending our cards and receiving permission to present ourselves at an appointed and early hour, we drove to the small, cosey [*sic*] house occupied by Liszt when here, on the outskirts of the garden of the duke of Saxe-Weimar, and were ushered by his Italian valet into a comfortable, cosey [*sic*] home-like apartment, where we sat awaiting the great man's appearance. Wide casements opened on a stretch of lawn and noble old trees; easy chairs within and writing tables, MS music with pens lying carelessly beside it, masses of music piled up on the floor, a row of books there, too, a grand piano and an upright one, a low dish of roses on the table, a carpet, which is not taken for granted here as with us – altogether the easy, friendly look of a cottage drawing room at home, where people have a happy use of pleasant things.

He entered the room after a few minutes and greeted us with a charming amiability for which we warmly blessed the absent friend. Of course, everybody knows how he looks – tall, thin, with long white hair; a long, black, robelike coat, being an *abbé*; long, slight, sensitive hands; a manner used to courts and a smile and grace rare in a man approaching seventy. He spoke of Anna Mehlig and of several young artists just beginning their career whom we personally know. Very graciously he mentioned Miss Cecilia Gaul, of Baltimore, spoke kindly of Miss Anna Bock, one of the youngest and most delicate of artists, and, most forcibly, perhaps, of Hermann, like Anna Mehlig, a pupil of Lebert in the Stuttgart Conservatory. 'There is something *in* that young man,' he said with emphasis. So he chatted in the most genial way of things great and small as if he were not one of the world's great ones, and we two little insignificant nobodies sitting overcome with a consciousness of his greatness and our nothingness, yet quite happy and at ease, as everybody must be who comes within the sphere of his gracious kindliness. (!) [The inserted exclamation mark is Davison's.]

Suddenly he went to his writing table and with one of his long, sweet smiles, so attractive in a man of his age – but why shouldn't a man know how to smile long, sweet smiles who has had innumerable thrilling, romantic experiences with the sex that has always adored him! – he took a bunch of roses from a glass bowl on his table and brought it to us. Whether to kiss his hand or fall on our knees we did not quite know, but, America being given less than many lands to emotional demonstration (!!) [two more of Davison's intrusive exclamation marks], we smiled back with composure and appeared, no doubt, as if we were accustomed from earliest youth to distinguished marks of favour from the great ones. But the truth is, we are not. And these roses, which stood on Liszt's table by his MS music, presented by the hand that has made him famous, are already pressing and will be kept among our Penates, except one perhaps, and that will be distributed leaf by leaf to hero-worshipping friends, with date and appropriate inscriptions on that sheet where it rests. How amiable he was, indeed! The roses were much. But something was to come. The Meister played to us! For this we had not even dared hope during our first vist. No one, of course, ever asked him to play, and whether he does or does not depends wholly on his mood.

It was beautiful to sit there close by him, the soft lawns and trees framed by the open casement making a background for the tall figure, the long peculiar hands wandering over the keys, the face full of intellect and power. And how he smiles as he plays! We fancied at first in our simplicity that he was smiling at us, but later it merely seemed the music in his soul illuming his countenance. His whole face changes; it gleams and grows majestic, revealing the master spirit as his hands caress while they master the keys. With harrowing experiences of the difficulties of Liszt's compositions, we anticipated as he began something that would thunder and crash and teach us what pigmies we were; but, as an exquisite, soft melody filled the room and tones came like whispers to our hearts and a theme drawn with tender, magical touch brought pictures and dreams of the past before us, we actually forgot where we were, forgot that the white-haired man was the famous Liszt, forgot to speak when the last, faint chord died away, and sat in utter silence, quite lost to our surroundings, with unseeing eyes gazing out through the casement.

At last he rose, took our hands kindly and said: 'That is how I play when I play badly. I am suffering from a cold at present.' We asked if he had been improvising or if what he played was already printed. 'It was

only a little nocturne,' he said. It sounded like a sweet remembrance.
'And *was* one,' he replied cordially. Then, fearing to disturb him too
long and feeling we had been crowned with favours, we made our
adieux, receiving a kind invitation to come the following day and hear the
young artists who cluster round him often here, some of whom, he
informed us, played *famos*. And after we had left him he followed us out
to the stairway to repeat his invitation and say another gracious word or
two. And we went off to drive through Weimar and only half observe its
pleasant, homely streets, its flat, uninteresting, yet friendly, aspect, its
really charming park – *Lisztified* we are, as a friend calls our state of
mind. The place has, indeed, little to charm the stranger now, except the
memories of Goethe and Schiller and all the literary stars who once made
it glorious – and the presence of Liszt. – B.W.H.

While such 'high falutin' as this is allowed to pass current, how
can the taste for genuine music in America be nourished? If ever
there was an enemy to the art in its purest significance, that enemy
is Franz Liszt; – and an enemy all the more formidable because of
his great natural abilities. Our sage and sober J.S. Dwight, the
Boston (U.S.) aristarch, ought to blush for shame at transferring
such arrant rubbish to his pages. Talk of 'petticoat pianists'!
'Lisztified' pianists of any sex are insupportable – long-haired or
short-haired.

12

TCHAIKOVSKY

For *Romeo* Read Rubbish

Musical World, 18 November 1876

On the 4th instant . . . the Saturday afternoon programme – Peter Von Tchaikovsky's overture to *Romeo and Juliet* . . . is not the only Shakespearean subject set by Von Tchaikovsky, as he has also *The Tempest* for a fantasia . . . The general tone of the overture is so stormy that the tale of *The Tempest* seems to be illustrated rather than the love strains of *Romeo and Juliet*. It may be assumed that the street combat of Montagues and Capulets, the *fête* at the mansion of Juliet's father, and a dirge at the ending of the tragedy, were predominant in the fancy of the Russian composer. There is, in fact, more power than pathos in the overture. Programme music it is, of course. If the technical treatment be examined, the evident resolution to be original – the determination to assert individuality – cannot be mistaken . . . Both the piano concerto played at the Crystal Palace the preceding March and the overture are the evidence of the existence of an original thinker, who defies rule and rote when he has effects to achieve. His overture does not terminate in the starting key of F sharp minor but ends in B major; this is not without good precedent but is still not orthodox . . . The overture is unusually long, and there is this peculiarity, that often when a close is expected a fresh imagery is heard, as if the composer had some additional incident of the tragedy to treat, so that the overture comes to a sudden termination after more than one seeming coda. Mr Ebenezer Prout, in the *Academy* speaks as follows:

The second novelty was Tchaikovsky's overture *Romeo and Juliet*, which had not been previously heard in England. The

233

Russian musician is undoubtedly one of the most original living composers. His overture, which is of symphonic proportions, taking nearly twenty minutes in performance, is avowedly an illustration of Shakespeare's tragedy. It is full of most practical and charming ideas; but it is so absolutely novel in thought and treatment that, except by a minority of the audience, it altogether failed to be appreciated and was received coldly and even with signs of disapproval. Special praise ought to be given to Mr Manns for securing a really magnificent rendering of a most difficult work. No such performance could have been heard elsewhere than at the Crystal Palace.

The fact is that . . . the overture was very ill received. That it came at the end of the concert is true, but the same place, with very different results, has often been given to masterpieces by Beethoven, Mendelssohn and others. For ourselves, we were not among 'the small minority of the audience' and failed to appreciate Tchaikovsky's work. The Russian composer may be possibly the Russian Beethoven; but, as Liszt makes 'coming Beethovens' by the dozen, we prefer to know something more of Tchaikovsky before venturing upon a decided opinion. What, by the way, is the opinion of 'G' on this same overture? We should like to know, because everything he does not himself choose to write about, in the admirable analytical programmes of the Crystal Palace, we are greatly inclined to suspect. We doubt, indeed, if 'G' would feel moved to dignify the subjoined *galimatias* [balderdash, gibberish] with the title of *theme*:

. . . To our ears it sounds hideous. Perhaps it is intended for a 'Leitmotif'. Oh Wagner! Oh, Wagner! Thy most devoted apostles must admit that thou hast led them astray.

Theophilus Queer [pen name]

Bibliography

All titles are published in London unless otherwise stated.

Anonymous, *Actors by Daylight, or Pencillings in the Pit*, Vol. 1, [ref. Laura Honey] (Lambeth, 1838)

Anonymous but ascribed to the Rev. John Edmund Cox, *Musical Recollections of the Last Half Century*, 2 Vols (Tinsley Bros., 1872)

Anonymous, *Memoirs [of] the Extraordinary and Secret Amours of Mrs Honey*, (J. Thompson, 1838)

Anonymous, *The History of The Times. The Traditions Established, 1841–1884,* London (Written and published at the office of *The Times*, 1939

Bache, Constance, *Brother Musicians. Reminiscences of Edward and Walter Bache*, (Methuen, 1901)

Banister, Henry C., *Macfarren, George Alexander*, (George Bell, 1891)

Barnett, John Francis, *Musical Reminiscences and Impressions*, (Hodder and Stoughton, 1906)

Barzun, Jacques, *Berlioz and the Romantic Century*, 2 Vols (Columbia University Press, New York and London, 1969)

Beale, Willert, *The Light of Other Days Seen Through the Wrong End of an Opera Glass*, (Richard Bentley, 1890)

Bennett, Joseph, *Forty Years of Music, 1865–1905*, (Methuen and Co., 1908)

Bennett, J.R. Sterndale, *The Life of William Sterndale Bennett by his Son*, (Cambridge University Press, 1909)

Berger, Francesco, *Reminiscences*, (Elkin, Matthews and Marrot, 1931)

Boschot, Adolphe, *Une Vie Romantique, Hector Berlioz*, (Plon-Nourrit, Paris, 1919)

Berlioz, Hector, *Mémoires de Hector Berlioz*, 2 Vols (Calmann-Lévy, Paris, 1926)

Bernard, Daniel, *Corréspondance inédite de Hector Berlioz, 1819–1869,* (Calmann-Lévy, Paris, 1879)

Brockway, Wallace and Weinstock, Herbert, *The World of Opera*, (Methuen and Co., 1963)

Bunn, Alfred, *The Stage Both Before and Behind the Curtain*, 3 Vols, (Richard Bentley, 1840)

Carse, Adam, *The Orchestra from Beethoven to Berlioz*, (W. Hueffer and Sons, Cambridge, 1948)

Chorley, Henry Fothergill, *Thirty Years' Musical Recollections*, 2 Vols (Hurst and Blackett, 1862)

Chorley, H.F., *Musical Recollections of the Last Half Century*, (Tinsley Bros., 1872)

Cox, Bertram and C.L.E., *Leaves from the Journals of Sir George Smart*, (Longmans, Green and Co., 1967)

Davison, Henry, *From Mendelssohn to Wagner, being the Memoirs of J.W. Davison, Forty Years Music Critic of* The Times, *Compiled by his Son*, (William Reeves, 1912)

Davison, James William, *An Essay on the Works of Frederic Chopin* [without author's name], (Wessel and Stapleton, Music Sellers to Her Majesty, HRH the Duchess of Kent the Court and the Army, 1843)

—*Chopin's Mazurkas in Eleven Books, complete with a Biographical and Critical Introduction and Portrait*, (Boosey and Sons, 1860)

Ella, John, *Musical Sketches Abroad and at Home*, revised and edited by John Belcher, (William Reeves, 1878)

Ellis, William Ashton, *The Letters of Richard Wagner*, edited with notes by John N. Burk (Victor Gollancz Ltd., 1951)

—*Life of Richard Wagner*, (Kegan Paul, Trench, Trubner & Co., 1906)

—*Prose Works of Richard Wagner, Opera and Drama*, Vol 2, (Kegan Paul, Trench, Trubner & Co., 1893)

—*Richard to Minna Wagner . . . his first Wife*, letters translated and prefaced, (H. Grevel & Co., 1909)

Finck, Henry T., *Wagner and His Works*, (H. Grevel and Co., 1893)

Graves, Charles L., *The Life and Letters of Sir George Grove, C.H.*, (Macmillan, 1903)

Gruneison, Charles Lewis, F.R.G.S., *Sketches of Spain and the Spaniards, a Lecture*, (The Literary Association, 1874)

—*The Opera and the Press*, (Robert Hardwicke, 1869)

Hipkins, Edward J., *How Chopin Played . . . from the Notebooks of E.J. Hipkins*, (Dent, 1937)

Hueffer, Francis, *Half a Century of Music in England*, (Chapman and Hall, 1889)

Hunt, Leigh, *Critical Essays on the Performers of the London Theatres*, (London, 1807)

Lumley, Benjamin, *Reminiscences of the Opera*, (Hurst and Blackett, 1864)

Macfarren, Walter, F.R.A.M., *Memories, An Autobiography*, (Walter Scott Publishing Co., 1908)

Mackenzie, Sir Alexander Campbell K.C.V.O., *A Musician's Narrative*, (Cassell and Co., 1927)

Mapleson, Henry, *The Mapleson Memoirs, 1848–88*, (Remington, 1888)

Moscheles, Charlotte, *Life of Moscheles, with Selections from His Diaries and Correspondence.* By his wife, adapted from the original German by A.D. Coleridge, 2 vols (Hurst and Blackett, 1873)

Moscheles, Felix, *Letters of . . . Mendelssohn to Ignaz and Charlotte Moscheles from the Originals in His Possession,* (Trubner and Co., 1888)

Newman, Ernest, *The Life of Richard Wagner,* 4 Vols (Cassell and Co., 1933–47)

Niecks, Frederick, *Frederic Chopin as Man and Musican,* (Novello, 1888)

Osborne, Charles, *The Complete Operas of Verdi,* (Victor Gollancz, 1969)

Phillips, Henry, *Musical and Personal Recollections during Half a Century,* 2 Vols (C.J. Skeat, 1864)

Praeger, Ferdinand, *Wagner as I Knew Him,* (Longmans Green and Co., 1898)

Reeves, J. Sims, *Life and Recollections Written by Himself,* (Simpkin, Marshall and Co., 1888)

—*My Jubilee or Fifty Years of Artistic Life,* (The London Music Publishing Company Ltd., 1889)

Rockstro, W.D., *Mendelssohn,* (Samson Low, Marston, Searle & Rivington, 1884)

Rosenthal, Harold, *Two Centuries of Opera at Covent Garden,* (Putnam, 1958)

Scholes, Percy A., *The Mirror of Music, 1844–1944, a Century of Musical Life in Britain as Reflected in . . . The Music Times,* (Novello & Co Ltd. and Oxford University Press, 1947)

Stratton, Stephen S., *Mendelssohn,* (J.M. Dent, 1904)

Sydow, Bronislas Edouard, *Corréspondance de Frédéric Chopin,* annotated and translated in collaboration with Susanne and Denise Chainaye, 2 Vols (Richard-Masse, Paris 1960)

Toye, Francis, *Giuseppe Verdi, His Life and Works,* (William Heinemann Ltd., 1931)

Tiersot, Julien, *Hector Berlioz, Le Musicien Errant,* 1919

—*Au Milieu du Chemin,* 1930, (Calmann-Lévy, Paris)

Periodicals

Musical World, 1836–1891, weekly, published from Dean Street, Soho, London, J.W. Davison being its Editor from 1843 to approx. 1883.

Musical Examiner, an Impartial Weekly Record of Musical Events. 'Fair Play to All Parties.' London, Wessel and Stapleton, 1842–43)

Musical Magazine, F. de Porquet and Cooper, Covent Garden, London, monthly from 1835, J.W. Davison writing for it under pen-name Arthur Pendragon.

Index